GENDER AND LANGUAGE

GENDER AND LANGUAGE

Towards a Feminist Pragmatics

Christine Christie

Edinburgh University Press

Edinburgh University Press Ltd
22 George Square, Edinburgh

Typeset in Sabon 10 on 12$\frac{1}{2}$pt
by Initial Typesetting Services, and
printed and bound in Great Britain by MPG Books Ltd, Bodmin

A CIP Record for this book is available from the British Library

ISBN 0 7486 0935 0 (paperback)

CONTENTS

1

INTRODUCTION

1.1 PRAGMATICS AND FEMINISM: AN INTRODUCTION

The primary aim of this book is to demonstrate, for an interdisciplinary readership, what feminist research that focuses on language use has to gain from an awareness of work in the field of pragmatics. My particular concern is that scholarship in pragmatics is not widely recognised across the range of disciplines within which feminist research on language use is carried out. Possibly due to the opacity of its terminology, the fact that it does not fit neatly within disciplinary boundaries, and misconceptions about its aims and assumptions, pragmatics is not as accessible as it should be to the wide range of students and scholars across the humanities who have an interest in analysing language. What I hope to illustrate in writing this book therefore is that studies that address naturally occurring language use, including those within the broad range of approaches covered by the term *discourse analysis*, or those that adopt methodologies based on *conversation analysis* are often premised on unexamined and occasionally untenable assumptions about what it means to use language. In particular, where studies lack a pragmatic perspective such research cannot adequately account for the relatu nship between the functions carried out by language and the socio-culturally situated users of that language. While accounting for this relationship is a problem for studies of language use generally, the particular concern of this book is that feminist studies of gender and language use should be able to recognise and explain potentially significant patterns in their data. As David Graddol and Joan Swann (1989) and Robin Lakoff (1995) have suggested, certain problems faced by studies of linguistic phenomena can be avoided if those phenomena are approached from a pragmatic perspective. However, no published work has yet adequately demonstrated what a pragmatic approach to the study of gender and language use would entail, what analytical tools it would generate or what its specific benefits might be. This book is designed to fill that gap.

1

In the following chapters I show that current assumptions about language use and language users that underlie both pragmatics and feminist research are in many ways compatible, and that there are benefits for both in recognising the common ground they share, and the progress each has made in describing and explaining issues of gender and language. I also show that there are, however, some significant areas of controversy where both pragmatics and feminism have something to learn from one another. Although in the course of this book I therefore argue that both fields can benefit from a greater awareness of the research that has taken place in the other, my specific concern is with the methodological implications for feminist research that would arise out of a closer engagement with pragmatics. My primary aim is therefore to lay the foundations for a prag-matic approach that will benefit feminist research by demonstrating what, precisely, would be gained by adopting such an approach. Since I am not assuming that readers will have a detailed knowledge of either pragmatics or feminism the opening chapter provides an introduction to both these fields. In Chapter 2 I provide a background to and outline of some of the concerns of feminist scholars before showing the methodological conse-quences of not approaching linguistic date from a pragmatic perspective. In Chapter 3 I begin to provide insights into the phenomena that come into view when a pragmatic perspective on language use is adopted. In Chapters 4, 5 and 6 I introduce a range of pragmatic theories: speech act theory, Grice's theory of conversation, politeness theory and relevance theory, and illustrate their relevance to studies that focus on issues of gen-der and language use. In Chapter 7 I draw together the points made through-out the book to argue that pragmatics, if it is to have the relevance for empirical research that I believe it warrants, needs to take into account theories of identity that have been developed through feminist scholarship and needs to build on the findings of studies of gender and language use generally, both within and outside of pragmatics. In that chapter I also consider the direction that a specifically feminist pragmatics might take. To begin with however, since this book does not assume a high level of familiarity with either of the fields I focus on, in this opening chapter I offer a brief introduction to both pragmatics and feminism.

I am aware that attempting a *brief* introduction to either of these fields is fraught with problems. When a term such as *feminist* or *pragmatic* is used to describe a piece of research it is likely to be seen by individuals outside of either field as implying that such research is based on a stable and coherent set of practices with a specific set of aims, interests and methodologies. However, scholarship that might be categorised as falling within either of these areas is engaged in the investigation of a set of complex and wide-ranging phenomena, the boundaries of which are constantly being renegotiated. Inevitably therefore there are ongoing internal controversies over how scholars who see their work as either pragmatic or feminist might best describe and explain the object their research focuses on, and just as significantly, controversies over which phenomena are relevant to their research and what the purpose of that research might be.

This internal controversy, and the resulting self-questioning that characterises any thriving area of academic inquiry often works against attempts to use the insights gained in one field to address questions posed by another. As Kitzinger's (1998) argument illustrates, scholars outside of a discipline are rarely fully aware of the complexity or significance of the issues addressed within that discipline, and interdisciplinary work can often result in an inappropriate use or simplification of terms and concepts. In spite of these difficulties, and with a strong awareness of possible pitfalls, the point I want to make in this book is that research in both pragmatics and feminism would benefit from the insights into gender and language use that the other can provide. In this chapter, therefore, after offering provisional answers to the questions 'What is pragmatics?' and 'What is feminism?' I go on in section 1.2 to make a case for my claim that any study of language use needs to take into account the insights that have been generated by pragmatics scholarship. In section 1.3 I conclude this chapter by suggesting some reasons for supposing that feminism and pragmatics have something to offer each other in relation to the study of gender and language use, and consider why they have a particular significance for each other at this moment in time.

1.1.1   What is pragmatics?

In a British television programme on politics and feminism screened in 1990, Emma Nicholson, who at that time was a Conservative MP, related the following anecdote. It took the form of a voice-over to a shot of Nicholson walking towards and then through the gates of the Houses of Parliament.

> I remember when I was a child going into the Carlton Club to find my father. And I walked in at the front door and I looked left and saw my father, my uncle who was Lord Chancellor, another uncle who was a Member of Parliament, all sitting together in a lovely room. And I just went through that door to say 'Hello, here I am.' All three rose to their feet and my father rushed forward and they all shouted 'Get out, get out. This is men only.'[1]

Even though a reader might feel that the *point* that Nicholson is making here might be open to debate, to competent users of English, the 'literal' meaning of this anecdote appears to be self-evident. However, being able to understand a piece of language use is quite distinct from being able to explain how that understanding came about. In this section I begin by detailing some of the problems that surround the explanation and description of what goes on in the process of constructing and interpreting utterances by suggesting some questions that an analyst taking a pragmatic approach to meaning might ask in relation to this anecdote. My aim here is to introduce an argument that is developed throughout this book, namely, that such pragmatic questions are central to *any* research that focuses on language use and, therefore, given current trajectories evident in the study of gender, that such questions are of particular interest to feminist research. I begin with an account of how a specific group of people made sense of the anecdote transcribed above.

1.1.1.1 Utterance interpretation: An example

A common-sense explanation of how English language users are able to understand Nicholson's anecdote might be that we understand it because we are able to understand the words that she is using. As English speakers we feel confident that we know what items like *I*, *remember* and *father* signify. It also seems obvious that we understand the anecdote because we understand both the words and the way in which they are strung together. In linguistic terms, what such an explanation would be proposing is that we understand Nicholson's meaning because we understand the sentences (that is, the structured way in which the words are strung together) that make up this anecdote. That is to say we know, even though this may not be a conscious knowledge, how English syntax works and we also know the meaning of everyday English words and, therefore, we understand what Nicholson is saying. This type of knowledge is, within the discipline of linguistics, referred to as linguistic or grammatical competence. It is the tacit knowledge we have about the language system (the words our native language consists of and the way the words function in relation to one another) that enables us to construct and interpret sentences. There are, however, many reasons for questioning the assumption that we, as readers or hearers, simply draw on our knowledge of the English language when we interpret 'utterances' (uses of language by speakers or writers) such as this anecdote. Indeed, it is axiomatic to pragmatics that our linguistic knowledge does not provide us with sufficient information to be able to understand examples of language performance, that is to say, actual uses of language such as the Nicholson anecdote. A pragmatic approach begins with the assumption that interpreting even the simplest of utterances calls on a range of processes which draw on both linguistic and on extra-linguistic knowledge.

One way of demonstrating that linguistic knowledge alone does not explain how we come to understand an utterance such as Nicholson's story is to focus on the final sentence, where she reports her male relations' use of the words:

(1) This is men only.

As part of a study of discourse comprehension I carried out some time ago (see Christie 1994, 1998a), I played a video recording of the programme that contained Nicholson's anecdote to two groups of women, all of whom were native speakers of English, but who had had quite distinct cultural experiences. I then asked them to tell me what they thought Nicholson meant by the word *this* when she was recounting this moment of her childhood. Some of the respondents said that they thought Nicholson was using the word *this* in her anecdote to refer to:

(2) Somewhere in Parliament.

Others thought she was using the term to refer to:

(3) Some kind of boardroom

or

(4) The Carlton Club.

The range and characteristics of these responses suggest that the audience members were drawing on information from both within and outside of the linguistic context when trying to assign a referent to the word *this*. For example some respondents appeared to be drawing primarily on the visual images that were being broadcast during the voice-over, and for them, what the men in Nicholson's story appeared to be indicating was:

(5) Females are not allowed to enter this part of Parliament.

Others appeared to have been drawing on a range of associations that the language and the visual images invoked for them when they perceived the word *this* to be referring to 'some kind of boardroom'. For them the final words indicated:

(6) Females are not allowed to enter this boardroom.

For those who picked up on the linguistic context to make a link between Nicholson's description of herself as a child entering the Carlton Club and the men's speech, the words indicated that:

(7) Females are not allowed to enter the Carlton Club.

I use this example to show how interpreting an utterance calls on more than an understanding of the language that is used. Although each of the three possible interpretations can be said, in this case, to be based on the same perception of the 'sentence meaning' in that all of the audience members appeared to have a common understanding of the words and how they were functioning in relation to one another, they did not share an understanding of the 'utterance meaning'. According to the referent they assigned to the word *this* the audience members offered very different interpretations of this single use of a single string of words.

It might be tempting to dismiss interpretations (5) and (6) as simply wrong in that, particularly for readers of this anecdote, it probably seems pretty obvious that (7) is the meaning that Nicholson intends her audience to take. But there are three major reasons why these interpretations should not be ignored. Firstly, they indicate that even apparently simple and straightforward utterance interpretations vary. Secondly, they indicate what people actually do in the process of interpreting utterances. To dismiss this evidence according to judgements about whether or not an interpretation appears to agree with the speaker's intended meaning would be to ignore vital information about the dynamics of communication therefore. For example this evidence implies that referents appear to be 'inferred' by the audience members. That is to say, these interpretations appear to be based on deductions that the audiences have made on the basis of available evidence. Thirdly, and perhaps most significantly, they show that these inferences are based on not just linguistic but also visual and cultural evidence. Responses such as the above are interesting to pragmaticians therefore even though they appear to be 'misunderstandings' in that they indicate something of the way in which utterance interpretations come about, and what they tell us has implications for how language use might be explored and explained in that they indicate just how hazardous communication can be. If it is the case that, even when hearers are engaged in working out what they tend to experience as the 'literal' meaning of a simple utterance, they are required to draw on different types of knowledge, a number of questions about language use arise. For example, even if we felt it was common sense to suppose that a speaker and hearer will share a knowledge of the particular language they are using, how can we be sure that these other types of knowledge are also shared by all users of a given language? And if they are not, given the significant role they appear to play in acts of utterance interpretation, how can we be sure if and when a speaker 'successfully' communicates a meaning to a hearer?

These questions have in turn led to other questions, such as: What do we mean when we talk of 'successful communication'? How might we characterise the sort of meaning that is communicated by speakers? What part does linguistic knowledge play in the process of communication? What other sorts of knowledges do speakers and hearers have to share in order for communication to occur? What is the source of these different types of knowledge? How can this 'sharing' of knowledge be conceptualised and explained? Over the last fifty years, as surveys such as those offered by Levinson (1983) and Verschueren et al. (1995) show, pragmaticians have built up a considerable body of scholarship that has addressed these questions, and many other questions that they in turn have generated. Specifically, pragmatics has developed a descriptive base that enables analysts to demonstrate that implied meanings can take many different forms. It has developed a vocabulary that facilitates the discussion and exploration of the many different ways in which the meaning of a given utterance can be under-determined by the linguistic component of that utterance. It has also developed ways of describing and explaining the interaction between linguistic and non-linguistic components that seem to be necessary to meaning generation in particular and to acts of communication generally. Most pertinently, for the purposes of this book, pragmatics has begun to theorise the relationship between language use and the impact of socio-cultural factors on the different types of knowledge that play a role in interlocutors' attributions of meanings to utterances. In the process of developing these accounts of what language in use consists of, pragmaticians have pointed to a number of distinctions that need to be made if we are to understand the processes involved in communication. These include the distinction between communicating and saying, and between speaker meaning, utterance meaning and sentence meaning. Although, as I show in later chapters these distinctions are not clear cut and are often problematic in many ways, I use them at this point because they provide a useful means of bringing into view something of the complexity of language use.

1.1.1.2 Sentence meaning, utterance meaning and speaker meaning

I have already suggested that understanding what goes on in the interpretation process initially requires a recognition of the difference between sentence meaning and utterance meaning: where sentence meaning appears to be largely explicable in terms of the language system, utterance meaning clearly requires an engagement with contextual phenomena. So for example, if I wanted to argue that the sentence meaning of the phrase *This is men only* can be captured largely by an appeal to our linguistic knowledge, I might discuss such meaning in terms of verbal equivalents or paraphrase by saying that the phrase means 'the place inhabited by the speakers is prohibited to females' or 'females are not allowed to enter the area where the speakers are'. If the meaning is accounted for in this way, I could say that I have understood what is 'said' even though I may not be aware of which specific thing in the world the word *this* is pointing to when Nicholson actually uses the phrase. From this perspective, it does not seem to matter whether the words are being used to refer to the players' changing rooms at a local football club or the Forbidden City in Beijing, the sentence meaning remains the same. On the basis of their responses, it would appear that the audience members I interviewed shared an understanding of this phrase at this level of meaning.

In contrast, utterance meaning can be seen as the meaning that these strings of words have for the hearers *within their specific context of use*, and one of the things that this sort of meaning will depend on is the relationship between the language and things in the world, that is to say, it will be dependent on an act of reference. Intuitively, the concept of *reference* appears to be straightforward – it is the thing in the world that a speaker is pointing to through her use of specific words. In fact, as many theorists (see Recanati 1993, Verschueren 1999, Yule 1996 for surveys) have shown, reference is a great deal more complex than this. For the purposes of this discussion however, I will address reference in very general terms and use it as an example of one factor that plays a part in a hearer's interpretation of utterance meaning. The point I want to make in relation to the interpretations of the Nicholson anecdote is that where reference assignment varied, the respondents came up with the different utterance meanings indicated by examples 5–7:

(5) Females are not allowed to enter this part of Parliament
(6) Females are not allowed to enter this boardroom.
(7) Females are not allowed to enter the Carlton Club.

What this illustrates is the way in which each utterance meaning is generated by the active synthesis, by the hearer, of their understanding of the sentence meaning and their understanding of other types of contextual meaning, one of which is based on the act of reference assignment.

Many pragmaticians would argue that a third distinction also has to be made: the distinction between sentence meaning, utterance meaning and speaker meaning (for example, Sperber and Wilson 1995 and Thomas 1995). Indeed some would argue that the goal of any act of communication is not the hearer's understanding of sentence meaning, or of utterance meaning, but rather his understanding of what the speaker intended her utterance to mean.[2] For example, an aspect of the anecdote I have not so far discussed is Nicholson's meaning: what point she is trying to make by relating this story. It is important to stress at this stage that for most pragmaticians the concept of speaker meaning is not premised on the assumption that speaker meaning is directly accessible to a hearer, or indeed that any verbal act of communication can guarantee access to speaker meaning. To say that a hearer's goal is to understand speaker meaning means in practical terms that the hearer is engaged in the process of making hypotheses about the speaker's meaning. In the above example, it is clear that Nicholson's meaning is not directly accessible to the audience members that I interviewed in that, on the basis of the differences in their interpretation of the utterance meaning, these respondents are clearly going to have different notions of what point Nicholson is trying to make. Although each of the interpretations I have listed above might lead the hearer to assume that Nicholson is trying to make a point about the institutionalised exclusion of females that her upbringing exposed her to, because of the different understandings of utterance meaning that are indicated above, it is likely that the *specific* meaning attributed to Nicholson by these audience members will also vary. The utterance meaning implied by example (5) above indicates that this audience member is likely to have understood Nicholson's point to be one about the exclusionary practices of Parliament. It may be quite obvious to you as a reader that this last interpretation is an inappropriate one, the point is, however, that for at least one audience member, this is what Nicholson appeared to be communicating.

What this variation highlights is the need to distinguish between what is 'said' and what is 'communicated'. It also highlights how a speaker's construction of an utterance requires her to take into account the knowledge that she believes her hearers will have access to. It may be, for example, that Nicholson or the programme editors would have altered the form or the visual context of Nicholson's speech if they had seriously thought that the choices they made would have led to their intended meaning being misinterpreted by audience members. The variation also highlights something about 'context' that I will address in more detail in Chapters 6 and 7. Generally context is seen as an *a priori* feature of an utterance in that it seems to be uncontroversial to claim for example that in the 'context' of a political discussion, the word *green* would signify a political allegiance, while in a discussion of paint, it would signify a colour. What the responses to the Nicholson anecdote indicate is that what constitutes 'context' appears to be generated by the hearer in the process of interpretation. Indeed it appears to be the visual images that are being broadcast at the same time as the verbal cues that produce interpretation (5), while it is the reference to the Carlton Club that produces interpretation (7). To that extent, context appears to be dynamic and inferred rather than static or pre-given. While the act of interpreting sentence meaning appears therefore to call primarily on our knowledge of language, interpreting utterance and speaker meaning calls on our ability to synthesise our knowledge of language with other types of knowledge. This latter ability and the processes it involves fall within the domain of language use that is studied by pragmaticians. Pragmatics focuses on how speaker intention can be indicated through linguistic choices, how context might be theorised as a social, cultural or cognitive set of phenomena, and it sets out to explore the processes that lead to utterances being produced and interpreted.

I am conscious that I have not actually defined pragmatics yet. Partly because of the range of theoretical and empirical material that pragmatics scholarship engages with, definitions of pragmatics are always troublesome. Introductory texts on pragmatics often spend a whole chapter weighing up the range of available definitions (Levinson 1983 is the classic example) or else they purposely avoid providing a definition at all in order to get on with the business of applying pragmatics in the analysis of language use (for example, Grundy 1995). At this stage I will adopt one of George Yule's (1996: 3) definitions *Pragmatics is the study of how more gets communicated than is said*. Although this choice is somewhat reductive, it does enable me to make some initial points about pragmatics and feminist research before going on to define the aims and methods of pragmatics in more precise terms.

1.1.2   What is feminism?

Although non-feminists often appear to know exactly what the term 'feminist' means, this issue has always been less clear for people who identify themselves in this way. Writing in 1913 for example, Rebecca West comments: 'I myself have never been able to find out precisely what feminism is: I only know that people call me a feminist whenever I express sentiments that differentiate me from a doormat' (cited in Coppock et al. 1994: 184). The problem with defining feminism perhaps stems from the fact that it exists both as a set of political practices and as a set of theories concerned with the conceptualisation of gender relations. Van Zoonen (1994) describes feminism as a social movement that has 'the double edge of being both an interest group lobbying and struggling for social and legal changes beneficial to women and of challenging cultural preoccupations and routines concerning femininity and gender' (152). Although, as these introductory comments indicate, feminism seems to be characterised by diversity, one way of pinning down feminism as an academic field of interest would be to consider in what ways its focus and aims distinguish it from other fields of interest. Broadly speaking, I would argue that this distinction arises from the fact that the focus of academic feminism is gender and its aims are emancipatory.

The emancipatory project arises out of the shared belief that, across virtually all known societies, a systematic hierarchy is in force that works against women as a group. Evidence in support of this belief comes from feminist research which, over a number of decades, has pointed to a range of cultural, social and economic inequalities of gender across categories such as class, race and age (see, for example, Bryson 1992, Ashworth 1995, Basu 1995 and Corson 1997). More recent feminist studies have shown that these inequalities remain in spite of the mainstream belief that equal opportunity legislation and changed work and child-care patterns over the last twenty years or so have now led to a 'post-feminist' society charac- terised by gender equality (see, for example, Walby 1990, Coppock et al. 1995 and Walter 1998). A wide range of feminist scholarship has also un- covered the extent to which such inequalities permeate and are perpetu- ated by the academic world (see Kramarae and Spender 1993 for a comprehensive review of this issue). Indeed, Adrienne Rich has commented: 'There is no discipline that does not obscure and devalue the history and experience of women as a group' (cited in Arianrhod 1993: 46). These issues are addressed in more detail in the second chapter. Here my aim is to point out that feminist scholarship, like any other form of feminism is primarily concerned to understand, and ultimately to eradicate inequalities that are based on gender, both within and outside of its own academic discipline.

1.1.2.1 The concerns of feminism

Although the above concerns might be seen as suggesting that feminism as an academic enterprise has a specific set of aims and methods, this is far from the case. The ways in which gender relations are theorised, what form social or political change should take, and what the point of such changes might be, are subject to constant debate within feminism. For example, writing from within the field of political theory, Bryson makes the following point:

> Feminist political theory . . . sees women and their situation as central to political analysis; it asks why it is that in virtually all known societies men appear to have power over women, and how this can be changed. It is therefore engaged theory, which seeks to understand society in order to challenge and change it; its goal is not abstract knowledge, but knowledge that can be used to guide and inform political practice. (Bryson 1992: 1)

Although she is pointing to the general aims of feminism here, Bryson's specific objectives, and the particular methodology that informs her work are inevitably determined by the intra-disciplinary debates taking place within political theory at the time she is writing. And these will be markedly different to the objectives and methods of a feminist scholar working at that moment within physics or sociology for example.

As well as differences in methodology, there are also marked differences in the way that feminists conceptualise gender, and therefore in the way in which inequalities of gender are perceived. It should be pointed out that feminist scholarship has, in the past, tended to work on the premise that gender is distinct from sex. So for example Graddol and Swann argue that 'gender, unlike sex is a continuous variable. A person may be more or less "feminine" and more or less "masculine"' (1989: 8). Moreover, as they also point out, accounts of inequality tend to be predicated on the assumption that gender differences rather than sex differences are at the root of the problem: 'men and women have different life experiences to an extent that cannot be satisfactorily explained by simply biological differences between the sexes' (Graddol and Swann 1989: 8). According to this view it is not physical or innate differences but the *constructed* differences that are built into the prevalent ideas of what it is to be masculine or feminine within a given society that lead to gendered inequalities in life experience. As Cameron (1998b: 16) points out, to say that differences are 'socially constructed' is not to say that they are imagined or can be wished away. She goes on to comment:

> How much I get paid is socially constructed – there is no law of nature which dictates my value on the labour market – but it still has real, material consequences for whether I can pay my bills at the end of the month, and I can't change it unilaterally. (1998b: 16)

Such an approach assumes therefore that the way in which men and women are perceived within a given society is predicated on a gender hierarchy in which differential values are assigned to the qualities, behaviour and experiences of males and females. Although, according to this view, gender inequalities within a given society are systematic, this is not the case for all feminist approaches.

Other forms of feminism (historically referred to as forms of 'liberal feminism') have argued that gender inequalities are simply a matter of the differential civil rights that are accorded to males and females as individual members of a given society. Such approaches tend to dismiss the argument that the way we conceptualise gender can be used to explain and combat gendered inequality. The concerns of this type of feminism are practical, focusing primarily on issues surrounding equality of opportunity, and may involve campaigns designed to give women and men an equal voice in decision-making, or campaigns designed to ensure that legal or employment practices do not discriminate against women. Coppock et al. (1995: 16) argue however that liberal feminist approaches reduce 'women's struggles against subordination' to a 'shopping list of single, self-contained issues'. Their point is that a failure to address the systematic nature of gender inequalities leaves fundamental power relations unchallenged.

These two types of feminism differ not only in relation to their perception of gender and their methods of exploring and fighting inequality, but also in terms of their conceptualisation of the individual in relation to society. Feminist approaches that engage with the systematic nature of gender inequalities tend to conceptualise the individual primarily in social terms and as having less autonomy than would be assumed by those approaches where equality of opportunity is the primary concern. At their most extreme point of difference it might be argued that, for adherents of the former approach, an individual's socially constructed consciousness plays a major part in the perpetuation of inequalities, while for adherents of the latter, individual consciousness is largely irrelevant. In the former case, it is assumed that as long as individuals (both male and female) perceive women as essentially less able or less significant than men, the power imbalances within society will not change. Simply changing legal practices or employment rights will not affect people's perception of women as fundamentally inferior to men. However, for the latter the assumption is that if people have equality of opportunity then the power differentials will gradually disappear as those opportunities are realised and women attain equal pay and equal status. According to this latter model, individuals are not as constrained by their histories as is supposed by the former. In practice, most feminist scholarship tends to fall somewhere between these two extremes (see Beasley 1999). However, a basic division between feminist approaches can be attributed to this difference in the conceptualisation of the autonomy of the individual in relation to society.

As I show in more detail in Chapter 2, the diversity of feminism does not end there. For example, feminist approaches that question the systematic nature of gender inequalities tend to focus on issues surrounding consciousness, ideology and the social construction of gender identity. But such scholarship draws on a range of different theoretical frameworks, including post-structuralism, postmodernism, Marxism and other materialist approaches to gender. And within each of these frameworks can be seen a number of debates where different scholars take up distinct positions over the extent to which identity generally, and gender identity in particular, can be seen as contingent upon historical and cultural factors including race and class. There are also constant debates over the implications of these various stances for the emancipatory aims of feminism.

As all of this should indicate, pointing to what is distinct about feminist research is often highly problematic. This is not helped by the fact that as well as there being *differences* within the category 'feminist', there are also strong *similarities* between feminist research and other (i.e. 'mainstream' or 'non-feminist') academic approaches. For example, post-modernist scholarship across a range of disciplines has actively questioned the validity of Western forms of knowledge. There is extensive overlap in both the method and the focus of feminist and non-feminist scholars who address issues of epistemology from this perspective. However, as Hennessy points out, there is a clear distinction in that: 'Unlike many post-modern discourses, feminism grounds its critique of Western knowledge in an emancipatory agenda' (Hennessy 1993: 2).

1.1.2.2 The focus of feminism

What the discussion so far should have indicated is that although feminism is realised in many distinct forms and employs many different methods, the theorisation of gender and the project of women's emancipation are the two central issues that characterise feminist research. Until recently the focus on gender has often, in practice, led to a focus on *women*. There are many reasons why the concept of 'gender' has tended to become conflated with the concept of 'woman'. Here I will illustrate this tendency by considering just one aspect of research on gender and language.

It has long been argued by feminists that women's uses of language have tended to be measured against male norms, and that this is evident even in approaches such as that of sociolinguistics which set out to address linguistic data as objectively as possible. In the specific case of sociolinguistic study, because the language use of men has been seen as 'normal', women's linguistic behaviour has often been seen as 'abnormal' and in need of explanation in ways that men's behaviour is not (for a survey of such accounts, see Cameron and Coates 1988). For some time, therefore, feminist research within sociolinguistics tended to focus on women's language in order to explore and challenge the bases of such claims. To this extent, a focus on gender and language in practice tended to mean a focus on women's use of language. Since the mid-1990s however, there has been a growing interest in men's use of language. The distinction between this and earlier work within sociolinguistics is that male linguistic behaviour is now addressed as specifically *male* linguistic behaviour and not simply as *normal* linguistic behaviour. However, as Johnson comments in her introduction to a collection of studies on language and masculinity, even where there is a change of focus from female to male behaviour, the emancipatory agenda remains:

> Though all feminist work is ultimately (and rightfully) concerned with the effects on women of life within a patriarchal world order, I would argue that to concentrate exclusively on women and femininity is insufficient. What is needed *in addition* is informed study of the mechanisms of oppression, that is, of the specific ways in which men construct a world which so manifestly excludes and undermines women. How else can such structures be contested? (Johnson 1997: 13)

The discussion of feminist research so far is designed to indicate a characteristic of feminism that I will develop further in Chapter 2: the awareness that what it is to carry out feminist research is constantly examined by feminist scholars in the light of ongoing research and changing social conditions. I conclude this introduction with two examples which indicate one such development.

It might reasonably be assumed that if issues of gender and emancipation are central to feminist scholarship, research within this field must be predicated on the assumption that there are clear distinctions between masculinity and femininity or at least that there is a clear distinction between males and females: in order to be able to argue that inequality exists between two groups of people, it would be reasonable to assume that there is a way of identifying these two groups. Recent feminist scholarship has questioned this assumption in a number of ways. For example, it has become increasingly evident that when the specifics of how gender is constructed across race, class and culture are studied, males and females *within* a given cultural group are often found to have more in common that do females *across* cultural groups, or males across cultural groups. Such evidence has led scholars to question whether the issues raised by feminist research can be addressed in terms of universals. It raises the question, for example, of what differences are being glossed over when we assume that there is a single coherent group that is sufficiently homogenous and which shares a specific set of qualities and a specific type of life-experience that can be called 'women'. Their point is that, if it is the case that what it is to be a woman is so different in different cultures, this raises questions about what we are assuming is shared when we talk about 'women' in generic terms.

A common sense response to such a question might be that what makes men and women different is, essentially, anatomic: what women across cultures share is their biological sex. However, feminist studies in recent years have argued that not only is *gender* a continuum rather than a category (some behaviour can be more masculine/feminine than others) and also a cultural construction (what it is to be masculine or feminine in the year 2000 in Britain is quite different to what it is to be masculine or feminine in 1890s Ireland or 1990s Thailand) but so too is *sex* a cultural construction and a continuum. Such studies point out that, historically, which specific biological factors have been seen to mark a person as 'male' or 'female' are quite different to those biological factors we point to today when we distinguish males and females (see for example Bing and Bergvall 1996). The argument that sex is also a cultural construction goes something like this: since theories of physiology inform the perception of sexual difference, if it is accepted that theories of physiology are culturally specific and subject to change, it can be inferred that so too are the factors that constitute sexual difference. What constitutes 'male' or 'female' should therefore be treated as historically specific, and a construction rather than a biological given. Eckert and McConnell-Ginet (1994) also makes this point:

> 'Female' and 'male' label distinctions in potential sexual reproductive roles: All cultures known to us sort people at birth into two groups on the basis of anatomical distinctions potentially relevant to those roles. Crucially however, what is made of those categories and relations emerges only in the historical play of social practices, including their link to such phenomena as medical and technological changes in reproductive possibilities. 'Defining' these various terms is not preliminary to but an ongoing component of developing a scholarly practice centred on questions of gender. (Eckert and McConnell-Ginet 1994: 434)

The notion that sexual difference can be explained by reference to ontologically prior biological 'facts' is further questioned by studies that point to cultures where the binary opposition male/female that is characteristic of Western thought is not valid and where there is a recognition that human beings exist within a range of states that cannot be captured by this dichotomy (see, for example, Bing and Bergvall 1996).

If biology cannot explain what it is that women share across cultures, a second response to the question of what it is that characterises *women* as a group, is that what women share is 'oppression' (for example, Bryson 1992: 1). However, feminist scholarship has long recognised that even if it can be shown that that section of the population labelled 'women' do share such an experience across cultures, the various forms that these inequalities can take are sufficiently distinct to raise questions about whether they can be accommodated within a single theoretical framework. I develop this point in Chapter 2 when I discuss in more detail the evidence for, and implications of, the feminist acknowledgement that on the one hand the term *women* signifies a highly diverse group of people with very different experiences and behaviours, and on the other the argument that male and female experience and behaviour is not as distinct as has previously been thought. At this stage, it is worth pointing out, however, that in spite of these developments, the aims of more recent scholarship tend to be the same as earlier accounts. What each is designed to highlight is the argument that it is not so much *actual* differences that underlie inequalities of gender but *perceived* differences. The aim of this recent development in feminist scholarship is to argue that even taken-for-granted differences, like those based on biological sex, can and should be subject to interrogation.

The question of difference is also subject to scrutiny in recent feminist scholarship for other reasons. For example, Bing and Bergvall (1996) and Cameron (1995, 1996) have suggested that previous research that emphasises difference is misguided not solely because it tends to exaggerate distinctions in gendered behaviour. They suggest that when earlier studies of linguistic behaviour have stressed the extent of gendered differences in order to re-evaluate female speech, this enterprise has often had unforeseen and unwanted results. These authors point out, for example, that the distinctions such studies have highlighted have often been taken up outside of academia and used as linguistic evidence of female inferiority. Bing and Bergvall assert for example:

> Attempts to prove difference are often attempts at gender polarization and one way to rationalize limiting the opportunities of women. For those who perceive no inequality of opportunity, difference does not signal an underlying pattern of dominance. (Bing and Bergvall 1996: 17)

They argue therefore that stressing diversity precipitates oppression since diversity is often used to justify inequality. As a result recent studies, such as West (1994) and those reported in Bergvall and Bing's (1996) collection, have argued that it is important to point out how far male and female uses of language overlap as well as the degree to which they differ. What such research has highlighted is the extent to which a great deal appears to be invested in the construction of difference by participants in a given linguistic interaction. This alternative approach therefore focuses less on gendered differences in behaviour and more on the difference that gender makes.

In this outline I have suggested that the aims of feminism are political in that they are concerned with eradicating inequality, but that the nature, extent and causes of existing inequalities, the measures needed to eradicate inequality, and the question of what equality would actually consist of varies widely across different forms of feminism. In the following chapter I explore these issues in more depth in order to show how feminist research across this wide range of interest has looked to language use in the analysis of gender. In the remainder of this chapter I consider the question of what feminism and pragmatics have to offer one another given the state of current research. In order to illustrate this I consider what it is that pragmatics adds to studies of language use.

1.2   WHY STUDIES OF LANGUAGE IN USE NEED A PRAGMATIC DIMENSION

The general claim I want to introduce here, and go on to substantiate in later chapters, is that any discipline which looks to language use in the form of speech or writing, and either implicitly or explicitly makes assumptions about the communicative functions of language and the dynamics of linguistic interaction, already engages at some level with issues that have been the subject of investigation within pragmatics for many years. My reason for making this claim is to be able to then go on to suggest that an understanding of scholarship within this field should be of wider interest than is currently the case. Indeed it has often been argued that pragmatics has much to offer disciplines as diverse as sociology, anthropology, cultural studies, social psychology and literary studies as well as being of particular interest to theoretical and applied linguistics, conversation analysis, discourse analysis, the ethnography of language and sociolinguistics (see, for example, Brown and Levinson 1987, Levinson 1983 and Verschueren 1999). My specific aim however is to consider what pragmatics has to offer *feminist* research within these disciplines. This section therefore addresses some general points about why research that focuses on language in use needs to engage with pragmatics. I conclude this chapter by drawing on this to argue that feminism and pragmatics have a particular relevance for each other.

1.2.1 Meaning and saying

In section 1.1.1 above I discussed Emma Nicholson's narrative, and the responses generated by different audience members, in order to highlight the fact that the meaning of an instance of language use (that is, an utterance) does not reside solely in the words the speaker has used, and nor does it reside in the meaning the speaker was trying to convey, or indeed in the hearer's understanding of either of these. I have said that a pragmatic approach would take it as axiomatic that meaning arises out of the interaction of all three. Here I want to indicate why it should matter that studies which address language use need to recognise this. It should be noted however that although I have argued that speaker and utterance meaning are not retrievable from an analysis of the language of an utterance, my point in doing so has not been to suggest that, as either language users or as scholars, individuals outside of pragmatics are not already aware that linguistic meaning is not self-evident. Neither am I suggesting that people are not already conscious that a given string of words can have a range of meanings according to the context in which it is used. Indeed for many readers these basic tenets of pragmatics might seem to be so obvious that their significance is not immediately evident. Most language users are very good at manipulating the context-dependency of linguistic meaning. We exploit the gap between saying and meaning in everyday usage when we use irony (*I just love these shoes*), when we use metaphor (*Money doesn't grow on trees*) or when we tell jokes that are predicated on polysemy (*What holds the moon up? Moon Beams*). Nor am I suggesting that this is necessarily an unconscious knowledge. Indeed this fact of language use has been the subject of debate in Western scholarship since the time of Socrates (see Harris and Taylor 1997 for an account of this). That meaning *can* be context-dependent is something that every language user knows and exploits, irrespective of how far they are actively conscious that they know and exploit it. However, there is little acknowledgement outside of pragmatics what the implications of this are for acts of communication, or the full extent to which contextual issues play a part in the generation of apparently straightforward and simple meanings. Here I want to illustrate this issue, and then show why it is significant.

Because we seem to be able to communicate our ideas without too many problems in everyday conversations, we usually have no reason to suspect that what is 'said' does not map directly onto what is 'communicated'. 'Indirect' forms of language use such as irony, metaphor or jokes that play on the ambiguity of word and sentence meanings seem therefore to be exceptions. A banal but serviceable example that indicates that such assumptions are misguided would be the response a speaker offers to the information that there is a phone call for her:

(8) I'm in the bath.

We derive meanings from utterances like this all the time. But what is communicated by such a response is clearly quite distinct from what has been 'said'. The string of words that the speaker is using here, if we consider how they combine to produce a sentence meaning, simply indicate her location. However, it is unlikely that the speaker's use of the words *I'm in the bath* would be seen by the hearer in this context as communicating anything other than:

(9) I can't come to the phone.

What is equally evident is that the words *I'm in the bath* in another context might generate an alternative meaning. It is not impossible, for example for them to imply:

(10) Bring me a gin and tonic.

In spite of this potential for generating alternative meanings, for all sorts of reasons, the chances are that when we hear an utterance like *I'm in the bath* in an everyday context, we are likely to interpret it according to the way that the speaker meant it to be interpreted. What this indicates is that even though it is clear that in everyday instances like this, what a speaker has 'said' is quite distinct from what she has communicated to the hearer, we have no trouble in finding what the speaker has said to be meaningful.

The evidence from pragmatics scholarship is that most, if not all, communication between interlocutors involves this degree of ambiguity and indirection. A corollary of this finding is that what a speaker means cannot therefore be explained by an appeal to our knowledge of the English language, and that most, if not all, meanings derived from language use are as dependent on contextual phenomena as this example. What is odd is how little interlocutors are aware of this gap. Indeed Graddol and Swann (1989: 169) argue that there is plenty of evidence to suggest that readers and hearers are very poor at distinguishing between information that was strictly given in a message and information that they had to infer on the basis of context. What they are suggesting is that we are rarely conscious that a response like *I'm in the bath* is actually different from *I can't get to the phone*. Because our interpretation of such utterances is so automatic, we rarely register that these two forms are not 'saying' exactly the same thing. It would seem that it is the apparent 'content' of the message rather than the 'form' of the message that we remember when we hear an utterance, whether this 'content' is explicitly stated or indirectly implied. It is perhaps because of the seeming obviousness of the 'content' that the question of how people get from what is said to what is meant is rarely recognised as a meaningful question outside of pragmatics. However, as has been pointed out by many pragmaticians, this is an oversight that should not occur in scholarship that focuses on language use. If meaning cannot be read off from 'form', how one comes to fill the gap between utterance and interpretation needs to be made explicit if that interpretation is to be seen as valid.

Brown and Levinson (1987) address this issue when they question the validity of sociological analyses that address acts of communication but do not also take into account this basic premise of pragmatics. They suggest that making explicit the interpretation process is a necessary step that sociologists need to take when discussing spoken data. In particular they argue that studies which take meaning as self-evident are flawed if they do not acknowledge that the meanings that are generated within a given communicative context are inferences (that is, hypotheses) and are therefore specific to that context.

> Until sociological methodology is explicit, descriptions will have uncertain status and must be taken on the assumption that other observers so placed would similarly observe. (Brown and Levinson 1987: 55)

Their point is that for an analyst to 'understand' a speaker is not enough, it is also necessary for the analyst to justify his or her interpretation of the speaker's language use by explaining how those interpretations were generated within that specific context. Indeed Brown and Levinson argue that the relationship between society and language remains speculative without such an explanation and go on to make that point: 'We identify strategic message construction as the key locus of the interface of language and society' (56). This raises the question of what 'strategic message construction' is and how it functions.

1.2.2   Strategic message construction

The significance of pragmatics to empirical studies of language use was pointed out by Levinson in the early 1980s. However, his point has remained largely unacknowledged by researchers engaged in such studies, and it is worth considering why that should be. The point that Levinson (1983) makes is in relation to sociolinguistic studies of language. He suggests that since sociolinguists are involved in trying to understand the social significance of patterns of language use it is essential that they understand the structural properties of language as well as the processes that constrain the use of language in a given verbal interaction. He makes the point that a failure to do this can lead to misguided explanations such as that of Bernstein who, in a study carried out some years previously, had attributed sociological causes to patterns of hesitation in speech behaviour without understanding the 'underlying conversational motivations for such patterns' (Levinson 1983: 374). What Levinson suggests is that studies which try to explain linguistic phenomena need to take into account the fact that any example of language use is just that: it is someone's *use* of *language*. This is not to suggest that linguistic and socio-logical phenomena are not connected, but rather that to look outside of the communicative event for an explanation without acknowledging that the subject of analysis *is* a communicative event is to ignore a primary determinant of why linguistic phenomena take the form they do, and have the significance that they do.

For example, a pragmatic approach would argue that if interlocutors who hear responses such as (8) above come to see the speaker's words as meaningful in spite of their apparent indirectness, an initial assumption that has to be made by each participant is that the other is using the language items they select in order to intentionally communicate some-thing. And for most pragmatic theorists, this recognition that com-munication is quite distinct from language, and that communication is just one strategic use that language, has led them to ask how and why language users come to employ language in this role. Different pragmatic approaches would address these questions in different ways. One way would be to consider that for a hearer to understand what an utterance such as (8) signifies requires him to work out how that utterance is func-tioning. Speech act theorists for example would argue that if one hears the words *It's for you* one would not simply take this as a piece of infor-mation. The utterance may actually be functioning as a command in that the speaker may be using that form of words to tell an interlocutor that she should come to the phone. Equally, we might say that a response like *I'm in the bath* is functioning as a refusal to obey that command. Part of our use and understanding of language might be explained then by our perception that in communicative events, speakers use utterances to perform acts.

But even with this level of explanation, it still is not clear exactly how we get to see the words *I'm in the bath* as a refusal in (8) in that it appears to be communicating something like 'I am not going to come to the phone' while in another context the very same words, with exactly the same intonation, might be interpreted as a request for a drink as indicated in (10). Most pragmaticians would account for the distinction in meaning by pointing out that the two interpretations of *I'm in the bath* are inferences made by the hearer. Theories that explain how inferences are drawn by hearers tend to propose that they are generated by the expec-tations we have about everyday uses of language in conversations. One of the earliest such theories is that proposed by Paul Grice who argues that we understand what a speaker means, not only because we make assumptions about what sorts of acts their speech might be performing in a given context, but also because we measure their speech against certain communicative (specifically conversational) norms (see Grice 1989). His point is that we expect our interlocutors to be rational and not to provide us with incorrect, inappropriate or irrelevant information. Grice is not suggesting that this *is* how interlocutors act in everyday conversations. He is suggesting that the expectations he points to constitute a set of premises that underlie, and trigger our interpretation of conversational turns. It is *because* we have these expectations that we are able to interpret an utterance as meaningful even though the linguistic choices a speaker has made do not appear to constitute, at the level of sentence meaning, a relevant or appropriate contribution to a conversational exchange. Grice's point is that the expectation itself acts as a mechanism that sets off the interpretative process that would lead to a speaker's contribution being perceived by the hearer as relevant and appropriate.

There are many problems with speech act theory and with Grice's theory that later pragmaticians have pointed to and addressed in their own accounts of communication and language use (these are discussed in Chapters 4, 5 and 6). However, Grice's work in particular indicates one way in which speaker and utterance meaning might be explained: he suggests that hearers need to make assumptions about *how* a specific string of words is being used, as well as about *why* that string of words is being used if they are to work out what is meant by a speaker on the basis of what that speaker has said. Moreover, what his work highlights is that the meanings that speakers and hearers come up with can only be explained in terms of the part they play in strategic acts of communication. Trying to explain them by calling on the system of linguistic meaning will not work. Grice's account also foregrounds the way that issues of *context* need to be addressed if we are to understand how communication works. For example in order to explain how *I'm in the bath* comes to be seen as a refusal to come to the phone rather than a demand for a gin and tonic, it would be necessary to show *how* context plays a part in the process and why assumptions about context should be brought into the mind of the hearer at all. Although Grice's account does not engage with these questions, later theories, which I will address in Chapter 6, do attempt to provide an explanation. At this stage however, my discussion is designed to show that, for pragmaticians, explaining what bits of language use mean is inevitably tied up with understanding the strategies that language users apply in the act of communication. These explanations have not always been sufficiently comprehensive, but each has contributed something to the overall question of how language is used in acts of communication. They also provide increasing evidence of the centrality of pragmatics for an understanding of linguistic data.

Before considering the advantages of a feminist application of pragmatics I address the question of why it is that, if as I am suggesting pragmatics has the potential to be as significant to studies of language use in a range of disciplines, this is not already widely recognised. If you are new to pragmatics, the relevance of this section may not be immediately evident, and you may prefer to ignore it. It is aimed primarily at readers who know something of pragmatics but who are not convinced of its usefulness.

1.2.2   Pragmatics in context

There are many factors that might account for the marginalisation of pragmatics. I will briefly summarise three: (1) the assumption that pragmatics is unable to address either the social or cultural contexts of language use (2) the assumption that pragmatics is predicated on a liberal-humanist conceptualisation of the individual and (3) the obscurity of pragmatic terminology. On the one hand this summary offers an opportunity to broaden the picture of pragmatics I am building up, but it is primarily designed to indicate that the problems with pragmatics that have been pointed to in the past, should not preclude the use of pragmatics in feminist research on gender and language use. In particular I argue that even though the first two objections might appear to have been partially valid in the past, they have never been entirely valid, and are even less so today. I hope that, after the introduction to pragmatics in the chapters which follow, this book will be one step towards removing the third objection.

1.2.2.1   Problems with pragmatics

Many scholars who focus on language use indicate that they reject pragmatics because the approach is incapable of engaging with the socio-cultural context of either language use or language users. Pragmatics has often been seen as too abstract to be relevant to studies that deal with 'real language use' such as sociolinguistics, discourse analysis, conversation analysis or the ethnography of language. For example Schiffrin, in her survey of approaches to discourse analysis, describes pragmatics in the following terms:

> Pragmatics focuses on meaning, context and the communication of constructed utterances in hypothetical contexts. The communicative meaning of a particular utterance is derived through general assumptions about human rationality and conduct; together with the literal meaning of utterances, these assumptions are the basis from which to draw highly specific inferences about intended meanings. (Schiffrin 1994: 12)

What is interesting about this account is that in order to be able to argue that this is all that pragmatics does, Schiffrin has to ignore a vast body of scholarship that has focused on 'real language use' and which has been reported in two international journals devoted solely to pragmatics research for more than a decade (indeed one of these journals, *The Journal of Pragmatics,* was upgraded from a quarterly to a monthly publication in the early '90s in order to be able to cope with the growing volume of this research).

In spite of such evidence, Schiffrin's account implies that pragmatics has not developed since Grice first formulated his theory of conversational implicature in the 1950s. Subsequent chapters will provide evidence that indicates how selective a view of pragmatics this is. However, in spite of the evidence to the contrary, Schiffrin's view seems to be shared by a range of scholars, and it is worth exploring what is at stake here. Clearly Schiffrin's view is shared by Goodwin and Duranti (1992) in that they use somewhat similar terms to discuss pragmatics in their introductory chapter to an edited collection of ethnographic studies of language and context:

> The work in this volume differs in significant ways from other approaches to the study of context. For example there is a long linguistic and philosophic tradition in pragmatics which invokes context to help account for aspects of meaning in language that go beyond the scope of semantics. Workers in this tradition typically use as data isolated sentences and descriptions of contextual features that have been constructed by the analysts themselves to illustrate the theoretical argument being developed. Within this tradition, processes of interaction between participants are rarely, if ever, examined. (Goodwin and Duranti 1992: 9)

The authors' point here is to argue that pragmatics is distinct from their own approach in that, unlike their own, it does not engage in 'processes of interaction between participants'. As with Schiffrin's account, this description does have some truth in it, but again it is tenable only so long as a great deal of pragmatic scholarship is ignored. For example it may indeed be the case that this description would have fitted many examples of pragmatic scholarship a decade or so before Goodwin and Duranti are writing in that such studies did tend to focus almost entirely on abstract problems that appear to have little to do with the dynamics of actual language use.

A case in point is the way in which some early accounts set out to explain the intuition that certain types of language use seem to indirectly communicate a set of unstated assumptions (a set of phenomena now termed 'presupposition'). In these early accounts (see, for example, Levinson's 1983 summary of the literature on presupposition) such phenomena were interrogated by considering how a sentence like *The King of France is bald* might be explained. To the extent that these accounts did not make explicit why presupposition might be a significant feature of communication, it is quite true that they appear to be far removed from the study of actual language use. However it is also true that it has long been recognised (as I show in detail in Chapter 3) that the concept of presupposition is a useful way of explaining how some utterances appear to smuggle in ideological assumptions that are difficult to contest (see, for example, Magalhaes 1995), and to that extent the concept offers a way of explaining how power relations are realised dynamically in acts of actual language use, and how they are related to broader socio-cultural conditions. What I am suggesting is that although the roots of some pragmatic concepts can be traced to abstract philosophical discussion, it does not mean that these concepts do not have a practical relevance, or indeed that they are not at any time tested out in the analysis of naturally occurring examples of language use. For this reason, although Goodwin and Duranti's description might equally apply to some current pragmatics scholarship, it does not on its own constitute a critique of such an approach. In exploring characteristics of language use at a theoretical level, it is quite often the case that an argument might draw on constructions such as my examples (8), (9), and (10) above. However, the whole point of such constructions is that they illustrate claims about language in a sufficiently explicit form for those claims to be explored and laid open to question. That is to say, such abstract discussions are developed in order to formulate testable hypotheses about language use that can be applied and qualified in the study of naturally occurring utterances.

As I indicate in later chapters, and as should be evident in the very act of my writing this book, the relationship between theories of pragmatics and studies of actual uses of language is a dynamic process. Theories of pragmatics are constantly being rethought in the light of evidence of actual language use. Moreover, I would argue that even if it is not often acknowledged, the reverse is also true: the methodological underpinnings of studies of language use are constantly being rethought in the light of developments in pragmatics. Indeed the contributors to Duranti and Goodwin's (1992) collection are part of that dialogue between theory and empirical study, as even the briefest glance at the index of that edition shows. The contributors draw on and apply terms such as deixis, coherence, speech act, context, inferencing and even presupposition. Each of these terms refers to a concept that has been developed and explored within pragmatics on the basis of abstract arguments that use constructed examples, and in the works in the collection, each forms the basis of a discussion of empirical data. So how are we to understand this? On the one hand the contributors to Duranti and Goodwin's collection are overtly using concepts developed by pragmatics, and indeed explicitly refer to and draw on the works of a range of pragmaticians in their discussions. On the other hand the editors are actively engaged in marginalising pragmatics in their introduction by suggesting that it is quite distinct from their own concerns. What are we to make of this? Why do the editors not simply acknowledge their engagement with pragmatics and make it clear that what their contributors are doing is applying and developing pragmatic concepts? This is a significant question in that it is not an uncommon phenomenon. Fairclough (1989) and Georgakapoulou and Goulsos (1997), for example, also apply pragmatic concepts, in their own analyses while also arguing that the pragmatics enterprise is fundamentally antithetical to their own approach. I would want to argue, however, that such assumptions and the distancing activities are both misguided and counter-productive.

My own feeling is that the incompatibility that such studies point to appears to be based on the assumption that pragmatics conceptualises the individual language user in a way which is antithetical to ethnographic or critical approaches. Possibly because many pragmatic concepts are explored in terms of the behaviour of hypothetical individuals within an isolated interaction, it is often inferred that pragmatic approaches *per se* are incapable of theorising the individual as a social being. Moreover, because pragmatics often approaches communication in terms of the strategies employed by individuals, and also theorises these strategies in terms of intentions, it is possible that this is seen to imply that a pragmatic approach inevitably entails a conceptualisation of the individual in liberal-humanist terms, that is, as the originator and controller of meaning. In spite of the evidence that many empirical studies have applied concepts that have been developed within pragmatics, it is possible then that the distancing manoeuvres I have pointed to are attempts to address perceived tensions between the different conceptualisations of the relationship between the individual and society. This is certainly the impression I take from Lavandera's (1988) account of pragmatics in a discussion premised on the claim that the social is subordinate to the interactional context within what she calls 'the subdisciplines' of conversation analysis, pragmatics and discourse analysis. She asserts that these 'subdisciplines' try to explain a given interaction in terms of psychological notions such as intentions, beliefs and rationality rather than in terms of the power relations that exist within the society in which the interaction takes place:

> To give an example, studies of politeness strategies tend to focus solely on the state of the relationship between the participants themselves, in particular to their state of psychological satisfaction or offence. The approach to personal relationships is a 'punctual' one: one or both of the participants are pleased or insulted by a single act. Yet they typically ignore the social fact that such strategies reflect the distribution of power in the society. How power is assigned and maintained linguistically in the society remains outside the scope of conversation analysis and pragmatics. (Lavandera 1988: 10)

While some parts of Lavandera's description may indeed apply to some aspects of pragmatic scholarship, it is questionable whether it is possible to claim that because pragmatics tends towards the 'punctual' it *cannot* address issues of power or that it is incapable of addressing language use in social terms. Indeed what Lavendera's opening sentence here ignores is the empirical, socially situated research that underpins the pragmatic concept of 'politeness' she discusses. Brown and Levinson, who have been primarily responsible for developing the pragmatic notion of politeness explicitly state the need for a symbiotic relationship between socially situated empirical research and the theoretical. Writing over a decade ago, they categorise the distinction in terms of approaches, arguing that 'sociolinguistics should be applied pragmatics' (Brown and Levinson 1987: 281), however while 'applied pragmatics' and 'pragmatics' might have been distinct in the past, there seems little point in making that distinction today. Pragmatics today *is* both theory and application.

1.2.2.2   Pragmatics and the socio-cultural context

What I have been suggesting is that there appears to be a tendency to assume, on the basis of certain types of pragmatic analysis that pragmatics is not relevant to, and either does not or can not engage with studies of socially situated language use. There is also a tendency to assume that, because pragmatics often focuses on the communicative strategies employed by individuals, it must be predicated on a naive liberal-humanist conceptualisation of the individual as an entirely free agent, able to create and control meaning quite independent of the constraints of the socio-cultural context. What I hope to show in the course of this book is that there is plenty of evidence to suggest that neither of these assumptions is tenable. Two examples should suffice at this point. I will however develop this point in subsequent chapters when I consider examples of pragmatic research that addresses gender and language use. The first example I focus on addresses one of the assumptions of pragmatics that I have been foregrounding: the assumption that utterance meaning is as dependent on context as it is on our sense of what words and sentences mean as part of the language system.

Eades (1993) in a study of police interviews indicates how pragmatics can address both the punctual and the socio-cultural context . She demonstrates for example that although a pragmatic analysis might be 'punctual', in that it focuses on a specific set of utterances that take place in a specific context between two interlocutors, any explanation of how these utterances function has to draw on the dynamics of the relationship between language use and the power differential that arises from the socio-cultural background of the interlocutors. Her study focuses on a transcript of an interview with a police witness whose first language is Aboriginal English. The interview was led and transcribed by a police officer whose first language is Australian English. Eades' point is that the syntactic structures of Aboriginal English and that of Australian English are distinct and that the syntax attributed by the police officer to the Aboriginal English speaker is highly unlikely to have been produced by a speaker with that sociolinguistic background. The aim of her analysis is to show that such evidence brings into question the accuracy of the police transcript, and to indicate something of the power relation that holds between the two racial groups in this context. She points out that her analysis could not have been made without the application of pragmatics in that it centres on the specific ways in which Aboriginal English speakers refer to time in certain communicative contexts. She shows, for example, that there is evidence that when Aboriginal English speakers are asked a direct question about when an event took place, they do not answer by providing specific times (for example, *It happened at 8.30 a.m.*) as might occur in Australian English speech. An Aboriginal English speaker would respond to such a question not by referring to time in numerical terms but in terms of a coinciding event such as *It happened just before the sun went down.* In the transcript of the interview however the officer attributes to the suspect answers to questions about time that do not follow this pattern of language use. Such an analysis is inevitably predicated on a pragmatic approach in that, it is not that the syntactic structures found in the interview transcript would *never* occur in Aboriginal English speech, but rather that in the specific communicational situation Eades' study focuses on they would never constitute an appropriate response.

A second example of a pragmatic analysis of naturally occurring language that links the punctual with the wider social context can be seen in Lane's (1993) study of the Polynesian English use of *yes*. She points out that if a Polynesian English speaker replies *yes* in answer to negative questions such as *You haven't done it have you?* the *yes* means 'yes, I agree with your statement' which is to say 'Yes, you are correct, I have not done it'. In contrast to this Pakeha English speakers (that is, New Zealanders of European descent) are likely to use and understand the word *yes* in such a context to mean 'I have done it'. Again, although this type of analysis does take a punctual approach, in that it focuses on a specific interaction between two people within a given context, the significance of the analysis only becomes evident in a wider socio-political context. Lane shows for example how this difference in understanding leads to problems in the context of a Polynesian law court where Pakeha English speakers' assumptions about what *yes* means are taken as the norm, and Polynesian uses of the term are misinterpreted.

Recent texts on pragmatics have increasingly stressed the social and political basis of language use. For example in his introductory text on pragmatics, Mey argues that what distinguishes his field from other approaches to language is that pragmatics places its focus on the *language users* and *their conditions of language use* (1993: 287). Moreover he describes pragmatics as the science of 'language as it is used by real, live

people, for their own purposes and within their limitations and afford-
ances' (5). Although he suggests that the sorts of question asked by
pragmaticians include 'Why would people say a particular thing on a
particular occasion?' and 'What are people trying to do with their language?' (14), the answers to these questions are not couched in terms of
the individual psyche, of the immediate relationship between two
interlocutors, or as though a speaker is in absolute control of his or her
meanings. They are addressed in terms of the way that meanings are
generated by individuals who have specific socio-cultural histories and who
act within specific socio-cultural settings when they make choices about
their use of language. Lane (1993) and Eades (1993) show one way in
which this can include an engagement with the conflicts of interest that
arise from power relations based on racial background within specific
cultural settings. My own interest is in how this is addressed in terms of
the conflicts that arise from the effects of gender within specific cultural
settings. And in particular my aim is to show that studies that address
gender and language use need to call on a theoretical framework that can
account for the relationship between the cultural setting, the language user,
the linguistic choices the user makes, and the factors that underlie those
choices.

I have argued that there is some evidence to suggest that scholars outside
of pragmatics appear to think that if pragmatics takes language use to be
strategic it must therefore be premised on the assumption that speakers
are in control of meaning, or on the assumption that individuals somehow
create meanings in a socio-cultural vacuum. I have also argued that both
of these assumptions are misguided. As I show in Chapter 3 an acceptance
that people use language strategically does not necessarily entail an
acceptance that the individual is in sole control of her meaning, nor does
it necessarily entail a dismissal of the social or the cultural. I am not however suggesting that scholarship within pragmatics *never* takes an entirely
punctual approach to the material it focuses on, or that there have never
been, and are not now some problematic assumptions about social and
cultural phenomena evident in pragmatics scholarship. As I shall go on
to suggest, such problems do exist, and they are often most evident in
relation to the absence within pragmatics of a theoretical framework that
accounts for social identity generally and gender identity in particular.
However, what I am arguing is that addressing interactions in punctual
terms, or addressing hypothetical interactions do not invalidate what is
claimed in a study. Such exercises are designed to make hypotheses about
actual behaviour – they are not necessarily an end in themselves. And
indeed unless these hypotheses are made, empirical studies of language
use will lack an adequate descriptive base and an explanatory framework.
My particular concern is that feminist research is not weakened by such
a lack. This concern is particularly pertinent in the light of the turn to

language taken by many feminist researchers within the social sciences. I address this issue in some depth in Chapter 2, here I will briefly summarise what my concerns are.

1.3 WHY ARE PRAGMATICS AND FEMINISM RELEVANT TO ONE ANOTHER?

To summarise my discussion of pragmatics so far: I have pointed to the need to make a distinction between language as a structured set of knowledges (that is, a system) and language use. I have also claimed that explanations of the meanings generated by specific examples of language use need to take into account a range of factors including the inter-locutors' tacit knowledge of the language they are using, and assumptions about what that language is being used for, who is using it, and what the context of use is. I have suggested that an engagement with these issues has implications for research in disciplines outside of pragmatics. My point is that the significance of material gathered in empirical studies of language use, whether it is in the form of conversation, court-room dialogue or interview transcripts, cannot be treated as self-evident be-cause the processes that underlie utterance meaning are not self-evident. Moreover, even where meanings are interrogated in such studies, they cannot be explained by theories of language alone or by theories that only explain social or cultural phenomena. While the former might provide a solid descriptive basis for analysis, and while the latter might offer rich insights into socio-cultural phenomena such as gender, I would want to argue that it is only when these two domains are linked in the form of pragmatic analysis that a sufficiently explanatory theoretical framework becomes available.

1.3.1 Why a feminist *pragmatics*?

As I indicate in more detail in Chapter 2, in recent years there has been a turn to language across the humanities. For the most part, such an engagement has been described in terms of 'discourse analysis'. Here I want to consider what this engagement with language has entailed. As Tannen (1989) has pointed out:

> The term 'discourse analysis' does not refer to a particular method of analysis. It does not entail a single theory or coherent set of theories. Moreover, the term does not describe a theoretical perspective or methodological framework at all. It simply describes the object of study: language beyond the sentence. (6)

The idea that discourse is 'language beyond the sentence' has at least two meanings. On the one hand it can indicate that rather than seeing grammatical relations between words *within* a sentence as the object of study, discourse analysis sees linguistic relations *between* sentences within a text as the object of study (see, for example, the sort of discourse analysis employed by Halliday and Hasan 1976 and which I discuss in Section 3.3.1). In this case both types of data are accounted for in terms of language as a system. On the other hand, 'beyond the sentence' can mean that the object of study is language in use (speaker/utterance meaning) rather than language as a system (sentence meaning). In this case both language and relevant phenomena *outside* of language are used to account for the data. The latter conceptualisation places such an object of study within the domain of pragmatics. Many discourse analysts from the social sciences who work within a post-Foucauldian or postmodernist paradigm would also recognise this subject matter as falling within their own field of interest. Indeed Tannen goes on to stress that the type of study termed *discourse analysis* will never be monolithic precisely because it does not grow out of a single discipline:

> Since discourse analysis embraces not just two disciplines but at least nine: linguistics, anthropology, sociology, psychology, literature, rhetoric, philology, speech communication and philosophy, and there are culturally different subdisciplines within each of these disciplines, the goal of a homogeneous 'discipline' with a unified theory, an agreed upon method, and comparable types of data, is not only hopeless but pointless. (Tannen 1989: 7)

However, although she acknowledges that discourse analysis can never be pinned down to a single approach, Tannen goes on to make the following point that is particularly pertinent to my own concerns in this book:

> To say that discourse analysis is not monolithic is not, however, to exempt individual works (or individual's works) from having, and having to make, clear theoretical, methodological and when appropriate empirical frameworks. (7–8)

As I show in Chapter 2, not all feminist applications of discourse analysis actually do this, and as a result they leave their claims vulnerable to criticism on a number of counts. I also show that such analyses often indicate a relative naivety about language use. Specifically then I am suggesting that it is crucial that feminist researchers interrogate the assumptions they have about language use when they apply their specific versions of discourse analysis. I am also suggesting that, no matter what specific type of discourse analysis is being applied, what this calls for is an explicit engagement with the phenomena that come into view when a pragmatic perspective is applied.

This is not a new claim. Cameron (1996) and Bing and Bergvall (1996) amongst others have pointed to the need for a more sophisticated account of the relationship between language and gender. Graddol and Swann (1989: 11) have also made the point that although many feminist studies have suggested that language is implicated in the mechanisms that lead to gender divisions, and specifically in those divisions that support social inequalities between the sexes, their own survey of feminist research makes it quite evident that:

> there exists no agreed and coherent theoretical framework which clearly and persuasively establishes how linguistic behaviour gives rise to social and economic sexual inequality. Furthermore the nature of the connection between language and inequality is a controversial one and many writers dispute the idea that language plays an active role. (136).

In exploring the connection between language and inequality, Graddol and Swan suggest that a pragmatic approach would be the most appropriate in that it allows specific questions to be asked about the mechanisms and types of knowledge that underlie acts of communication, and to that extent pragmatics allows a way of addressing the relationship between language use and language users in ways that can be overtly explored. Unfortunately, given the scope of their work, Graddol and Swan (1989) are only able to offer a brief outline of some of the applications that a pragmatic approach would have for feminist research on gender and language use. Their work provides a useful survey and evaluation of the claims made by studies of language and gender and, although they make many insightful comments about the use of pragmatics in this context, they do not have the space to explain precisely what pragmatics is and how it can actually be used in empirical studies. This book builds on Graddol and Swan's (1989) argument with the explicit intention of offering a more comprehensive account of what a pragmatic account can offer feminist research.

1.3.2   Why a *feminist* pragmatics?

Since the early 1980s there have been an increasing number of studies that apply pragmatics to the analysis of linguistic material ranging from court-room dialogue to casual conversation (see for example Blum Kulka 1997, Brown 1980, Harris 1995, and Sarengi and Slembrouk 1992). These empirical studies have led to an ongoing questioning of the original theoretical framework that was designed to enable a description and explanation of the processes involved in utterance production and interpretation. To this extent there has been a developing symbiotic relationship between pragmatic theories and empirical studies of language use. There are many recent examples of research that question the assertions that certain principles of communication are universal for instance (for example, Harris 1995 and Sarangi and Slembrouck 1992). Where these have been taken seriously by pragmaticians, however, tends to be in relation to studies that point to cross-cultural variations in patterns of language use (see, for example, Blum-Kulka et al. 1989). What research on gender and language use has shown in addition however is that there are intra-cultural variations in patterns of language use which appear to be based on gender-specific perceptions of what a normal conversation is, or gender-specific perceptions of what a particular linguistic choice might signify in a given context. Such studies take many forms however, and are based on a range of different assumptions about how language and gender interact, and how these two sets of phenomena might be theorised. As such they exist as a series of fragments at this stage, and the questions such research raises about current explanations of language use, the scope of certain pragmatic principles, and how to theorise the relationship between gender and language use have yet to be addressed.

Possibly because of this, the impact of research on gender and language use has not been strongly evident in pragmatics. As with many other disciplines the assumption within pragmatics has been that the central theories are essentially ungendered, but that they can be applied to studies that address gender. However, the question of how far the original theories that inform pragmatics are ungendered is open to question. For example, Rundquist (1992) raises this question when she applies a Gricean analysis to a corpus of data which includes interactions between children and their parents, and interactions between the parents. Reviewing this study Mey argues that her findings imply that:

> the classic theory of speech acts (as shaped by Grice and Searle) fails to recognise one of its own preconditions, the limited access to social power for women as compared to men . . . Such a breaking of maxims says less about their cognitive content or conversational importance in a given situation than about who is in control of that situation. (Mey 1993: 284)

Moreover, much of the work by Jennifer Coates questions the specifically masculine bias of original formulations of conversational structure by Conversation Analysts. The evidence Coates provides across a range of studies suggests that there seem to be measurable differences between male and female uses of language (see, for example, Coates 1997). This is evident in her studies of the process of turn-taking in informal conversation in which she argues that the original model of conversational structure was premised on a relatively narrow conceptualisation of conversation, and this seems to resemble the norms of male interaction, while ignoring the norms of female interaction. In her studies she points to evidence that there appears to be a quite different economy in force when women engage in informal conversation. As I indicate in Chapters 4 and 6, Janet Holmes makes similar points across a range of studies. These findings have many implications including the need to rethink the way in which differential usage and perception of speech acts is explained.

Studies of gender and language use call on pragmatic concepts in order to explore a range of different phenomena therefore, but they can be used to argue quite contradictory points. For example, some studies use pragmatics to argue that men and women use conversation for quite distinct ends, and are designed to re-evaluate feminine speech styles. Other studies have used pragmatics to argue that the speech of men and women is not significantly different in function (for example, Crawford 1995). There is currently, therefore, a need for an overview of this work that would allow the claims to be evaluated. In the final chapter I attempt such an overview. My point here however is to argue that irrespective of the diversity of this work, such studies raise a range of questions that pragmatics needs to engage with: specifically they suggest that gender plays such a fundamental role in language use that it would be untenable if a theory that claims to explain language use should ignore this factor.

As well as questions arising from pragmatic studies of gender and language use, feminist research generally poses questions that pragmatics should be able to address. For example, recent developments within feminist theory, have led to a move from a conceptualisation of gender as a social or cultural category, to a conceptualisation of gender as a verb (Eckert and McConnell-Ginet 1994). What this means in practical terms is a rejection of the methodologies that have characterised sociolinguistic studies in the past, where the use of specific language forms is correlated with factors related to the users, and where differences in language use are seen as arising from differences between language users' class, age or sex for example. Where gender is conceptualised as a verb, the use of specific language forms is seen as one way in which individuals construct themselves as more or less masculine or feminine. From this perspective individuals perform gender, and gender identity is perceived as an effect of language, rather than an *a priori* factor that determines linguistic behaviour. Pragmaticians need to consider whether they wish to, and indeed are able to, take part in current debates of this nature given that orthodox accounts (such as politeness theory for example) have tended to perceive identity as relatively fixed or else irrelevant. The question is then whether pragmatics can explain this form of meaning construction. I hope to show that a *feminist* pragmatics can.

NOTES

1 This extract comes from a programme entitled 'The Politics of Experience' which was screened by Channel Four as part of a series entitled *Ordinary People* in 1990.
2 I have followed Sperber and Wilson's (1986) convention of referring to the speaker as she and the hearer as he.

2

FEMINIST ACCOUNTS OF GENDER AND LANGUAGE USE

2.1 FEMINIST STUDIES: EXPOSING/EXAMINING/ REDRESSING GENDER INEQUALITIES

As I suggest in Chapter 1, it would be inappropriate to perceive feminist scholarship as a unified body of work where each piece of research neatly dovetails with the remainder to produce a single coherent theory of gender relations. I begin this chapter by arguing that it should not be assumed that this lack of coherence is either an accidental or a negative characteristic of feminist research. My aim in drawing attention to this heterogeneity is in order to provide a background for understanding why it is that feminist scholars do not address language or language use in a uniform way. The point I want to go on to make is that in spite of this diversity, and indeed, as I shall suggest later, possibly because of what this diversity indicates, feminist research that focuses on language use has much to gain from an engagement with pragmatics.

2.1.1   The diversity of feminist research

There is a great deal of evidence to suggest that feminist scholars have actively set out to embrace heterogeneity. For example, writing in 1986, on the subject of feminism and science, Harding argues strongly that feminism should be 'an open-ended evolving process of theory construction' (Harding 1986: 12). Rather than consisting of unified theories competing for master status, she suggests that feminism should remain open to new theoretical developments, be able to use tensions and contradictions productively, and be suspicious of apparently 'clear' solutions that have the effect of repressing dissonant elements (243). A more recent account is provided by Hennessy (1993), who interrogates the role of 'theory' in feminist research. She distinguishes between the notion of theory as a 'mode of intelligibility' and theory as a 'totalizing or master narrative' (7) in order to argue against the development of a feminist 'metanarrative'. Hennessy's point is that any analytical perspective is inevitably constrained by the specific historical conditions in which it was developed. To claim that a theory can transcend those conditions thus carries the risk that it will take on a spurious, unquestioned authority and its limitations may therefore be overlooked when it is applied. As she points out: 'Metanarrative escapes the critical gaze to the extent that it constitutes an (invisible) outside frame which establishes the terms of coherence for an empirical account' (7).

It could be argued then that the diversity that characterises feminist research is at least in part a function of the desire not to lose sight of the cultural and historical conditions that give rise to any theoretical standpoint, and the desire not to repress the tensions that arise from these different standpoints in the search for a spurious coherence. A corollary of this recognition of the dangers that arise from the adoption of an overgeneral theoretical framework is the feminist critique of universal categories such as 'woman'. As Lury (1995) has pointed out, much feminist debate has surrounded the question of whether it is valid to speak of 'womanhood' as though it referred to a set of experiences, behaviours or characteristics that was shared by all women:

> The acceptance of this historical definition of women as a universal category, it is argued, has the effect of excluding large numbers of women whose experiences are not made visible in this understanding of the social, including for example, Black women. (Lury 1995: 34)

Cameron (1998b: 17) argues that the problem with talking about women's experience in universal or global terms is that it has tended in practice to mean talking about the experience of the most privileged women as if it were shared by all women when clearly it is not.

The concern to embrace diversity has led some feminists to engage extensively with ideas generated by poststructuralist and postmodernist approaches which question 'essentialist' notions of gender. Essentialism is defined by Cameron (1998b: 15) as a 'belief in essences', which she goes on to describe as: 'the conviction that there is some essential, fundamental and fixed property or set of properties which all members of a particular category must share, and by which they are distinguished from the members of other categories' (15). Perceiving 'men' and 'women' as distinct categories whose members are 'essentially' different may be explained as either an effect of biology (sex) or of culture (gender). Cameron illustrates this distinction by referring to the argument proposed by some feminists that the psychological development of boys differs from girls. According to this theory, because women are more likely to be involved in childcare than are men, girls are more likely to be cared for and have their primary relationship with an adult of the same gender (usually their mother). And because of this, it is argued, girls tend to develop a more relational sense of self than boys do. A difference such as this is seen as 'essential' in that although childcare arrangements are entirely social phenomena (it is not a direct effect of biology that women tend to be the primary caregivers of young children) they nevertheless produce systematic and stable differences in the psychological disposition of girls and boys (16).

The anti-essentialist position calls into question conceptualisations of gender as characterised by a set of stable qualities that are acquired by women or men, whether these are biological or social in origin. A well argued example, that I discuss in more detail in Chapter 4, is found in Crawford's (1995) analysis of women's assertive behaviour. She points out that although 'unassertiveness' has been seen as a 'quality' that is characteristic of women, there is evidence to suggest that avoidance of assertiveness may be better explained as an adaptive choice. Drawing on a series of studies of gender and language use, she comments:

> When women were asked about their expectations of how others might judge their assertive behaviour, they expected moderately favourable judgements from other women, and less favourable ones from men . . . Thus these women were aware that women's assertion is not always positively regarded by others, and in fact their expectations accurately reflect the results of the studies I have described. As we have seen, there is no convincing evidence that women do not know how to speak assertively. (Crawford 1995: 68)

Her point is, then, that women are able to produce the type of behaviour that is generally categorised as 'assertive' but choose not to where they are aware that it will not be effective and may, moreover, have negative consequences.

More extreme proponents of the anti-essentialist position take the view that it is not just characteristics of gender that are unstable but that gender identity has no existence outside of the acts we perform. I discuss this position, which is characterised by the work of Judith Butler, in more detail in section 2.1.2 below. At this stage I consider the implications for the way in which gender relations are addressed. For example, as I indicated in Chapter 1, a consequence of assuming that 'womanhood' may be an fundamentally unstable concept, has been to question whether the oppression of women can be conceptualised in general terms if 'being a woman' cannot be perceived in general terms. As Hennessy argues, this has implications for the emancipatory aims of feminism:

> The question is whether postmodern knowledges, which have been so important in the development of western feminism's challenge to the humanist subject and rational-empiricist foundations of knowledge, have also made appeals to the objective condition of women's lives untenable as the ground for feminist theory. (Hennessy 1993: 68–9)

On the one hand, as Hennessy comments, postmodernism has been seen by materialist feminists as 'a powerful critical force for exposing the relationship between language, the subject and the unequal distribution of social resources' (5). On the other, postmodernism raises particularly difficult problems for materialist feminism. If gender identity is perceived as unstable, where does this leave a political stance that presupposes an ontologically grounded feminist subject? As Harding argues: 'Once "woman" is deconstructed into "women", and "gender" is recognized to have no fixed referents, feminism itself dissolves as a theory that can reflect the voice of a naturalized or essentialized speaker' (1986: 246). There are many works that have raised and addressed this question over the last decade or so by teasing out areas of conflict while avoiding the imposition of a master-narrative. Butler and Scott (1992), Harding (1986), Hennessy (1993), McNay (1992), for example, are all concerned to argue that the emancipatory aims of feminism should not be compromised by a preoccupation with theory and each represents an attempt to question essentialist notions of gender without foreclosing on the varied and fruitful directions a feminist interrogation of gender relations might take.

2.1.2   Feminism within the academy

As well as arising from a conscious rejection of metanarrative, the heterogeneity of feminism also arises from its unique relationship with other academic disciplines. For example, on the one hand, a given piece of feminist research, just like any other form of research, is both constrained and made possible by its relationship with the specific concerns of current scholarship in its own field: that is, feminism. On the other hand a given piece of feminist research is also constrained and enabled by its relationship with the concerns of current scholarship in the mainstream discipline that shares its specific focus. Such research as well as being 'feminist' therefore also engages with the way in which 'culture', 'the psyche', 'society' or 'language' are conceptualised and studied in, for example, cultural studies, psychology, sociology and linguistics. Any example of feminist research tends to be involved in debate on at least two fronts, therefore: with current feminist concerns and with the concerns of the mainstream discipline that addresses the same phenomena.

Celia Lury (1995) illustrates what this means for feminist scholarship in her account of the relationship between feminism and cultural studies. She points out that this relationship has been described in terms of an 'affinity or an 'overlap' of interests' (33), and her work foregrounds its dynamic and changing character. She argues for example that at the time of writing: 'current feminist cultural studies are repeatedly held back by the continued dominance of ungendered understandings of culture' and goes on to substantiate this argument by considering the ways in which conceptual and methodological issues are 'inextricably intertwined' (33). A similar argument is put forward by Kitzinger (1998) in her discussion of the relationship between feminism and social psychology. I briefly summarise both these arguments in order to illustrate some concerns of feminist scholars, and to show how such work involves a richly symbiotic relationship with mainstream disciplines.

2.1.2.1 Feminism and cultural studies

Lury's (1995) argument is that scholars within mainstream cultural studies tend to assume that 'culture' as a concept, is gender-neutral and therefore the models that mainstream scholars have developed in order to account for cultural phenomena are also essentially ungendered. As a result, conceptual categories such as *modernism* and *authorship* and the distinction between high and low culture are, as Lury points out, 'largely developed at an abstract level without reference to gender, only adding in "women" as a matter of historical description' (36). Lury argues that this belated concern with gender constitutes 'additive feminism' and she suggests that such an approach leads to a number of problems. For example, she argues that each of the cultural categories pointed to above is already predicated on historically specific conceptualisations of gender relations. One of the more accessible illustrations of this is the traditional predication of authorship on a masculine rather than feminine subject. As Kaplan (1998) has pointed out this results in different significances being attached to a female subject's use of 'high' language compared to a male subject's use of such language. As a result terms such as *poet* or *author* have different implications when they are applied to men or women as social subjects. Lury adds:

> This means, for example, that while much feminist cultural studies has been concerned to explore the interrelationship between gender and culture it has done so without explicitly problematising what is meant by the cultural itself. (Lury 1995: 35)

Lury addresses the implications for theories of identity of recognising that cultural concepts are already gendered. In the process she draws on Butler's (1993) work which rejects essentialist notions of sex and gender and which argues instead that identities are characterised by instability.

As Lury points out, Butler's argument is that identities are not at any point 'fixed' but are achieved only through the repeated performance of specific acts (I discuss this in relation to linguistic acts later in this chapter). She asserts however that this should not be taken to mean that, in carrying out these acts, individuals are free to create any identity they wish. Lury's point in drawing on Butler's argument is to suggest that although, according to this view, identity appears to be constantly in the process of creation in the sense that it consists only in the ongoing and repeated behaviours of an individual, there are constraints on what a given behaviour might signify. Lury offers the following summary of Butler's argument:

> She [Butler] thus points to the importance of locating what she calls the 'conditions of intelligibility' within which individuals come to assume a sex and [she] seeks to relate them to what she calls the heterosexual hegemony or imperative. In this way she points to the importance of recognising that culture, or what she calls the conditions of intelligibility, is not a gender-neutral resource for self-transformation. (Lury 1995: 41)

Lury's point is that if, as she proposes, that set of phenomena categorised as 'culture' is already gendered, and if, as Butler argues, it is culture that gives meaning to the acts of identity performance, given the different significance of males and females within a culture, it is questionable whether women can be seen to possess an identity in the same way as men. She goes on to state:

> The ability to be an individual, including the ability to own an identity as a resource, to display it as a performance, is thus necessarily gendered. But how it is gendered, and how this process of gendering is also raced and classed, can only be determined through investigation. (42)

My outline of Lury's argument introduces some of the concerns of feminism that I develop in the following section of this chapter when I consider how linguistic acts come to acquire meaning. The outline also introduces some of the issues surrounding the feminist problematisation of identity that I will relate to pragmatic theories in later chapters. At this stage however, this account of Lury's work serves as an illustration of the way in which feminist scholarship engages in two levels of debate. It shows how on the one hand Lury is engaged in debates within cultural studies about how culture can be conceptualised, and how existing concepts need to be problematised. On the other hand, she is also engaged with questions about what it means to carry out *feminist* research that addresses the cultural. The pertinence of Lury's argument at this stage, then, lies in her claim that feminist research that sets out to account for gendered identities needs to critique the ostensibly gender-neutral assumptions about culture and identity which underlie the mainstream discipline. A similar argument is put forward by Kitzinger (1998) in relation to the discipline of social psychology. She also points to the problems of 'additive feminism', and like Lury illustrates the problems that arise when feminist research accepts uncritically the premises that underlie mainstream academic approaches. Specifically, she contrasts the 'additive feminist' approach with critical feminist approaches to the psychological.

2.1.2.2 Feminism and social psychology

Kitzinger points out that feminist research in social psychology 'has fallen into line with both the individualism and the positivist empiricist methods of the mainstream of the discipline' (1998: 201). She shows for example how the notion of 'diagnosis', which is grounded in a positivist paradigm, has been central to mainstream psychology, and argues that feminist research, while questioning specific diagnoses, has often failed to question the validity of diagnosis *per se*. Kitzinger cites the work of Phyllis Chesler to substantiate her claim that feminists have long realised that 'there are systematic gender biases both in the diagnosis of "mental illness" and in psychological definitions of what counts as "mental health" (202). She points to Chesler's evidence that women have been hospitalised for transgressing norms of feminine behaviour including 'women who disobeyed their husbands or who bore children outside marriage; lesbians; and women who were unhappy and refused to do housework after the birth of a child' (203). Kitzinger's point is that much feminist research in psychology has centred around demonstrating that such diagnoses are 'not empirically valid' or that 'they fail to take into account the social context within which the individual is embedded' (203). Kitzinger's point, however, is that feminist research has generally failed to critique mainstream assumptions about the *role* of diagnosis:

> On the whole feminist psychology accepts the diagnostic enterprise in principle but argues with the sexist biases which mar it in practice. Empirically valid diagnoses, which pay due attention to the social context within which the individual is coping, would be entirely acceptable to most feminist psychologists. (Kitzinger 1998: 203)

Kitzinger contrasts this mainstream feminist stance with a critical feminist approach which challenges and deconstructs the principle of the diagnostic enterprise itself and which argues that this enterprise is 'based upon a culturally specific, historically contingent and socially constructed notion of what it means to be a 'healthy' human being' (203).

Like Lury, then, Kitzinger here is engaged in a debate that is enabled and constrained by current concerns within the mainstream discipline (that is, social psychology) and by current feminist concerns. And, like Lury, she is working to develop not just the direction of inquiry into issues of gender within the mainstream discipline but also within current feminist scholarship. These two examples indicate something of the scope of feminist scholarship in that they constitute evidence of the way in which feminism is fed by and feeds into a range of mainstream disciplines, and is able to develop insights gained from different areas of academic inquiry. They also indicate something of the centrality of feminism in that they illustrate how the ideas that arise from an interrogation of gender are of concern to all areas of academic thought. In Chapter 7 I develop the claims made by feminist scholars who critique the apparently ungendered assumptions that underlie mainstream academic work when I consider the questions raised by research on gender and language use in relation to mainstream pragmatics. Moreover, in the chapters that follow, I show that while identity generally, and gender identity in particular, have been interrogated by feminist theory these concepts have so far remained under-theorised within pragmatics. At this stage however the above illustrations of feminist scholarship function as an indication of two strands of feminist concern, and are discussed in order to indicate that diversity within feminism arises in part from its symbiotic relationship with other disciplines as well as from a concern to avoid over-general theorisations of gender.

2.1.3   Common concerns of feminist research

What I hope is apparent from this brief discussion is that because of the range of mainstream disciplines it engages with, and given the diverse interests of feminist theory itself, there are few blanket claims that might be made about feminist research. As I indicate in Chapter 1, possibly what these general claims amount to are the minimal observations that (1) all feminist research focuses on some aspect of gender, and (2) all feminist research has a political agenda in that it is aimed at exposing, examining or redressing gender inequalities. Therefore, although the forms and aims of this enterprise can be so diverse and apparently contradictory that they may appear bewildering to those who are unfamiliar with feminism, these two elements seem to be common to all feminist approaches. A final example, which points to a recent development in feminism, will illustrate this point.

The work I have discussed so far in this chapter is predicated on the assumption that feminists need to question the development and use of conceptual categories that are implicated in the construction of gender. It is evident that both Lury and Kitzinger take these categories to be significant in that the argument proposed by each is predicated on the assumption that there is a link between acts of categorisation and the various ways in which women are subordinated. There are feminist ap-proaches that reject this assumption however. For example, 'new feminism', as it is advocated by Natasha Walter, dismisses the preoccupation with consciousness and subjectivity that characterises much feminist scholarship, describing it as irrelevant to the emancipation of women. Walter argues that new feminism 'must unpick the tight link that feminism in the seventies made between our personal and political lives' (1998: 4). She goes on to make the point that 'identifying the personal and the political in too abso-lute and unyielding a way has led feminism to a dead end. This generation of feminists must free itself from the spectre of political correctness' (4).

However, in spite of this rejection of one feminist approach, and in spite of the fact that Walter acknowledges that women in the developed world now enjoy many previously denied freedoms, her aims, like those of the scholars discussed above, are still primarily political. Walter points out for example that:

> [B]eside women's freedom lies another truth: the truth of their continuing inequality. The constraints that operate upon women are still fierce, and those constraints can come as a terrible shock to those insouciant young women as they move out of school and into their adult lives. (Walter 1998: 3)

Even though Walter's proposed methods for redressing gender inequity are different to that of her predecessors and even though she sets out to reject many of the conceptualisations of gender that have preoccupied feminist theorists for three decades, the common concerns of feminism remain evident. Just as her predecessors have done, Walter cites a range of evidence that indicates the extent and scope of gendered inequalities. She points out for example that at the time of writing 40 per cent of women earn less that £150 per week compared with 10 per cent of men, and observes that:

> When a woman has children she loses, typically, more than half of the money she would have made throughout her lifetime if she had not had children; but having children typically makes no difference to a man's lifetime income. (3)

In spite of acknowledging that women have made many gains, Walter goes on to argue that women's power is still a potential rather than a reality when '93 out of 100 university professors are men; 96 out of 100 general surgeons; 96 out of 100 company directors' (3). Although, therefore, because of its rejection of the argument that the personal is political, the concerns of 'new feminism' are inevitably quite distinct from the concerns of many other feminists, the general aim of emancipation and a focus on gender remain common ground.

2.2 FEMINIST APPROACHES TO LANGUAGE USE

Because of the diversity that characterises feminist research in general, it follows that the ways in which feminist scholars engage with language use are equally diverse. This is partly because it is not just scholarship within linguistic disciplines that addresses issues of language use. Language use is addressed by disciplines as diverse as sociology, medicine, cultural studies, anthropology, politics, law, and science. For example, in surveying the relationship between gender and science Harding analyses a series of texts that rationalise and chart the development of current scientific methodologies. It is their linguistic nature that allows her to argue points such as the following:

> Even in such an abbreviated form, this familiar story of the emergence of modern science provides clues to the complex and contradictory meanings science has for modern cultures. We can follow these clues if we treat the story not as a transparent window into history but as an opaque surface that has its own forms and significances. (Harding 1986: 207)

And as Wilkinson and Kitzinger's (1995) collection shows there has, since the late 1980s been a general 'turn to language' across the range of social sciences. Burman and Parker justify this move in relation to social psychology in the following terms:

> Language contains the most basic categories that we use to understand ourselves; affecting the way we act as women or as men (in, for example, the sets of arguments that are given about the nature of gender difference deployed to justify inequality), and reproducing the way we define our cultural identity (in, for example, the problems and solutions we negotiate when we try and define who we are as a member of a minority group). (1993: 1)

Much of the variation within feminist approaches to language arises out of disciplinary differences, therefore, in that, clearly, studies of language and gender within linguistics are informed by linguistic debates and aim primarily to say something about language, while of course studies of language and gender within cultural studies are informed by that discipline and aim, ultimately, to say something about culture.

There are also however differences in the aims and focus of feminist studies of language within linguistics. As Wodak (1997a) shows, feminist researchers have long been concerned both with language as a system and with language as behaviour, and this is evident in their concern with two basic questions concerning gender: 'How are women represented in the existing language system? How does the linguistic behaviour of the group of women differ from that of men?' (8). Researchers concerned with the first question take it as axiomatic that language 'encodes' the values of a culture. As Cameron puts it:

> Many strands in the feminist critique of language have concerned themselves with what languages tell their users and their learners about gender and about women. On the whole, feminists have concluded that our languages are sexist. They represent or 'name' the world from a masculine viewpoint and in accordance with stereotyped beliefs about women, men and the relationship between them. (Cameron 1998b: 8)

45

How languages come to be sexist, what constitutes sexism, and how women come to be disadvantaged by the use of language remains an issue of controversy however, and where contrasting accounts occur these often arise from differences in the way that scholars theorise the relationship between social and linguistic phenomena. This is also the case with researchers who are concerned with the second question. For example, in any collection of studies that focus on differential uses of language, there will be those that take gender as a determinant of linguistic difference and those that see gender as an effect of language use (see for example Coates 1993, Tannen 1993, Roman et al. 1994 and Wodak 1997b). However, as collections such those of Hall and Bucholtz (1995), Bergvall et al. (1996) and Kotthoff and Wodak (1997) indicate, there is a recent tendency to focus more on the latter. Although therefore much has been written that suggests gender makes a difference to linguistic behaviour, how and why this should be remains controversial and much of this controversy is to do with differing theories of the social.

One basic difference between these theories is captured by the distinction between materialist and poststructuralist accounts. Materialist feminists across disciplines tend to address language use as symptomatic of existing social inequalities, and language use is often addressed from this perspective in terms of the ideologies it gives access to. From this perspective, language use is seen as *reflecting* and arising out of the social. Where an approach is premised on a poststructuralist or post-Foucauldian conceptualisation of language-in-use (that is, discourse) it is often assumed that, in contrast, language use affects, or even, it has been argued, constructs the social. Both these approaches are based on complex theoretical frameworks and it is beyond the scope of this current discussion to go into them in any real depth. However, since discourse theory in particular informs a great deal of current feminist research on language use, and in particular informs some of the studies that I go on to discuss in relation to pragmatics, it is worth at this point distinguishing between the premises, key concepts and applications of these two approaches.

2.2.1 Language and society in discourse theory

Mills (1997), who provides a comprehensive and accessible introduction to the various uses of the term *discourse*, makes the point that post-structural uses of the term are predicated on a distinction between the notion of discourse as (1) an overarching theory that is called on to explain how we come to have the beliefs and knowledges that are characteristic of a given society at a given point in history, and (2) the idea that there are distinct ways of speaking that inscribe sets of beliefs and values that can be categorised as 'discourses'. She cites Foucault's comments on his own varied use of the term:

Instead of gradually reducing the rather fluctuating meaning of the word 'discourse', I believe I have in fact added to its meanings: treating it sometimes as the general domain of all statements, sometimes as an individualizable group of statements, and sometimes as a regulated practice that accounts for a number of statements. (Foucault cited in Mills 1997: 6)

An example of an 'individualisable' group of statements proposed by Coates (1998: 301) is the group that would be labelled 'conservative' in contemporary society. What makes this group a discourse is that they are premised on a shared set of beliefs about the value of preserving the *status quo*. Coates cites Holloway's definition of such grouping as 'a system of statements which cohere around common meanings and values' (301).

2.2.1.1   Courtroom dialogue: a discourse 'type'

The discourse of the courtroom provides another example of a discourse as an individualisable group of statements and indicates how conceptualising language use in terms of discourse 'types' not only allows a way of explaining the value and meaning of words within a given context, but also explains how these values and meanings are connected to the social roles taken by the individuals who use them. The following extract from an article on pragmatics by Jenny Thomas provides a useful illustration of this form of discourse. It is a dialogue that occurred in a magistrates' court in which the defendant, a young man, was unrepresented. He was accused of resisting arrest and hitting a police officer. He had already admitted hitting the policeman, but claimed in mitigation that the policeman had hit him first. The data is reconstructed from solicitors' notes.

Court Official:	How do you plead – guilty or not guilty?
Defendant:	(Silence)
Court Official:	Did you do it or not?
Defendant:	Well, I did hit him, yes.
Court Official:	So that's 'guilty' then.
Defendant:	Yes, sir. (Thomas 1985: 774)

This extract illustrates the Foucauldian notion that a discourse can be seen as a 'regulated practice which accounts for a number of statements' in that the dialogue is constrained to such an extent that any deviation from what is sanctioned by the discourse might constitute a punishable offence. This example therefore shows one somewhat extreme way in which the practices that constitute a discourse are regulated. Other discourse types, such as mother-child interactions or seminar discussions, are also constrained but less overtly regulated.

The courtroom dialogue is a useful illustration of the regulated nature of discourse types in that it is possible to point to the constraints on (1) what the words signify, (2) what effects they have and (3) who can say what to whom. Compare, for example, what the word *guilty* signifies in the above courtroom context with what the word would signify in talk between friends over lunch where the topic is the choice of dessert. The word *guilty* in an utterance such as *I always feel so guilty when I choose this* in such a context both signifies something quite distinct from the word in the courtroom context and has different effects. Guilt in the context of choosing a sticky pudding does not generally lead to decisions about which court procedures will follow. Moreover the dessert eater, unlike the defendant, can chose to remain silent, or can refer to their behaviour using different words such as *I'm going to really regret this*. Alternatively the other interlocutor can say *You're going to really regret that*. The interlocutors in the court do not have this degree of choice.

2.2.1.2 Subjectivity

This constraint on who can say what to whom arises from a central tenet of discourse theory: that speakers must, in the very act of speaking, inevitably take up one of the subject positions made available by the specific discourses they engage in. The person who fills the role of defendant in the courtroom extract might, in other circumstances, for example in a talk with friends in the car park ten minutes later, or six months later in a conversation with his mother, or at any other point when he is not taking on the role of defendant in a courtroom, refer to his behaviour in a range of different ways. However when he takes on the role of defendant, he is taking on a specific subject position within a courtroom discourse. He can therefore only use the terms *guilty* or *not guilty* at the moment he is asked by the court official how he pleads. He does not have the option of remaining silent or of talking about something else instead. Equally, someone who does not have a subject position within a courtroom discourse simply cannot speak in that context, because they do not have a subject position within the discourse that sanctions their talk. Members of the press, for example, may be present during this dialogue, but they are not sanctioned to intervene in it.

What is suggested by this approach is that although any given individual may speak in a range of ways, this range is governed by the subject position that the individual takes on at a particular moment, and, since the subject position is socially constructed, what can be said is socially constrained. What this has been taken to imply is that as individuals we may take on any number of roles in our daily lives, and that which roles we take on depend on which discourses we are able to engage in. Most of these roles are not as overtly constrained as courtroom discourse, where transgressions can in certain circumstances carry the threat of being charged with contempt of court. Norman Fairclough makes the additional point that the subject positions we take up when we engage in discourses do not only constrain what we can do and say: they also provide the conditions that enable us to act and speak meaningfully. He illustrates this in relation to the discourses used in a range of institutional settings:

> The discourse types of the classroom set up subject positions for teachers and pupils, and it is only by 'occupying' these positions that one becomes a teacher or pupil. Occupying a subject position is essentially a matter of doing (or not doing) certain things, in line with the discoursal rights and obligations of teachers and pupils – what each is allowed and required to say, and not allowed or required to say, within that discourse type. (Fairclough 1989: 38)

Since it is also axiomatic to this model that each discourse constrains what a given language item will mean (*guilt* in a courtroom/*guilt* in psychoanalysis), what this approach also suggests is that when an individual takes up a specific form of language use she is also taking on a particular way of engaging with the world. As Coates argues, 'There is no neutral discourse: whenever we speak we have to choose between different systems of meaning, different sets of values' (1998: 302). What this indicates is that discourse theory addresses both questions asked by feminist researchers referred to by Wodak: How are women represented in the existing language system? How does the linguistic behaviour of the group of women differ from that of men? The possibilities of representation arise from the specific discourse that is being used, as do the possibilities of what can be said by whom. What Coates, along with many other researchers, then goes on to do with this insight is to show how it is implicated in the construction of different 'selves'. Coates uses it to show how women in friendly conversation actively construct themselves as 'women' through their language choices.

When these implications of discourse theory are considered, it is not difficult to see how the notion of discourse might offer insights into the relationship between language and social identity. If, in the course of our lives, we take on a series of linguistic 'roles' it raises the question of whether I, for example, am being my 'true' self when I use the different forms of language available to me when I take up the subject position of 'mother' or 'friend' or when I take up the subject position of 'university lecturer'. For discourse theorists, this raises the question of whether one way of speaking can be seen as more representative of a given individual's 'identity' than another, and this in turn then raises questions about the stability of the notion: is identity any more than the range of subject positions an individual can take up in within the discourses they have access to?

2.2.2   Language and power: Two models

Coates argues that one of the advantages of theorising language from this perspective is that the concept 'discourse' accommodates the 'value laden nature of language' (1998: 302). She also makes the point that these values are often 'hegemonic' in the sense that they serve existing power relations by appearing to be 'commonsense'. It is worth at this point comparing the discourse approach with the materialist conceptualisation of hegemony as an effect of ideology. Mills (1997) provides a useful comparison when she draws out the practical implications of theorising the relation between language and society as an issue of ideology and theorising it as an issue of discourse.

Mills uses as an example the way in which each approach would address the issue of sexism in language, and cites as a focus the tendency within the British media to refer to male presenters of weather forecasts on television as 'weathermen' while female equivalents are referred to as 'weather-girls'. As she points, out the former are assigned adult status, while the latter are referred to as children. She goes on to assert that this is a common strategy within sexism whereby women who are in a position of equality with men are represented linguistically as holding a less powerful position (1997: 43). She then shows how ideological critics and discourse theorists differ in relation to their approach to such language use by pointing out that although they would agree on which statements count as sexist, within an ideological view, sexism would be seen as a form of false consciousness (a spurious representation of *real* gender relations), while in a discourse theory model, sexism is the site where gender relations are constructed and contested. Mills goes on to argue that discourse (in its sense as 'a general domain of all statements') is 'the arena where some males are sanctioned in their attempts to negotiate a powerful position for themselves in relation to women, but it is also the site where women can contest or collaborate with those moves (45). One basic distinction between the two approaches therefore is that seeing language use in terms of ideology would entail seeing an utterance as a way of *representing* gender relations, seeing it in terms of discourse would entail seeing an utterance as a way of *realising* gender relations. This distinction has further implications for the way that identity is theorised, and again, it is worth drawing this distinction out at this stage because of its relevance to current feminist concerns and to pragmatic approaches to gender and language use in particular.

Theories of ideology that adopt Althusser's (1971) notion of interpellation (the process by which individuals come to recognise their place in society) would argue that, by accepting sexism within language, social subjects are called upon to recognise themselves as taking up a position within a hierarchised system of gendered differentiation. And it is through repeated acts of recognition that the hierarchy comes into being. Butler describes the process thus:

> In the famous scene of interpellation that Althusser provides, the policeman hails the passer-by with 'hey you there' and the one who

recognizes himself and turns around (nearly everyone) to answer the call does not, strictly speaking, pre-exist the call. Althusser's scene is, therefore, fabulous, but what could it mean? The passer-by turns precisely to acquire a certain identity, one purchased, as it were with the price of guilt. The act of recognition becomes an act of constitution: the address animates the subject into existence. (Butler 1997: 24–5)

It is in this way, as Mills argues, 'sexism forces subjects into an acceptance of the *status quo* and of prevalent views of women as inferior . . . to men' (1997: 43–4). The act of recognising oneself as the subject of sexist language therefore has implications for one's sense of identity according to this approach: an ideological analysis would see women as victims of sexist language, unable to intervene in the process whereby they are op-pressed.

In contrast, as Mills points out, discourse theorists question the passivity that such a process implies:

The debate around sexism has been a struggle to change words, a struggle over language, at the same time it has been a struggle over legitimacy and about who has the right to define the usage of language as well as who has the right to decide what is studied in schools and universities. (Mills 1997: 44)

For feminist discourse theorists, the role of language in the construction of social categories in general and its role in the construction of identity in particular are seen to be key areas of gender conflict. An example of scholarship that explores this area is Hepworth and Griffin's (1995) meticulously argued account of the development of the term *anorexia nervosa* in which they consider the conditions within which a broad and diverse set of cultural and semantic phenomena came to be categorised as constituting a specific syndrome. And as they also show, this categorisation process has a range of material effects. They describe their agenda thus:

We are not engaged in a search for the causes of AN [anorexia nervosa]. Rather, we are examining the construction of the category AN and the discursive practices and subject positions which are made available through the complex process of that construction. (Hepworth and Griffin 1995: 69)

They go on to argue that the treatment of anorexia nervosa as a 'pre-given medico-psychological entity' constructs the range of problems experienced by women who have been diagnosed as 'anorexic' as grounded in, and arising from, the individual concerned (83). As such it suppresses the role of socio-cultural factors in producing these problems. As they point out 'the concepts we use and the ways in which we use them are equally important, since they shape what we (can) say and do about women's relationship to food and eating' (82). For Hepworth and Griffin then, to challenge language use is to challenge power relations in that it is through language that power relations are realised.

There are alternatives to the ideology and the discourse based accounts of the relationship between language and power. Some works, for example Fairclough (1989) and Fairclough and Wodak (1997) attempt to integrate the two positions in the development of a critical approach to language, and Hennessy (1993) attempts to build on the insights into gender and identity offered by postmodernist and poststructuralist accounts by synthesising them with a materialist approach. From these perspectives, language tends to be seen as symptomatic of the social but it is also seen as having material effects on the culture to the extent that language use is implicated in the construction of identity and in the realisation of power relations. The point I want to make in the following section is that adopting the ideology approach, the discourse approach or integrated approaches will have different methodological consequences for research on language and gender. I also want argue however that in spite of this, each approach has something to take from pragmatics.

2.3   WHY FEMINIST STUDIES OF GENDER AND LANGUAGE USE NEED PRAGMATICS

In this section I discuss two feminist studies that address language use. In section 2.3.1 I discuss an example of feminist research into audience reception of media texts that addresses language use in the form of interview data in order to explore the ideological impact of television light entertainment programmes. In 2.3.2 I discuss an example of feminist research in social psychology which analyses the speech of children in order to explore the impact of discourses of the body on the construction of identity. Language use in the first constitutes a medium for accessing the object of analysis while language use in the second constitutes the object of analysis. In the former, it is the material (ideas, thoughts, perceptions, interpretations and so on) that language makes available to the analyst that is foregrounded, in the latter, it is the materiality of language use itself that is foregrounded. The aim of my discussion is to illustrate the limitations that result in each case from the absence of a pragmatic perspective. In particular I want to point to two premises that appear to result from a failure to problematise meaning generation: the assumption that the meanings the analyst finds in her linguistic data are self-evident, and the assumption that the processes of meaning construction are self-evident whether these are the processes of interpretation that the analyst is involved in or whether they are the processes of interpretation that her subjects are involved in. In claiming that such assumptions are evident in feminist analyses of linguistic data, and arguing that they have unwanted consequences, I hope to illustrate why a pragmatic perspective is needed in studies of language use. This is particularly pertinent given the number of feminist studies that currently focus on language use across disciplines. Because of this, I have selected two studies that are outside the discipline of linguistics in order to show that the 'turn to language' that has occurred across the social sciences and the humanities generally and which feminist scholars within these areas appear to have found particularly useful can be weakened by under-theorised models of language use. My aim in selecting studies outside of the discipline of linguistics is also to illustrate the relevance of pragmatics across disciplines.

I should also point out that my selection of these specific studies is based primarily on the ease with which they allow me to point to the issues that arise when studies that address linguistic material fail to problematise language use. This is not to suggest that these two studies have nothing of interest to say about language and gender, but rather that although they ask some useful and insightful questions their methodologies do not allow them to substantiate the answers they propose to these questions. Partly my choice of these two studies has been determined by the way in which these two writers openly acknowledge the problems they face in their research, in that this, therefore, allows me to point to issues that are of interest from a pragmatic perspective with a minimum of explanation.

2.3.1 Language use as access: An example from media studies

The turn to language within the social sciences and the humanities has led on the one hand to the problematisation of the language of socio-cultural texts (the language use as object approach). On the other it has led to a focus on linguistic data such as interview material and transcriptions of naturally occurring talk where this material is analysed for the access it provides to other phenomena (the language use as access approach). In this section I follow a trajectory within media analysis that has tended to adopt this latter approach. Within media analysis and film studies (traditionally quite separate academic enterprises) an engagement with language arose from a growing interest in ethnographic approaches in that such approaches are characterised by a focus on interviews with audiences and on other linguistic representations of audience experience (see Moores 1993, 1994 and Graddol and Boyd-Barrett 1994 for useful surveys of this shift in focus). The growth of interest in audience experience itself can be traced to a paradigm shift evident in media analyses at the beginning of the 1980s which was directly related to the problematisation of language. This shift (which is traced by Collins 1990) hinged on the recognition that cultural texts, whether they be Hollywood films, television soap operas or newspapers are, like any other texts, polysemic. The term 'cultural text' in this context refers to the product that is categorised as 'a film', 'a television programme' or 'a newspaper article', and which is the result of a process that brings together linguistic, visual and aural phenomena. The recognition that cultural texts are polysemic tends to be explained in two ways. On the one hand it has been seen as arising from the premise that the significance of a given sentence, visual image or sound is inevitably open to interpretation in that there is never a simple one to one fit between a signifier and a signified. On the other hand, texts are seen as polysemic because any given representation in a film or a television programme draws on the juxtaposition of distinct forms (visual, aural, linguistic) and these forms do not necessarily cohere to produce a unitary meaning (see Meinhof 1994 for a clear summary of this argument). At the time, the recognition of textual polysemy was a particularly difficult idea to assimilate for those strands of media analysis that were grounded in a materialist framework . This was because such studies had often been premised on a strongly deterministic model of media effects, which took as axiomatic the existence of a single, text-immanent meaning. Collins puts the case thus:

> The dominant ideology thesis attributes to a unified body of erroneous ideas – ideology – causal status in what is defined as a systematic and pervasive mystification of people's understanding of society and social relations. The mass media are customarily understood to be at least a major agency, and often the decisive agency, in the propagation and reproduction of ideology. Implicit in the dominant ideology thesis is a notion of a strong media effect. (Collins 1990: 3)

Within this early work therefore 'the media' tended to be conceptualised as a monolithic entity that disseminated hegemonic messages throughout a given society, perpetuating and legitimising existing power relations. This process was perceived to be sufficiently automatic for it later to be termed the 'hypodermic model' of media effects. Although the use of this term implies a lack of sophistication that is not really justified, it is certainly evident that this strongly deterministic view of media effects became increasingly untenable as a result of the growing recognition that media texts are polysemic.

The acknowledgement of textual polysemy has had a number of practical consequences for media analysis. For example, although an analyst might argue very convincingly that a film or television programme carries a specific ideological message, if the textual phenomena that constitute the film can have a range of meanings the relevance of pointing to just one reading becomes questionable. This has given rise to a range of questions: What status does an analyst's reading of a media product have if alternative readings are also possible? And if audiences have to do some sort of interpretative work when they produce one rather than another

reading of a media text, can they be perceived as simply the passive recipients of the hegemonic messages an analyst has discerned within the
text? This line of questioning has led towards a reconceptualisation of the
audience within media studies and in particular it has precipitated a change
of focus in media analysis so that the question of what 'real' audiences
actually do with media texts has become increasingly significant. Audience
interviews have become one way in which this issue is addressed and
throughout these developments within media analysis, questions surrounding gender raised by feminist scholarship have both fed into and built
on this turn towards the use of linguistic data.

One example of feminist interest in this issue can be seen in the work
of Jackie Stacey, who focuses on film. Within film studies the developing
interest in textual polysemy did not lead to a focus on audience reception
as quickly as it did within media studies. Many feminist film scholars
tended to address this issue from a poststructuralist perspective, drawing
on Lacanian and Foucauldian accounts of discourse (see for example the
articles in Pribram 1988). Such studies aimed to uncover the range of discourses evident in a film, and to theorise spectatorship in terms of the
subject positions that these discourses made available to audiences. To this
extent, although it was recognised that different audiences would respond
to and understand a film text in different ways, audiences were addressed
primarily as theoretical constructs within such studies. In an article that
traces the development of her own engagement with film, Stacey describes
her dissatisfaction with this type of approach in the following way:

> While convinced by many of the feminist criticisms of the patriarchal
> character of Hollywood cinema, I saw three main problems with this
> approach: the universalisms of its claims (especially those based on
> psychoanalysis); the emphasis on sexual difference as the central (and often
> only) signifier of cinematic meanings; and the dismissal of audience (in
> favour of text) as having anything important to say about popular cinema.
> (Stacey 1995: 98)

Stacey's account describes how she came to question this 'dismissal of
audience' and the assumptions about 'textual determinism' that tended to
dominate film studies and how she instead turned to a consideration of
what spectators bring to films from their own backgrounds. In particular
she illustrates her interest in the way that spectators' cultural backgrounds
might inform their readings of films.

Stacey is, however, conscious of the methodological problems such an
approach gives rise to, and in particular is concerned with the question
of what status audience accounts of film might have and what they can
actually tell the analyst about a given film. Moreover, Stacey acknowledges
the fact that, because these accounts are *linguistic* representations of
audience experience, there is some question about how they should be

interpreted. To that extent she does not assume that their meaning is self-evident, and indeed acknowledges that the form of the data itself raises a number of problems. However, she goes on to assert: 'The role of the researcher is to interpret the material that audiences produce within a critical framework which is appropriate to the material and which is made explicit and can therefore be contested' (112). Stacey's account draws out many of the questions that face feminist researchers who, for a range of reasons, feel that a focus on the articulated experience of actual audiences is essential to an understanding of cultural products such as film and television, whether it is in terms of what these products 'mean', what effects they might have or how these texts might relate to their social and cultural context. Moreover, in pointing to the analysis of the articulation itself (whether it is transcribed discussions, interview data or letters) as crucial to an engagement with these questions, Stacey foregrounds two issues that I want to develop here. Firstly, there is the question of what exactly is lost if an analyst fails to problematise the interpretation of interview data, and secondly, the question of whether it is possible to make the process of interpretation explicit without recognising that this is a pragmatic process. In order to show what is at stake here I discuss in some detail an example of a materialist feminist study of audience reception that addresses issues of class and gender by drawing on linguistic data in the form of interview material.

The academic context of this study is the debate over textual polysemy I refer to above. The debate centres on the issue of how far it is possible to assume anything about the media's ability to disseminate ideologies if (1) a media text can have a range of meanings, and (2) there is evidence that different audiences (according to class, age, political affiliation and so on) interpret media texts in different ways. As I indicated earlier, these questions raised particular problems for materialist approaches which were premised on the assumption that media texts are largely hegemonic in effect. While there was, during the 1980s, some degree of consensus amongst scholars throughout the field of cultural studies that media texts were hegemonic in terms of *content* in that what appeared to be their 'intended' message worked to reinforce the status quo, the question of how this might be substantiated was a problem. For example, claims about a text's message might be supported by drawing on an analysis of the media text but explaining the text's impact becomes more difficult in the face of growing evidence from reception studies that that when people watch television or read newspapers they are actively engaged in a sense-making process, and that this often leads different people to come up with conflicting interpretations of a text. One solution to this dilemma, offered by Press (1991) is that variation in audience response can be accounted for in terms of a differentiated hegemonic effect which is contingent upon the class position of the audience.

Premising her work on both theories of hegemony and on the conceptualisation of the audience as 'active', and drawing on scholarship within American cultural and gender studies, as well as within British cultural studies, Press's aim in her study is to explore the role of the media in the formation of female identity. She argues that the formation of an individual's sense of self occurs 'within a massive sea of various and conflicting images of gender, many of which are propagated in the mass media' (1991: 6). She also asserts that since the 1950s there have been a series of contradictory developments in how 'femininity' is generally perceived and goes on to ask: 'How do the mass media represent these developments to women? How do women themselves conceptualise this confusion? Do the mass media have an impact on the way women are responding to these ideological developments?' (5). Press sets out to explore the effect of the mass media on women's sense of self by uncovering women's resistance to or acceptance of the hegemonic messages disseminated by television texts. Her argument is that the mass media in general perpetuate both class and gender oppression by their unwillingness to address the difficulties that are an intrinsic feature of many women's lives.

In order to illustrate the way in which the media mask women's oppression Press outlines a number of discrepancies between women's experience and their representation on television such as the following:

> On television, all single mothers are middle-class or wealthier and almost half of all families are at least upper-middle-class; there are no poor families. This contrasts with our society, in which 69 percent of all homes headed by women are poor, and the annual median income for a family with two working parents is just over 30,000 dollars. Also, more than half of all television children in single-parent families live with their fathers, who experience few financial difficulties in being a single parent; in society, on the other hand, 90 percent of all children in single-parent families live with their mothers, whose average annual income is under 9,000 dollars. (28)

Press relates this to three moments in the representation of women on television: *prefeminist, feminist* and *postfeminist*. Her argument is that women's lives are (mis)represented differently in each of these periods and she illustrates features which make the representations distinct. She suggests for example that in prefeminist family television it is quite normal to see some solidarity between women characters in opposition to male characters (Press cites the *I Love Lucy* show as an example) while in the postfeminist period this does not occur. Press substantiates her claims about the hegemonic effects of postfeminist television programmes by offering an analysis of *The Cosby Show* in which she argues that one of the principle characters, Clair Huxtable, is presented as able to unproblematically fulfil both the domestic role of wife and mother and the professional role of lawyer. She points out for example:

> Conflicts between Clair's roles are minimised, although for real women today such conflicts prohibit, in most instances, the fulfilment of both . . . Clair Huxtable's role on the *Cosby Show* illustrates well the hegemonic view that families need not change to accommodate working wives and mothers. (Press 1991: 80)

Although she analyses specific hegemonic messages in a wide range of programmes, Press argues that these messages do not simply 'interpellate' a female audience. That is to say these messages do not simply work to instil, by a process of 'recognition', a specific pattern of femininity in the audience. Her point is that the messages are mediated by the class position of audience members.

Basing her argument on a series of interviews with working and middle-class women that focus on how they perceive a range of light entertainment programmes Press asserts that both class and gender affect the formation of a woman's sense of self (64). However the mass media play a crucial role in this process in that it is Press's hypothesis that although according to their class position different audiences apply different criteria to their judgement of television programmes, a television programme will have a specific hegemonic effect on a woman's sense of self according to the extent to which it meets these criteria. For example Press argues that her data show that for working-class women the primary criterion employed in their judgement about a programme's worth is whether or not it offers a realistic representation of a given situation. In contrast, for middle-class women a major criterion for enjoyment is the ease with which they find it possible to identify with a character. Press's argument is that the differential application of these distinct criteria leads audiences to engage with media texts in different ways. She claims for example that a perceived lack of realism prevents working-class women from identifying with many television characters. For middle class women however, whether or not a character is realistic is rarely an issue, and a lack of realism does not prevent them from identifying with a character (175). Her argument is that middle-class women, in tending towards character identification, are 'vulnerable in a deplorably direct way to the set of representations that constitutes the feminine in our culture' (96). Press does however record an instance of middle class 'identification' with a character which is not perceived as hegemonic. She describes the character of Lucy in the *I Love Lucy* show as having 'feminist qualities' and argues that her middle class respondents 'pick up on the power within the family which Lucy appropriates from her husband' (77).

Primarily however, Press's claim is that an audience's 'identification' with a character and their perception of a programme as 'realistic' are the two most significant mechanisms of hegemony. She suggests that working-class women, who search for realism, are resistant to the mechanism of identification but are susceptible to hegemonic effects of another form. She demonstrates this by showing that the criterion of 'realism' her working-class informants applied was not a judgement based on their own experience. For example a working-class respondent perceived a depiction of a television character who was both a waitress and a 'strong person' as unrealistic and argued that in real life such a woman 'would start her own restaurant, she would go out and do something different, go to night school' (117). Press argues that comments such as this indicate that her respondents' judgements about realism were actually judgements about how closely a programme approximated a set of beliefs which perpetuate the class system. She sums up her finding thus:

> In large part, working class women criticise television content for its lack of reality; yet the concept of reality used here corresponds to television's portrayal of middle class life. The potential resistant thrust of their critique therefore is blunted by television's hegemonic impact itself. (175)

In her analysis, then, Press accounts for the variation in response indicated by her data as an effect of audience expectation. Within her analysis a television programme appears to contain a range of potentially hegemonic messages, only some of which will have an impact, and the variable controlling which messages will take effect is the set of expectations that arise from belonging to one class rather than another. To this extent Press manages to accommodate the notion of textual determination with evidence of varied responses, and evidence of audience activity. What I want to argue, however, is that, in accommodating these notions Press addresses both the text and the audience at such a general level, her claims cannot be substantiated. The point I want to make is that this is a methodological consequence of premising an analysis on an undertheorised model of language use and communication.

One consequence is that data are addressed at a very general level. This is evident in both Press's approach to the media and her approach to her interview data. For instance, although she produces a series of interesting and very convincing analyses of a range of light entertainment programmes in which her claims about the hegemonic messages they contain are well supported by discussion and example, she then goes on to use these detailed analyses as a basis for making a series of very general claims about light entertainment across diverse genres and over a span of a decade or more. To go on to make claims about how television programmes interact with the audience when the programmes themselves are addressed in such general terms causes a number of problems for Press that her methodology does not allow her to resolve. She often comments for example that her findings are ambivalent: 'For middle-class women, therefore, television is both a source of feminist resistance to the status quo and at the same time a source for the reinforcement of many of the status quo's patriarchal values' (96). Most significantly however, although her study is based on the assumption that media texts are essentially polysemic *because* they are texts, her analysis does not take on board the idea that her interview data is also a text and therefore also polysemic.

There are many problems that arise from the latter elision. Specifically, when carrying out her interviews, Press does not allow for the possibility that a single term may have more than one possible referent. This is clear from Press's presentation of one of the pieces of evidence upon which she bases her argument that working-class women tend to accept the images of reality constructed by television even where their own experience would contradict this image. In the following quotation Press cites two responses (from separate interviews) to a question about how realistic her informants found the character Alexis in the soap opera *Dynasty*. The first response is provided by Seline, a working-class woman, the second is provided by Estelle, a middle-class woman.

> Interviewer: Do you think there are women like Alexis? . . .
> Yes I'm sure there are (Seline) . . .
> No-one could be like an Alexis (Estelle). (112)

The way in which this question is posed suggests that Press is not conscious that the terms *like* and *Alexis* may have such a wide range of meanings that the respondents may in actuality be answering very different questions. The former response, from the working-class woman, may be implying that she believes that there are women who are as rich and who dress as extravagantly as the character of Alexis, while the latter, middle-class response may be implying that this character's behaviour towards other characters is unrealistic. Or then again they may not be implying either of these things. Without more explicit questioning it is not possible to argue that either of the interpretations I have suggested is actually what the informants were trying to convey. It is questionable therefore how far such responses can be seen as evidence to support Press's argument that class positions can explain differential engagements with texts.

Press often describes her findings as contradictory in some way, and I would argue that this again is a consequence of a methodology that is not premised on a recognition that the meaning of utterances is not inevitably self-evident. For example in summing up her analysis of her middle-class respondents' comments she states:

> It is paradoxical that middle-class women both speak more distantly of television than do working class women and, at the same time, seem to identify more closely than working-class women with many of television's images of women. (96)

This could well be the result of a pragmatic problem that Press acknowledges but, in the absence of an adequate theoretical framework, does not seem able to resolve:

> Sometimes even the very language involved in my questions – asking women whether they 'identify with' or 'relate to' specific television characters – seemed confusing to members of both groups which caused me to wonder whether the meaning of these terms was actually different for different groups of women. (95)

Without a more theoretically aware approach to linguistic data Press's aim of addressing the hegemonic effects of television in the construction of female identity, while raising a number of interesting issues, cannot provide the evidence which would make her account explanatory.

I should stress that this problem is not specific to Press's work. For example, in a general discussion of data analysis within media studies van Zoonen refers briefly to some problems with Press's study and points out that it is indicative of a wider problem. She suggests that 'methods of analysing qualitative data are not well formulated and very few generally applicable guidelines exist' (van Zoonen 1994: 140). As a result, she argues, the meaning of much data is addressed as though it was self-evident and explanations of how interpretations are arrived at are frequently omitted altogether. Van Zoonen points out that this is not helped by the editorial policy of many publishers which, she argues, 'discourages the inclusion of "tedious" methodological sections' (140). In the case of Press's study however, the problem is not explained by a failure to include an *account* of her methodology. I would want to argue that it appears to be a problem that lies at the core of this approach to linguistic data. The problem lies in the lack of awareness of the complexity of meaning generation. Specifically what is missing is a theoretical framework that would lead an analyst to expect and to be able to accommodate incidences of reference variation and which would, moreover, provide a means of explaining aspects of the data that otherwise appear to be contingent.

I discuss this issue further in subsequent chapters. At this stage, the point I want to make is that Press may well have uncovered some interesting issues in her work. Indeed West et al. (1997: 122–3) point to research which appears to support Press's claims about the material effects of television representations when they cite evidence from Patricia Palmer Gillard's work in Australia that indicates that girls are 'wont to make decisions about their own socio-economic futures based on the characterisation and actions of the women they see in television soap operas' (West et al. 1997: 122). Clearly then, these issues are worth exploring further. However, there is equally clearly a need for such an exploration to adopt a theoretical framework that can address language use with more precision.

2.3.2   Language use as object:
An example from social psychology

The second study I consider in relation to its approach to language is premised on a poststructuralist conceptualisation of the relationship between language and gender. Therefore, although this study and the above overlap in their focus on the relationship between language and gender identity, they approach the issue in quite distinct ways. Press addresses language use as a means of accessing the way in which audiences engage with media texts, theorising this engagement with media representations and the *a priori* class position of the women involved as primary determinants in identity formation. The study I address in this section focuses on examples of language use, and theorises language use itself as a factor in identity formation. The following study therefore foregrounds the role of language, or more specifically, *discourse* in the construction of gender identity. The academic context here is the debate between mainstream and critical approaches to social psychology referred to briefly in my above discussion of Kitzinger's (1998) work. In the study I focus on here, Kathryn Matthews Lovering (1995) sets out to critique the positivist approach to menstruation and adolescence that is generally adopted in mainstream social psychology by applying a critical feminist methodology. Her aim is to show that adolescent girls' experience of the menarche is largely constructed by the discourses of the body (that is, the ways of speaking about the body) that they have access to. In particular she is interested in exploring the reasons that underlie the negative perceptions that girls have towards menstruation – both before and after its onset – and also the perceptions that girls and boys have about what it is to 'grow-up'.

Lovering argues that issues such as this have been analysed by social psychologists in terms of the 'attitude' that an individual has towards an ontologically prior set of phenomena. She points out for example that such approaches take as axiomatic that a set of phenomena like those that constitute the menarche exists as a 'pre-given object of biology' (1995: 14). Lovering's argument is that the orthodox approach does not capture the extent to which such apparently autonomous phenomena are 'constructs' in the sense that what they are seen to consist of, and what they signify are culturally specific. She describes the post-Foucauldian approach that she adopts, and which has led her to question mainstream approaches, as being premised on the following assumptions:

> The psychology of the menarche and adolescents' experiences are seen as produced by particular discursive practices located in history and society; not by the 'truth' of an independent, materially given object which psychologists 'discover'. (14)

In her study therefore, Lovering aims to locate these discursive practices by analysing the language that girls and boys aged between the ages of eleven and twelve use when they discuss 'growing up'. Her rationale is that, since none of the boys, and few of the girls, at this age would have had personal or direct experience of menstruation, both the 'content and context' of their learning about menstruation would constitute its meaning for them. With the intention of uncovering the ways in which this meaning is articulated, she therefore carried out separate interviews with six groups of children across the ability bands of a single school year: three groups consisting of boys only and three consisting of girls only.

On the basis of her analysis of her interview data Lovering makes the claim that discourses that are used both within and outside of the classroom environment construct male maturation as 'normal' and the maturation of the female body as in some way alien. This leads female maturation to be seen as risible in the eyes of adolescent boys, and shameful in the eyes of adolescent girls. Based on the interview data, Lovering makes the following claim:

> From my own experience I would argue that the female body was experienced by these girls as embarrassing and somehow shameful. Here it is what is absent from the text rather than what is present which identifies the implicit theme of shamefulness. The girls cannot bring themselves to name the parts of a woman's body. (22)

The evidence Lovering points to in order to support this claim is an extract from her interview with the girls. The following section comes after a group of girls have been asked whether boys had been present during sex education classes that the girls had previously attended [GGG indicates giggling]:

Q: Didn't you like that?
A: They showed women's GGGGG
Q: Which bits?
A: GGGGG. (22)

Based on her application of Foucault's account of the relationship between language and identity, Lovering's claim is that the examples of language use she uncovers constitute distinct types of discourse in that she takes them to be 'an individualizable group of statements' (Mills 1997: 6) that require interlocutors who engage in them to take on one of a limited range of subject positions. For the girls, use of these discourses has the effect of alienating them from their own bodies:

> The girls talked of their distress when the female body and menstruation were the subject of laughter by boys, and their words captured how their subjectivity was constituted. It made the girls 'really self-conscious', 'puts us off' and 'makes us hide it all inside'. (Lovering 1995: 27)

Lovering concludes her account with the following piece of transcript – and she includes it in order to demonstrate the pervasiveness of 'this patriarchal sexist discourse'. Although it is rather long, I include it in full in order to illustrate her approach. Lines marked *Q* are the interviewer's speech while lines marked *A* are the undifferentiated responses of a group of boys she is interviewing. Material within round brackets indicates points at which the speech is inaudible, empty square brackets indicate that some transcript has been deliberately omitted, material within square brackets is classificatory information.

Q: Do any of you know why girls have those (periods)?
    [*The discussion quickly becomes chaotic and for me difficult*]
A: I don't know
A: GGG (not clear) [ ]
A: What did he say?
A: Tell us (not clear) come on tell us.
A: I'll tell it (not clear)
A: Come on tell me
    [Several boys start talking loudly all at once]
[*A disjointed discussion about menstruation and sex education followed during which I asked the boys*]

Q: What do you think is good about being a boy as opposed to being a girl.
A: [Loud exaggerated COUGH COUGH loud talking]
A: You don't have to have billiards [breasts]
A: GGGGGG
A: You don't have to have tits
A: GGGGG [loud talking]
A: They call them bosoms [they are called bosoms (unclear)]
A: Mam, mam, they knock you out
A: GGGG
A: Well you say that (not clear)
A: No [no]
[*The boys' behaviour was smutty, sexist, and oppressive. My next intervention was intended to shame them into better behaviour but only encouraged them to exploit the power of this patriarchal discourse further.*]
A: I can see why girls wouldn't want to have sex education with the boys.
A: GGGGG HaHaHa [loud laughing] [loud talking]
A: Oh don't be so disgusting
A: [loud talking] GGGGG
A: The boys don't have to have fannies
[*All I wanted to do was to get out of the room as fast as possible!*] (28)

Lovering makes the point that it could be argued that this event was an empirical problem in that she may not have handled the discussion particularly well. However, she asserts that her response was not due to inexperience on her part but rather that in this context she became 'a woman in the company of a group of young men using a patriarchal sexist discourse' and that she experienced it as 'oppressive and distressing'. She goes on to argue: 'It is these sexist discursive practices and gendered power relations which constitute girls' and women's subjectivities and give the female body and menstruation its particular meaning' (29). I would not for a moment dispute the impact this encounter had on Lovering, and nor would I want to dispute the inferences she draws from the interview data, that is, that the girls in her groups were indicating that they perceived certain aspects of growing-up as embarrassing or shameful in some way. However, what I do want to question is the claim that the form of data analysis applied in this study is able to support her argument that it is the *discourse* that is producing these effects. As I have indicated, claims about the material effects of discourses are not specific to Lovering's work. They form the basis of much poststructural scholarship. At least in part, what makes Lovering's study a useful focus for the questions I want to address is her awareness that there are problems with her approach. She points out, for example, that she is aware that discourse analytical conceptualisations of language are often open to question, stating: 'poststructuralist discourse analysis as influenced by Foucault has a central concern with content and therefore is a 'step away from language' (12). However, having acknowledged that a concern with content is a problem, Lovering does not actually specify what that problem is or how it might be resolved by stepping back *towards* language. What 'language' is, how it is different to 'content', and indeed how it is different to 'discourse' is never made explicit. What Lovering appears to mean by 'content' is linguistic data that has already been interpreted with a context. If this is the case, the problem here is that the processes that led to that interpretation, what exactly is meant by the term *context* and what phenomena might constitute the context remain unexamined. What I want to point to here are some issues that arise from this failure to problematise the processes that render the 'content' available for analysis, and to consider how this failure affects arguments that set out to understand mechanisms of gender oppression through the analysis of language.

The primary issue I want to focus on is the consequence of assuming that 'language' and 'content' are autonomous in some way. For example, such an assumption implies that it is possible to analyse and explain linguistic content without an engagement with the question of what, exactly 'language' is, or how it comes to produce 'content'. This assumption also elides the extent to which content is, amongst other things, a function of context. In practice then, the assumption that it is possible to focus on content in isolation when addressing the meaning of a text leads discourse analysts away from a need to theorise language or language use.

This has some unfortunate consequences. For example, few, if any discourse analysts address the distinction that most linguists would want to draw between language as a system and the uses (communication being just one) that human beings put this system to. In eliding these distinctions, poststructuralist analyses often fail to go on to make any distinction between meanings that are part of human acts of communication and meanings that are not.

That this occurs across poststructuralist approaches to gender and language is evident in a summary of such work provided by Hennessy (1993) as well as in her own arguments. For example, in arguing for a synthesis between materialist and poststructuralist approaches to gender and identity, Hennessy at one point argues that acts of interpretation are inevitably ideological in that they reflect the social conditions of their existence. However, in discussing these acts, Hennessy conflates the treatment of written texts with any social phenomenon that can be interpreted as meaningful:

> Understanding the practice of meaning-making as ideology implies that this activity is the effect of struggles over resources and power that are played out through the discourses of culture and the modes of reading they allow. The texts in which these discourses circulate are not just written documents, of course. They are all of those social productions that intervene in the process of sense-making by being *made* intelligible. (Hennessy 1993: 14)

What is significant here is that Hennessy appears to share with Lovering the assumption that meaning that arises from acts of human agency (written documents) can be addressed in the same way as any other type of meaning that arises from an act of 'sense-making'. A text is simply anything that can be 'read' as meaningful.

In the chapters which follow I will argue that meanings that are generated by language are quite different from other types of meaning. They are distinct, for example, from the type of meaning implied by the sentence: *smoke 'means' fire*. Of course, it is perfectly possible to argue that what we do when we see smoke is a form of reading. We 'read' the meaning of smoke to be that there is a fire. But there is a difference between smoke as the basis of an interpretation and language use as the basis of an interpretation: when language is being used to communicate, it always, at some level, involves an engagement with human intention and human agency. As should become increasingly evident in discussions of linguistic interactions throughout this book, a hearer always and inevitably, whether she or he is conscious of this or not, makes sense of an act of communication by attributing intention to the speaker. Now this point is a problematic one for many discourse analysts in that it is often assumed that if human intention is invoked then the only paradigm that can be in force is a liberal humanist one that is premised on the idea that human beings are in control of the meanings their language use generates. I hope to show that this is an erroneous assumption, and that one effect of making this assumption is that large areas of data remain closed off from analysis in studies that adopt it. I also want to point out that, whether it is acknowledged or not, poststructuralist analyses draw on speaker intention when they interpret linguistic data.

For example, Lovering's evidence that girls experience growing up as shameful takes the form of the following piece of transcript of the girls' speech:

A: They showed women's GGGGG
Q: Which bits?
A: GGGGG (1995: 22)

The process by which Lovering gets from this linguistic data to the claims she makes about what these utterances indicate about the girls' perceptions of themselves is not addressed. This is an unfortunate omission given that at times it echoes the boys' linguistic behaviour, for example here, where they have just been asked if they know why girls menstruate.

A: I don't know
A: GGG (not clear) [ ]
A: What did he say? (28)

At both these points, the informants appear to be avoiding acts of naming, and possibly exhibiting embarrassment, but in the former case the utterances are seen to signify shame, in the latter, sexism. Although it could be argued that the boys' meaning becomes clearer in the light of their subsequent utterances, that still indicates that the meaning of individual utterances is not self evident, and that context and speaker intention play a part. In particular, the question that needs to be asked is whether it is possible to specify what these strings of words signify without some hypothesis on the hearer's part about why *these* specific speakers are using *these* specific words in *this* specific way?

It seems to me quite clear that although she does not overtly acknowledge it, the sense that Lovering makes of these utterances is based on her perception of them as individual acts of communication that are motivated by a specific set of intentions, and that they are meaningful only to the extent that she has attributed these intentions to these speakers. Although looking at the whole transcript, it seems obvious that the boys' utterances can be read as sexist in *this* context, what if this whole series of utterances by the boys had been addressed to a male interviewer? Or what if they had been spoken by a group of girls and addressed to either a male or a female interviewer? It seems obvious that if the linguistic strings were to remain the same, but were used in an alternative context (that is, with different speakers and hearers), the significance of these strings of words would be entirely different. It is also the case that these same strings could have a different significance if they were used by other boys, in a different context, or by the same boys to a different female hearer.

What I am suggesting is that if it is accepted that meanings cannot be read off from the words alone, they must therefore be the result of inferential work that incorporates contextual factors. I am also suggesting that the theoretical framework that informs this type of discourse analysis does not enable Lovering to acknowledge or explore what this inferential work consisted of in the case of her own interpretation of the boys' linguistic behaviour as 'smutty, sexist and oppressive' (29). Although she refers obliquely to 'gendered power relations', she does not explain how these interact with linguistic meaning to construct the subject position she sees herself as having to take up when she becomes 'a woman in the company of a group of young men using a sexist patriarchal discourse' (29). Meaning construction is never explicitly explored in this study, and in not explaining how the language that is used leads to the specific meanings she finds there, one can only assume that as far as Lovering is concerned it is possible to move from the string of words to the meanings of the speakers without considering any mediating interpretative processes because she assumes the meaning to be intrinsic to the utterance. These points are significant in that, because her methodology does not enable her to justify her interpretation, Lovering's data cannot provide adequate evidence for the claims she wants to make about 'the ways in which discursive practices and meanings constitute girls' subjectivities' (26). She states that she experienced the boy's use of language as oppressive, but without an explanation of how it comes to be oppressive her claims that the 'discourse' caused this are meaningless. All her present framework allows her to point to is a correlation between the words the boys used and the threat she felt. She has no evidence that allows her to explain how they are linked and therefore no evidence to support her claim that a causal relationship obtains.

Now to an extent, I agree with Lovering's claim, in that I do believe there is, at some level, a causal relationship here. What I don't agree with is her choice of methodology. Poststructuralist methodologies tend to address language use in such vague terms that they are unlikely to ever produce a convincing case that there is a causal relationship involved in such cases. The data might be used to argue that specific ways of speaking appear to indicate specific ways of perceiving certain phenomena, but they do not, and can not, produce evidence that the discourse is *constructing* subject positions that lead girls to experience menstruation negatively. Indeed my own studies, which I discuss in Chapter 6, indicate the limitations of applying theories of discourse as an explanation of hegemonic phenomena in that they show that a speaker may perceive herself to be speaking within a given discourse but this carries no guarantee that a hearer will share this perception of the speaker's meaning. Within a pragmatic framework this is uncontroversial to the extent that it is taken as axiomatic that a hearer, in the process of interpreting an utterance will make hypotheses about the speaker's intentions. It is only where there is sufficient overlap of knowledge between a speaker and hearer that the meanings the hearer infers are likely to approximate those the speaker was attempting to convey. What makes this significant in this context is that if it is accepted that the meanings Lovering finds in these utterances are primarily inferential rather than, as her analysis suggests, immanent to the content, it locates the processes and knowledge that produce the sense of threat or oppression in the hearer as well as in the words and intentions of the speakers. Now I am not suggesting for a moment that this was an inappropriate inference – or that Lovering had a free choice about her interpretation of the boys' utterances. What I am saying, however, is that it is necessary to locate the assumptions that led to this interpretation appropriately if we are to understand how speech comes to have the power that Lovering and other poststructuralist analysts attribute to it. If we take it for granted that this power is in the 'discourse', without taking into account what discourses are and how they relate to language resources, the use of those resources in acts of communication, and the relationship between these factors and language users, it seems to me that we are failing to engage with crucial elements of the process.

2.3.3   Conclusion: Towards a feminist pragmatics

The two studies discussed above can be seen as engaged in a similar debate about emancipation in that each attempts to unpack the determinants of gender identity and each calls on linguistic evidence to explain the relationship between gender identity and female disempowerment. In the first, language use constitutes the focus of analysis to the extent that the study is premised on the idea that the interviewees' utterances offer access to extra-linguistic determinants of gender identity. In the second, language use itself is perceived as a determinant in that the study is premised on the assumption that the specific language-choices the analyst points to have an impact on the way in which the female respondents experience the process of becoming an adult. My point in discussing these has been to indicate the extent to which each addresses linguistic data as already interpreted. Specifically, in Lovering's account the utterances that make up her data are addressed as though it was self evident that they either constitute examples of sexist and oppressive discourse (in the case of the boy's speech) or examples of the effects of sexist and oppressive discourse (in the case of the girls' speech). In Press's account the utterances are taken as self-evident indications that middle-class women judge programmes according to their ability to identify with characters while working-class women judge programmes according to their assessment of how realistic they find the representations.

That it may be problematic to address utterances as already interpreted or as though an interpretation is self evident has been pointed out by many linguists in the past. Writing over ten years ago, Graddol and Swan (1989: 167) argue, for example, that poststructuralist approaches leave obscure the process by which a context will endow words with a particular sense within a given discourse. This is significant to the extent that where an interpretation is taken as self evident, this tends to go along with a failure to engage with the interpretative processes that produced that meaning. My point is that this failure is often a direct consequence of adopting a discourse analytical methodology that does not make overt the extent to which meaning construction is a pragmatic process. Although I have taken some time to point out that these studies do not engage adequately with issues of meaning generation, it may not be clear why it should matter. As I shall argue, what is at issue here is the loss of potentially significant forms of data and the absence of a theoretical framework that would explain the significance of that data even if it were somehow made available. My contention is therefore that leaving the act of interpretation un-problematised closes off potentially fruitful areas of inquiry. In the remainder of the book my intention is to show that the act of investigating what has led to an interpretation often holds the key to the questions that feminist research has set out to address.

3

LANGUAGE USE AND THE
GENERATION OF MEANING

3.1 PRAGMATICS AND THE
PROBLEMATISATION OF LINGUISTIC MEANING

In this chapter I begin my account of pragmatics by pointing to some of the phenomena that come into view when research on language use takes on this perspective, and by demonstrating the relevance of this approach to feminist research. In particular, I argue the necessity of taking on board the implications that arise from the recognition that the meanings generated by all uses of language (whether these are structured interviews, intimate conversations or spoken or written media texts) are neither self evident nor derivable from linguistic 'content'. In particular, what an acceptance of this premise should foreground is how far the meanings attributed to data are generated by analysts themselves. My primary aim in this chapter, therefore, is to argue that, although assessing the meaning and function of utterances is inevitably an act of interpretation on the part of the analyst, by applying a pragmatic framework it is possible to interrogate the grounds for that interpretation and to offer appropriate evidence and argument in support of it.

I am not suggesting, in pointing this out, that feminist scholarship that does not recognise the analyst's own role in meaning generation will have nothing whatsoever of value to say about a particular example of language use. However, what I am suggesting is that where the process of meaning generation is left unproblematised, the claims about content and utterance meaning that are made by an analyst tend to depend on unarticulated appeals to native-speaker intuition. And if what is intuited is not articulated the claims that are made cannot be substantiated. Any argument an analyst proposes on the basis of such claims is therefore considerably weaker than it might be. My point is that claims about meaning, therefore, need a theoretical framework that (1) opens up the interpretation process to interrogation; (2) indicates what type of evidence constitutes valid support for a given interpretation; and (3) can explain the significance of the evidence called on in support of an interpretation. Without such a framework, the scope and validity of research that addresses language use is limited in that what the analyst may be attempting to represent as having a general significance can be dismissed as a purely subjective response to the data. It is this that my discussion of Press's (1991) study and Lovering's (1995) study was designed to illustrate. While what I pointed to in the previous chapter indicates some general problems that are faced by all scholarship that addresses linguistic material, my particular concern is that the exploration of gender and language use by feminist scholarship should not be weakened for want of an effective model of language use.

In this chapter I am suggesting therefore that what is needed is a model of language use that can account for the interaction between language as a resource, the (socio-culturally situated) uses that resource is put to, and the (socio-culturally situated) users of that resource. And, as I shall show in my discussions throughout this chapter, such a model is needed because utterance meaning cannot be taken as self evident. In what follows therefore, I introduce some basic analytical tools that have been developed by pragmaticians for analysing and explaining utterance meaning. I also show that this type of analysis both enables pragmaticians to show why it is that meaning generation is always under-determined by language and enables them to suggest something about the role that language does play. In order to illustrate these arguments, I draw on an example I used in the first chapter: Nicholson's televised anecdote in which she recounts how as a child she attempted to enter a room in the Carlton Club to join her father and other male relations and was told by them: *Get out. Get out. This is men only.* In Chapter 1, I pointed out that this utterance (which took the form of a voice-over of a shot of Nicholson walking in front of the Houses of Parliament at a time when she was an MP) was interpreted differently by different audience members. Given that the language items heard by all the audience members were the same but that the interpretations varied, in this and subsequent chapters, I consider pragmatic responses to the following questions that this example raises:

- If the language of an utterance does not determine the meanings it generates, what factors other than language might explain meaning generation?
- If the language of an utterance does not determine the meanings it generates, what role does language play?
- If both linguistic and non-linguistic elements play a role in the generation of meaning, how do these distinct elements interact?

I also consider what the methodological consequences of the responses might be for feminist approaches to language data.

3.1.1 The scope of pragmatics

One of the problems with analysing the meanings generated by everyday uses of language is that readers and listeners more often than not experience these meanings as entirely self evident. Even where there is a potential for ambiguity, it also seems quite obvious that this is resolved by 'context'. So it would seem to be the 'context' that would lead an utterance of a sentence like *This is a pupil* in a discussion about eyes to generate one meaning and the utterance of that same sentence in a discussion about school children to generate quite another. However, over the years pragmatics scholarship has raised a number of questions about what exactly is being referred to when the term *context* is used and what does invoking it allow one to say about utterance meaning. For example, if I applied the term in the above, somewhat loose, way as a means of explaining the variety of interpretations generated by Nicholson's use of the words *this is men only*, it would not be very informative: the context, according to my above usage, did not vary. Both the linguistic context (the sentences that went before and after the phrase) and the visual context (the televised shot of Nicholson walking in front of Parliament) were the same for all audience members. The situational context was also the same for each audience member: each was one of a group of friends sitting together in a room, watching television. And yet the interpretations were not the same.

So if invoking a loose notion of 'context' would not appear to be able to explain the type of variation in interpretation the audience members came up with, what would? One rather obvious factor that seems to be playing a part in these specific interpretations is an audience member's existing knowledge about and experience of certain aspects of British culture. And this knowledge and experience does not seem to be separable from the social experiences of these audience members in that social factors relate directly to the way in which some people come to acquire specific forms of cultural knowledge and experience while others do not. Moreover, these different forms of experience and knowledge seem, in turn, to be playing a part in the active sense-making processes being carried out by the audience in that when they produced different responses the respondents appear to be drawing on a range of cues: the visual images on the screen, a knowledge of British culture, a knowledge of who Nicholson is and what she is likely to say. Clearly then, if invoking the notion of context is going to be able to explain the way that language use generates meanings, it is necessary to draw on a model of context that can accommodate these user-related factors. It is also necessary for that model of context to be able to accommodate the notion that although meaning is generated dynamically and is not simply a property of the language used in an utterance, the language system does play a significant role in the generation of meaning.

If, as I am arguing, language does play a part in meaning generation, but is only one factor, and if, as I suggest, context is a significant factor, but a complex one, how then can an analyst negotiate the complexities of meaning generation? Verschueren (1999: 6) argues that pragmatics does this by exploring the links between 'language and human life in general'. He points out that pragmatics has sometimes been seen as a 'component' of linguistics, and argues that the component model is premised on the idea that pragmatics addresses issues that cannot be accommodated by the linguistics of 'language resources'. According to this model, theories about linguistic meaning (semantics), linguistic structure (syntax) and linguistic sound (phonology), cannot on their own explain how language as a resource comes to have the range of functions that human beings put it to in everyday acts of communication. The component model sees pragmatics as able to add an extra layer of explanation to the linguistics of language resources that would accommodate language in use. Verschueren's argument however is that pragmatics is best seen not as a component, but as a perspective that links the linguistics of language resources to disciplines that address whatever other factors (social, cultural, psychological) are involved in the generation of meaning. When pragmatics is conceptualised as a perspective rather than a component it is no longer possible to attribute to it an exclusive sphere of interest. Pragmatics is seen instead as concerned with integrating scholarship in all relevant spheres of interest in order to understand how language resources are used. According to such a view then pragmatics would be:

> a general cognitive, social and cultural perspective on linguistic phenomena in relation to their usage in forms of behaviour (where the string 'cognitive, social, and cultural' does not suggest the separability of what the terms refer to). (Verschueren 1999: 7)

Verschueren goes on to make the point that pragmatics seen in this way would not be concerned with the question of how language resources are used, but would be more likely to ask: How does language function in the lives of human beings? (8). In developing a feminist pragmatics, my aim is to enable a consideration of how this question can be addressed so that it brings into view the way in which the functioning of language interacts with, arises from, or is constitutive of gender.

3.1.2 Language choices and the generation of meaning: Words

Although each of the factors I pointed to above (social, cultural, psychological) give some indication of why different meanings were generated by the audience of Nicholson's anecdote, there is a danger that, in acknowledging that the linguistics of language resources has limitations, the analysis of language use will, as a consequence, tend to dismiss or fail to engage adequately with the role that the language system does play in meaning generation. In this and the following section I illustrate some of the ways in which the role of language is both significant and highly complex and then go on to show how pragmatics has addressed this complexity. I begin with a discussion of lexical choices and then discuss syntactic choices.

3.1.2.1 Word and meaning

On one level it may seem obvious that language choices matter in that if Nicholson had reported her male relations as saying

(1) This is adults only

or

(2) This is women only

these choices are likely to have generated quite other meanings to those generated by Nicholson's use of the words

(3) This is men only.

But this is not as obvious as it seems. Although there are of course conventional associations between words and things, and for the most part we assume these conventional associations are being called on when a word is used, as has long been recognised across a range of disciplines, these associations are essentially unstable. For example, although the word *adults* and the word *men* would in most circumstances appear to have quite distinct senses in the English language, as do the two words *men* and *women*, it is also possible to cite instances that undermine the apparent clarity of this distinction. Indeed it is a commonplace to observe that the word *men* can often be used to incorporate the referent 'women'. Examples of the latter abound in feminist critiques of the generic use of male terms (see for example Bodine 1998 and Braun 1997), and would include, for instance, uses of the phrase *cave men* to refer to both males and females of the Palaeolithic era. Moreover, although the dictionary definition of the word *adult* is something like 'a person who has attained maturity' in some contexts of use the term *adults* can refer to 'men but not women who have attained maturity', as the following extract from a *Sunday Times* article indicates:

(4) The lack of vitality is aggravated by the fact that there are so few able-bodied young adults about. They have all gone off to work or look for work, leaving behind the old, the disabled, the women and the children. (cited in Cameron 1992: 121)

Although such usage might seem objectionable, the fact that the above example could have ever been seen as a meaningful statement in the English language indicates that the term *adults* does have the potential to be read as referring to 'men but not women'. What this tells us then is that, although we use language as though our choice of words matters, how and why that choice matters is not self evident. A brief consideration of how we use words indicates the complexity of this issue.

3.1.2.2 Using words

Linguists have long realised that although semantic accounts are able to make a case that words have a 'sense' when the relationship between a word and its meaning can be shown to be relatively stable, and where that meaning can be paraphrased using other words in the language system, there is a particular set of words that would include terms such as *there*, *here*, *him*, *it* and *today* whose meanings cannot be explained in semantic terms. Meaning of this type is referred to as deixis, and it appears to be a pragmatic rather than a semantic process that generates deictic meaning in that such meanings are primarily a function of the context in which the word is used. For example, intuitively it seems that a word like *here* appears to have a relatively stable meaning in that it can be explained by drawing on other elements of the language system such as the words: *a place close to the speaker*. But compare the meanings generated by these two very similar uses:

On a holiday postcard I write:
(5) Wish you were here. [Where *here* implies 'in Lanzarote']

Someone holds out a cup of coffee and I say
(6) Put it here. [Where *here* implies 'on the table']

So although *here* indicates proximity to the speaker, what type of proximity is not determined by the meanings conventionally associated with the word itself but by taking into account the conditions in which that language item is used: who is speaking, what they are saying, and to whom they are speaking.

There are a range of introductions to pragmatics that give good accounts of the different types of word that are classified as deictic (see, for example, Blakemore 1992, Grundy 1995, Levinson 1983, Verschueren 1999), and which indicate that this type of meaning has long been judged as requiring a pragmatic explanation. On the basis of this work, deictic expressions tend to be seen as having only a meaning *potential* and an awareness of their existence is useful when approaching linguistic material generally in that it alerts an analyst to the fact that when utterances contain such words (such as Nicholson's anecdote) they should not be taken as haven a self-evident meaning. However, more recently pragmaticians have questioned whether it is only deictic words whose meaning cannot be explained by semantic accounts of meaning. There is evidence to suggest that even innocuous little words like *on* are problematic. For example, if I say *There's a woman on the phone* I am using the word *on* to invoke a concept that is quite distinct from that which I want to invoke when I say *There's a scratch on the phone*. And the sentences *There's a spider on the floor* and *There's a spider on the ceiling* also indicate that quite distinct spatial relations can be implied by the same word. This type of observation may indicate that not only deictic words but all words should be approached as meaning potentials. And if this is the case, then semantic models of word meaning, and research that implicitly adopts a semantic model by taking linguistic 'content' as indicative of utterance meaning, need to be reconsidered.

3.1.2.3 The pragmatics of word meaning

A clearly argued case for this position is outlined by Cicourel (1991) who points out that traditional semantic accounts tend to be premised on the assumption that the meaning system of a given language, such as English, consists in a set of 'standardised meanings that are assumed to be accessible intuitively or directly but whose clarification need not go beyond normative descriptions of hypothetical environments' (38). As an example, he discusses the use of semantic concepts such as 'hyponymy' in descriptions of the core meanings of words. Hyponymy is described by Cicourel as the relation that holds between a specific or subordinate and a general or superordinate concept, so 'spaniel' would be an example of a subordinate, and 'dog' an example of a superordinate concept. This relationship is described as one of a 'containment', and Cicourel cites the following definition: 'if a concept *c* contains another, C, *c* is said to be a hyponym of C' (42). He illustrates this by suggesting that if 'boy' contains the concept expressed by 'male' then 'boy' is a hyponym of 'male'. According to this approach the concepts expressed by 'man', 'brother' and 'father' are also hyponyms of 'male'. Cicourel's aim in outlining this account is to argue that although the concept of hyponymy is a useful analytical tool, the way that it is used in semantics fails to capture how far word meaning is worked out on the spot by interlocutors.

Cicourel (1991: 51) asks for example under what conditions we can say that 'mother' is a hyponym of 'parent', and he draws on the work of George Lakoff to show that there can be quite distinct models invoked by different uses of the term *mother*.

Birth model: a woman who has given birth to a child;
Genetic model: a female who has contributed genetic material;
Nurturance model: a female who gives nurturance to a child;
Marital model: a wife of a father;
Genealogical model: the closest female ancestor.

Cicourel then goes on to show how Lakoff proposes that the term *mother* can be rendered problematic in everyday discourse in uses such as the following:

I was adopted and I don't know who my real mother is;

I am not a nurturant person so I don't think I could ever be a real mother to a child;

I had a genetic mother who contributed the egg that was planted in the womb of my real mother, who gave birth to me and raised me.

Cicourel's point in citing the above set of examples is to argue that analysts who address language use should reconsider the semantic model that explains words in terms of their 'core' meanings. His argument is that such a model conceals the way in which words gain meaning within contexts of use, and, in assuming that word meaning can always be accounted for in terms of core meanings, elides the necessity of justifying one's interpretation of the data. As he points out:

> Lakoff's examples illustrate the kinds of contingencies that can mitigate or weaken normative conditions associated with a compositional semantics that avoids routine local discourse or exchanges in daily life settings in which structural elements of a kinship term like 'mother' can in practice express problematic conditions. (Cicourel 1991: 51)

What Cicourel is arguing, therefore, is that a recognition that word meanings are subject to modification in everyday uses of language should lead researchers who focus on language use, no matter what their discipline, to raise to a self-conscious level the tacit knowledge that all competent language users have about phenomena such as hyponymy. His point is that such phenomena should become a part of the analyst's research tools.

In this and the next three chapters I consider a range of such tools that have been developed within pragmatics scholarship, and address the notion of hyponymy in particular in section 3.2.1 below. My aim in this section has been to suggest that the way in which word meanings are dependent upon contingencies of use indicates why studies of language use need a pragmatic perspective. In the following chapters I consider how pragmatics addresses some of the questions that arise from the above evidence, such as how, if meaning is so unstable, we ever get words to mean what we want them to mean, and how we know when we hear an utterance which, out of all the potential meanings a word can have, is the one we should be assigning to it. Before that however, I will briefly summarise what a pragmatic perspective has to say about the meanings generated by uses of sentences.

3.1.3 Language choices and the generation of meaning: Sentence structure

As well as making lexical choices in the production of utterances, speakers also have to make decisions about syntax. If, in her anecdote, Nicholson had chosen not to report her relations' words verbatim but had referred to them indirectly, again it is possible that different meanings would have been generated by her utterance. She could for example have phrased the final part of her anecdote in the following way:

(7) My male relations all jumped up and told me to leave because females were not allowed to enter the Carlton Club.

By phrasing the report in such a way that the place of exclusion (that is, the Carlton Club) is named, Nicholson could have lessened the likelihood that the anecdote would generate the interpretation that it was *Parliament* that did not admit females. I suggest that it would only have been less likely and not actually impossible because, as with word choices, the use of one rather than another sentence structure cannot entirely determine the meaning an utterance will generate for an audience. For example, a ten-year-old native British English speaker who understands the sense of these words, may have an awareness that a place called Parliament exists, may recognise the location of the shot as Parliament, but may not yet have acquired the cultural knowledge that Parliament and the Carlton Club are distinct places. It is therefore possible that in spite of this distinct phrasing, a similar process to that which led one of my respondents to assign the referent 'Parliament' to the word *this* could, within certain conditions of reception, lead another English speaker to assign the referent 'Parliament' to the phrase *the Carlton Club*.

As I pointed out in the first chapter, although it is tempting to simply dismiss such a response because it is 'wrong', to ignore the potential for such a response is to ignore the amount of inferential work that is required in reference assignment, and the extent to which different types of know-ledge are drawn on even when the referent is explicitly named. Again, the point I am making here is that, as with word choice, although choices about phrasing and syntax that are made available by the language system do matter, they cannot be described as having *determined* the generation of a particular meaning. Moreover, it is worth noting that although the indirect report of the speech that I posited as an alternative in (7) is more informative, in that it enables the Carlton Club to be named, it is a far less effective as a way of ending the anecdote than that actually used by Nicholson. So although linguistic choices matter in the generation of meaning, so too do communicative choices. Although a speaker's choice of syntax may make more information available to a hearer, there are clearly rhetorical issues involved here that also impact on what is communicated: if a message is not constructed so that it re-tains the interest of the hearer then his attention may not be captured, and nothing will be communicated anyway. Again, this issue will be addressed further in subsequent chapters and particularly in relation to relevance theory in Chapter 6.

3.1.3.1 Using sentences: Propositional meaning

The point I am making is that in order to understand what is meant when a particular string of words is used, it is necessary for hearers to actively make decisions about which things in the world those words might be referring to. This is significant in that although one can intuit, at an abstract level, what is meant by a string of words like *this is men only* (whether or not it is used in a context) by drawing on one's knowledge of the English language, when it is viewed at this level of abstract meaning, the string of words cannot generate the sort of meaning that would allow a hearer to relate what is being 'said' to anything outside of language. For example, without a referent for the word *this* I have no idea which thing in the world is being described as 'only for men', and I have no idea whether the term *men* is being used generically or in a sex specific-way. If the string of words is interpreted within a context of use, however, then the type of meaning that is generated can be related to the world. An example would be when an audience member hears the string of words uttered by Nicholson in a television programme, and, because of the conditions under which it was uttered, the member can assign the referent 'Parliament' or 'The Carlton Club' or whatever to the word *this,* and can disambiguate the meaning of the word *men*. At this point, it could be argued that the hearer has assigned to the sentence a 'propositional meaning'. A sentence can be said to have been assigned a propositional meaning when it is possible to make judgements about whether it is a 'true' or 'false' representation of a state of affairs.

The relationship between 'truth' and 'meaning' has been seen as a significant one within semantics, and it is described by Recanati as follows:

> We understand the French sentence *La neige est noire* because we know what state of affairs it represents, and we know this because we know the sentence would be true if (and only if) snow were black. But we do not know what 'The avatars pick apart the eye of the canvas' means, because we are unable to imagine what sort of circumstances could make this sentence true. (1987: 1–2)

The extent to which our ability to understand a sentence is tied up with our ability to assess the conditions under which it might be considered to be a true or false representation of the world is a tenet of what is generally referred to as 'truth conditional semantics'. In the next chapter I consider this approach in more detail in relation to speech act theory. Here the point I want to make is that even semantic approaches need to posit a context of use when accounting for word and sentence meaning (even though that context is a hypothetical one) and to this extent it could be argued that propositional meaning is essentially pragmatic.

This is evident in that the propositional meanings that the audience members indicated they were assigning to Nicholson's words could not have been simply 'decodings' of the sentences she uses: they were meanings assigned to Nicholson's use of the words on the basis of ideas that they, the audience members, had supplied, and were clearly not attributable to the *content* of what was said. This is a crucial distinction to make in that, if it is accepted that propositional meanings are inferred and are not determined by the language system, then I, as an analyst or interlocutor can only ever make a claim that a speaker has 'said' something, insofar as I have gone through the process of enriching and disambiguating what I see that speaker as having implied through her use of linguistic resources. Recognising the contribution of the hearer or reader in the generation of propositional meaning has many implications for the analysis of linguistic data in that it raises questions about how far propositional meaning can be attributed to the language a speaker has used, the socio-cultural conditions within which an utterance was made, or, given his own contribution to this sense-making process, how far it is attributable to the interpreter.

3.1.4   Strategic uses of language resources

The point I have been making here is that recognising that cultural, social and psychological factors have an impact on meaning generation should not be taken as implying that the resources of the language system can be ignored. Linguistic choices matter, but it is not obvious how and why they do. Therefore recognising that they matter raises far more questions about how meanings are generated than it answers. If linguistic resources play a part in meaning generation, given the instability of word and sentence meanings, in what way do they contribute to utterance interpretation? And if contextual factors play a role in meaning generation, what model of context would explain that process? Within pragmatics, responses to these questions have traditionally been framed in terms of expectations that interlocutors have about the communicative situation they are engaged in, the ability of speakers to use linguistic resources strategically so that their intentions are optimally accessible to hearers, and the ability of hearers to draw on linguistic and other forms of evidence in accessing those intentions.

Seen from some academic perspectives, this may make pragmatics seem an epistemological minefield, and one best avoided. However, I hope in the course of the remaining chapters, to show that describing communication in terms of intentions and expectations is not the same thing as arguing that people are entirely in control of what their utterances signify, or the same as indicating that they are the 'source' of the meanings generated by their utterances. Moreover, describing language choices in terms of *strategies,* is not to suggest that language use is deliberately planned or controlled to the degree implied when that term is used in the phrase *military strategy*. Tannen (1994: 47) describes linguistic strategies as 'ways of speaking' that may not be consciously thought through but which are motivated to the extent that where people are questioned about why they spoke in the way that they did, they are, to some degree aware of what they were trying to accomplish through their linguistic choices, and can moreover rationalise and justify those choices.

3.2 EXPLAINING INFERENCES BASED ON WORD AND SENTENCE CHOICES

The above account has indicated that the meanings that hearers generate on the basis of a speaker's use of language are, even at the basic level of working out what is 'literally' meant, based on inferences. Just what triggers inferences, however, or how much of utterance meaning is inferential is open to debate. Some earlier models of pragmatic meaning, such as those proposed by Grice and Searle, tend to assume that utterance meanings are by and large encoded within the language system, but that there are some exceptional types of language use that call on the addressee to make inferences. Later models, such as that proposed by Sperber and Wilson posit that *all* utterance meanings are inferred, but the language system, given the conventional links between signal and message it offers, makes it a particularly efficient resource for the generation of inferences. I will address these two models in later chapters. At this stage, my aim is to show two ways in which the conventional meanings of words and phrases appear to interact with pragmatic processes in the generation of meaning.

3.2.1 Entailment

One way in which linguistic meaning has been explained by semantic approaches is by considering what propositions would necessarily be implied by a given assertion. For example, if I assert:

(8) I have a spaniel

you might think it would be reasonably safe to assume that

(9) I have a dog.

One way of describing this relationship between the propositions generated by the above two uses is to say that *I have a spaniel* implies that *I have a dog*. This particular type of 'unstated' relationship between two propositions is traditionally referred to as 'entailment'. Specifically, the term *entailment* tends to refer to cases where the truth of one proposition necessarily follows from the truth of another, and this tends to be dependent upon the adoption of a semantic view that words have 'core' meanings. According to this view, if after saying *I have a spaniel* I later said:

(10) I do not have a dog

I would appear to be contradicting my earlier statement. This contradiction would be explained from a semantic perspective as arising from the fact that the concept 'spaniel' contains the concept 'dog', which is to say that 'spaniel' is a hyponym of 'dog'. Because of this semantic relationship between *dog* and *spaniel* if you accept the truth of statement (10), that is if you believe I do not have a dog, you would have to have to judge my earlier claim (8) about having a spaniel as false.

To check whether one proposition entails another would be to analyse the 'truth conditions' of what is being asserted. This involves asking the question: if it is true that this is a spaniel, is it also *necessarily* true that this is a dog? According to truth conditional semantics if, because of the meaning *spaniel* has in the English language at the time that question is asked, the answer is yes, then it is possible to say that the statement *this is a spaniel* entails *this is a* dog. Note that it does not work the other way round. The proposition *this is a dog* does not entail *this is a spaniel*. Again, to check, you would ask: If it is true this is a dog, does it necessarily follow that it is also true that this is a spaniel? If the answer is no, then the first proposition does not entail the second.

From a pragmatic perspective, the concept of entailment raises some interesting questions in that, if it is accepted that meanings are attributed to words within the dynamics of communication, then although it is possible to point to what appears to be *conventionally* meant by a word by considering its 'core meaning' and scope within general usage, it is also possible to point to the way that a given meaning is actively generated by a conversation or a piece of writing. The analysis of entailment from a pragmatic perspective would engage with the way in which words can be seen, on the evidence of the interlocutors' linguistic behaviour, to gain emergent or negotiated meanings that hold for the purposes of the conversation only, or sometimes only for part of that conversation. An illustration of the way in which such an emergent meaning is generated can be seen in the extract from the television news programme *Newsnight* cited below. What I want to point to in the following analysis of the extract is the way in which the meaning of the item *closed circle* is an effect of the argument process rather than something that entirely pre-exists the argument. In particular I want to show that the term's conflicting meanings are generated in an indirect way, and particularly by the speakers' tacit engagement with the relationship between propositions that I have described above as being one of entailment.

3.2.2 Analysing entailments in naturally occuring speech

In the extract below, Derek Draper, a former aide to a British government minister, and Anna Coote, a former ministerial adviser, are debating the relative merits of the current procedures for appointing special advisers to members of the government. The issue is of topical interest at the point of broadcast because earlier that day an employment tribunal had ruled against the Lord Chancellor, having found him guilty of indirect sexual discrimination against a specific female solicitor because she was, as a result of the selection procedures in force, denied the opportunity to apply for the post of special advisor. The tribunal found that, because the post had not been openly advertised, and the appointment was, according to the *Newsnight* report that preceded the discussion, made purely on the basis of people who were well known to him, the Lord Chancellor had discriminated against women in favour of men. At the beginning of the debate Anna Coote makes the following point about the type of people who typically make up the pool of special advisors or who are potential candidates for that post:

> AC: These special advisors and the Downing Street Policy Unit make up quite a powerful little coterie and it is a closed circle of · very predominantly · YOUNG WHITE men.

Some time later in the discussion, she goes on to give the following account of the impact of the current selection procedures:

> AC: You can't even GET to the point where you MIGHT be OBSERVED trying to get a job because you don't know the right people / this is all [about the
> DD: [GET to know them / GET off your arse and GET out there and [GET to know them
> AC: You can't
> DD: It's [politics
> AC: [you CAN'T /because it's a closed circle =
> DD: =No it's not =
> AC: =It is/it's a closed circle=
> DD: =No it's not / it wasn't closed to me / I was a working class lad from Chorley and I worked for ten years in the Labour Party . . . (*Newsnight* 20 May 1999)

In the above transcription, pauses of less than a second are indicated by a full stop; strongly emphasised words are in capitals; the end of tone groups are indicated by a slash (e.g. /); the onset of overlapping speech is indicated by square brackets ([) and where there is no discernible gap between turns this is indicated by an equals sign.

In my own interpretation of the above account, the referent I am assigning to Coote's initial use of the word *you* is 'women who want to become special advisers'. On the basis of this I infer that what she is arguing is that this group of women do not get to the point where they can be considered as candidates for the post of special adviser because the set of people involved in the selection process constitute a *closed circle*. It is not obvious from the above whether she is referring, through the use of the term *closed circle,* to both the selectors and the set of people who constitute potential candidates or to just one of these groups, but what does seem evident from the above exchange is what is entailed by her use of the term. For Coote the assertion:

(11) It's a closed circle

would appear to entail

(12) It [whatever *it* is] excludes female candidates.

What I want to show here is that Draper, in disputing Coote's claim that there is a closed circle, does so by contesting what is entailed by his understanding of the term rather than explicitly engaging with Coote's (implied point) that women are being excluded from the selection process. What I am suggesting, therefore, is that in order to explain the way in which this term is assigned a meaning in this debate it is necessary to look beyond what is 'said', and to consider this discussion in terms of what the speakers mean by what they say, that is by addressing what their assertions entail. In particular, I want to demonstrate that because a discussion of entailment enables an analyst to articulate some of the factors that contribute to a given interpretation, the claims about meaning that are being made in the analysis of linguistic material can be opened up to debate in a way that intuited interpretations cannot. For example, I would want to argue that in the above extract Draper is using the tacit knowledge that the truth of some propositions automatically follow from the truth of others to try to refute Coote's claims about the existence of a closed circle. This is evident in that he makes the point that 'it' is not a closed circle by stating that he was not excluded from this circle. This suggests that the model of the term *closed circle* that Draper is using is one where assertion (11) *It's a closed circle* would entail

(13) It [whatever *it* is] excludes people like Derek Draper.

In arguing that this entailment is demonstrably false since he 'got in', Draper is therefore attempting to show that Coote's assertion (11) is false. What is interesting, however, is that what he is demonstrating is that this proposition would be false only according to his own, rather than according to Coote's, understanding of the term. His refutation of the entailment is therefore a refutation of what he is assuming the assertion to mean, and not what Coote assumes it to mean.

That the point Draper is making here is entirely irrelevant to the point being made by Coote, which is that the circle is closed to women and not to people like Derek Draper, does not seem to be considered by Draper in his attempt to redefine this term according to his own rather than Coote's understanding of it. Moreover, the fact that his denial of what (11) would entail for him, actually supports Coote's overall point (that it is only young, white males like Draper who are not systematically excluded by the selection process) is not picked up by either Draper or the interviewer. And although Coote tries to indicate that Draper's point actually supports her case, the interview continues as though Draper has made a valid point. And indeed when I have shown this interview in informal discussion groups, this is how his point tends to be interpreted by audience members. By addressing the notion of a *closed circle* in general rather than sex-specific terms (whether this is deliberate or purely a misunderstanding on his part) Draper manages to deflect Coote's main point: that the exclusion of women from the post of special adviser is an effect of systematic sex discrimination. His evidence that a closed circle does not exist is what structures much of the remainder of the interview. As far as I can see, the only route available to Coote at this stage that would have prevented this direction being taken would have been to overtly bring into question the validity of Draper's understanding of what is meant by a *closed circle* by disputing the relevance of his denial that people like him are excluded. Within the dynamics of a televised debate where point scoring and pace are paramount, to take the debate to this level of subtlety is not easy to achieve however, and for many reasons (some of which I address in my discussion of Grice in Chapter 5) may not be successful even if it were achieved.

What the concept of entailment allows an analyst to show therefore is the extent to which interlocutors draw on and exploit implied meanings when they engage in talk. The meanings that Draper and Coote are negotiating here are not going to affect what is conventionally meant by the term *a closed circle*, and to that extent it is not some 'core' meaning of the term that is being addressed here. However, what the above analysis indicates is that the same tools that have been used for analysing conventional word meanings can be applied from a pragmatic perspective to analyse the way that meanings are generated dynamically and at the level of implication within conversations. A second type of implied meaning that appears to be generated by specific linguistic choices made in the utterance of a proposition, but which has tended to be seen as primarily a pragmatic phenomenon is presupposition.

3.2.3 Presupposition

A presupposition is, like an entailment, an implied proposition. But unlike an entailment, which is an implicit proposition whose truth necessarily follows from the truth of something that is asserted, a presupposition is a proposition whose truth needs to be taken for granted if an assertion is to be interpreted as meaningful. Verschueren (1999: 28) uses the example:

(14) A time of peace and prosperity will return.

He argues that the use of the iterative verb *return* presupposes that there has been a time of peace and prosperity before. He makes the point that languages provide numerous conventionalised carriers of implicit meaning such as this which link explicit content to relevant aspects of background information (27). Other useful introductory accounts of presupposition are provided by Green (1989) and Grundy (1995). Both of these show that there are different types of presupposition, and both show for example that presuppositions appear to be triggered by the use of particular terms such as *realise, forgot, understood*. So an assertion such as *I forgot I was going to call you back* presupposes the truth of the proposition *I was going to call you back*. In this section I want to build on the insight that in order to accept an asserted claim as meaningful it is sometimes necessary to accept a range of unasserted claims as true. My aim is to show how it is possible to apply this insight in the critique of an argument.

The following extract from a review of Tannen's best-seller *You Just Don't Understand* illustrates the way in which an argument can be dependent upon presupposition. Tannen's book posits that there are differences in the way that men and women approach conversation, and this can sometimes lead to miscommunication. The reviewer at one point comments in relation to this:

(15) Although Tannen, despite her heroic efforts to do so, has not (in my male view) completely freed herself from the worldview of her genderlect, she clearly recognizes that men often feel aggrieved by what goes wrong in intersex interaction. (Murray 1992: 508)

There are many propositions that need to be taken for granted if Murray's comments here are to be understood and found to be relevant. I point to just two below, and I choose them because they are highly controversial in that they assume a degree of homogeneity within genders and also within gendered uses of language that I would want to dispute. They are:

(16) Genderlects exist.

(17) Genderlects have worldviews.

In pointing to the above propositions and claiming that they are presuppositional, I am arguing that these are premises that need to be accepted *as uncontroversial truths* if Murray's claim about Tannen here is to be accepted as meaningful. Specifically, Murray's comments only make sense if the reader takes for granted that there is such a thing called a genderlect that Tannen is using (I am assuming that what Murray means by a genderlect here is 'a gender-specific language') and that this genderlect inscribes a particular way of perceiving the world. What this implies moreover is that because her language is distinctly female so, too, is Tannen's 'worldview'.

What I hope to show is what can be gained by recognising that although Murray's critique of Tannen's work at this point is dependent on the reader taking (16) and (17) as uncontroversial truths, both are highly contentious. For example, one of the problems with confronting an argument such as Murray's is that a reader may be aware that it is fallacious, but, because the argument works at the level of implication rather than assertion, it is difficult to contest. And even if it is perceived that controversial propositions are being implied, how is it possible to claim that they are actually *there* if they are not expressed? At no point does Murray actually assert 'women see the world differently to the way that men do because their language is different to the language of men'. So if I wanted to make a case that these propositions are what he is implying, how can I support that claim? The way in which pragmaticians have characterised presupposition as distinct from other types of implied meaning indicates one way of providing evidence that would substantiate a claim that this type of meaning is being implied. For example, according to Strawson's (1998: 6) analysis, propositions that are perceived as presuppositions are propositions that must be accepted as true as a necessary precondition 'not merely of the truth of what is said, but of its being *either* true *or* false'. Since, as I have already suggested, knowing the conditions under which an assertion can be judged as true or false has been seen as a crucial part of understanding the meaning of what is asserted, what Strawson is suggesting is that accepting what is presupposed as true is a precondition for the assertion to be seen as having any meaning whatsoever.

Essentially, then, putting a case for the existence of a presupposition is similar to putting the case for an entailment in that it involves making explicit the conditions under which it is possible to say that what is implied or asserted is true or not true. The process is different to that of making a case for entailment however in that, as I have shown, to say an assertion entails a given proposition (whether this is a semantic or pragmatic application of the concept) is to claim that the truth of what is implied follows from the truth of what is asserted (if it is true this is a spaniel, it is necessarily true that it is a dog; if it is true this is a closed circle, it is necessarily true it excludes people like Derek Draper). The significant thing about entailment is that since this relationship is dependent upon these truth conditions, if what is asserted is shown to be false, the entailment is lost (if it is not true it is a spaniel, it is not necessarily either true or false that it is a dog; if it is shown that it is not true that this a closed circle, it is not necessarily either true or false that it excludes women).

With presuppositional phenomena, however, what is asserted can be shown to be false without losing the implication. For example the following assertion presupposes (16) and (17) above (that genderlects exist and that genderlects have world views):

> (18) I assert that Tannen has completely freed herself from the worldview of her genderlect.

While a denial of what is asserted would lead to the loss of what is entailed, presupposed elements such as (16) and (17) still hold even if I deny what is asserted:

> (19) I am wrong, Tannen has not completely freed herself from the worldview of her genderlect.

These elements would also still be presupposed by the following question and conditional construction:

> (20) Has Tannen freed herself from the worldview of her genderlect?

> (21) If Tannen freed herself from the worldview of her genderlect she would be a better scholar.

And they are evident in the specific construction used in Murray's argument:

> (22) Although Tannen . . . has not completely freed herself from the worldview of her genderlect. . .

What is special about presuppositions then is that they are a set of implied meanings that remain whether something is asserted, whether what is asserted is denied, whether one asks questions about it or whether one supposes something about it.

There is another way of arguing that an implied meaning is presuppositional, and that is by showing that, although as (19) indicates, what is *asserted* can be denied without losing the presuppositions, the *presupposed elements* themselves cannot be denied without self contradiction, as the following rewriting indicates:

> (23) Tannen, despite her heroic efforts to do so, has not (in my male view) completely freed herself from the worldview of her genderlect. In fact there is no such thing as a genderlect, and genderlects do not have worldviews.

However, an indication that presuppositions are only propositions that are taken for granted and are not essential to the *sense* of what is being argued can be seen from a third characteristic of presuppositions: although they cannot be denied without self-contradiction, it does appear that they can be suspended:

(24) Tannen has not completely freed herself from the worldview of her genderlect. If indeed there is such a thing as a genderlect, and if genderlects do have worldviews.

As Green (1989: 75) points out, a presupposition is a proposition that is taken for granted or assumed but not asserted in a declarative sentence. The above discussion should have indicated how, in spite of the fact that such a proposition is not asserted, an analyst can make a case that it is playing a part in the meaning generated by a given utterance. Engaging with presuppositional material can also explain why it can be difficult to contest certain ideas. For example, if I wanted to contest what is being argued by Murray, the simple denial (26) would enable me to register an objection to what is being explicitly asserted in (25):

(25) Tannen has not completely freed herself from the worldview of her genderlect.

(26) That's not true, she has.

Contesting what is asserted is relatively straightforward therefore. However, uttering (26) would not allow me to register an objection to what is presupposed by (25). Contesting presuppositions requires a more detailed and sustained critique. I would have to show that what is *asserted* is meaningless because it is predicated on *presupposed* propositions that cannot be taken as self-evident truths: specifically, that it is questionable whether women speak in a way that is sufficiently distinct from men, but sufficiently similar to each other for it to be claimed they use a gender-specific language; and it is questionable how far a language within a language might 'hold' a worldview.

On the one hand, then, being able to recognise a presupposition enables me to point to what a writer is taking for granted. But on the other hand, I can only contest presuppositions by a detailed critique of the argument. While this may be possible and useful within the context of academic writing, where it is expected that the assumptions scholars make will be questioned, the extent to which presuppositions can be challenged in every-day interactions, and in particular where those interactions are spoken, is limited. As Graddol and Swann point out:

The incorporation of contentious material into the presuppositional rather than the propositional [asserted] part of utterances or texts is a well-known ploy of propagandists and advertisers. Presuppositions can, in principle be taken up by listeners but pragmatic constraints on the discourse make this difficult. Attempts to deny presuppositions are, for example usually heard as hostile acts (since it suggests that the speaker's assumptions are in error) and may be a difficult activity for a speaker in a subordinate position. (Graddol and Swann 1989: 166)

Graddol and Swann use the phrase *I see you two women have stopped gossiping* to indicate the sort of everyday assertion that it is difficult to challenge without appearing hostile to the speaker. Their example is also a useful illustration of the way that what is presupposed draws on conventional ways of seeing the world that can be difficult to contest: the presupposition *you have been gossiping*, which would be implied by a given use of the above sentence would (where the term *gossiping* is taken as labelling the speech as trivial) be one that the female addressees of such an utterance might want to challenge. However, it is not just the implication that their speech is trivial that would make this an offensive assertion for female addressees, it is the way in which such an assertion places the addressees as *typically* female because it locates them in an ideology of gender that tends to associate all women's speech with both gossiping and triviality. This is evident in that a use of the phrase *I see you two* men *have stopped gossiping* would imply the same basic presupposition (you have been gossiping) but because there is no stereotype that associates all men's speech with gossiping and triviality it would not have the same implications for the way in which the male speakers' behaviour is being downgraded because it is seen as typical of their gender. Why this should be the case will be explored in the discussion of Grice in Chapter 5.

3.3 EXPLAINING INFERENCES BASED ON TEXTUAL MEANING

I have been arguing that the meanings of utterances are generated dynamically by interlocutors: that even though the lexical and grammatical elements that contribute to meaning generation may have a relatively stable set of conventional meanings, because there is no one-to-one relationship between a linguistic signal and the message that a reader or hearer will attach to that signal, the linguistic elements of utterances always have to be disambiguated and enriched if a reader or hearer is to assign to that language use a propositional meaning. My aim has been to show that meanings are implied as often as stated, that speakers and hearers both have a part to play in meaning generation, and that language items do not 'contain' meaning but are best seen as triggers that generate meanings. So far I have focused on this in relation to the roles interlocutors play in the generation of meanings that seem to be triggered by specific word choices or sentence constructions. Here I want to point to the way that stretches of language use that are longer than a sentence generate meanings. A useful place to start in illustrating the complexities involved in the generation of meaning across extended linguistic strings is to consider the inferential work a reader has to do in order to generate links between propositions.

3.3.1 Textual connections

What is evident from the analysis of longer stretches of language is that we tend to perceive the propositions generated by a text to be linked in some way. And indeed this sense of connectedness is what leads Halliday and Hasan (1976) to characterise 'text' in terms of unity:

> If a speaker of English hears or reads a passage of the language which is more than one sentence in length, he can normally decide without difficulty whether it forms a unified whole or is just a collection of unrelated sentences. (1)

Their point is that where a passage is seen to form a unified whole, it is because it has 'texture' (the characteristics that make the item a 'text'), and it in turn derives this texture from 'the fact that it functions as a unity with respect to its environment' (2). Their seminal work *Cohesion in English* sets out in detail the resources that English has for creating 'texture'.

However, there is much evidence to suggest that the 'connectedness' that is attributed to phenomena that we see as 'text' appears to be achieved by more than the resources provided by the language system. This is evident in relation to connections that are perceived to hold between the set of propositions implied by the use of a single sentence, and the connections that hold across sentences, in that neither of these links can be explained by appeals to either grammar or semantics alone. Consider for example the links between the two propositions likely to be inferred from a use of the following sentence:

(27) I was tired and the cat was tired.

Although the use of the word *and* here seems to have an additive function in that it is implying that both the speaker and her cat share a particular state, how far it is the use of the word *and* that would lead an utterance of this sentence to generate this connection is open to question. This is evident given that the use of the word *and* in the following string of words appears to be implying quite a different type of connection:

(28) I was tired and I went to bed.

Here the use of the same word can also be seen as implying that a causal relationship holds between these two states of affairs. That is to say, the sense of this sentence could be captured by the paraphrase: *I was tired and therefore I went to bed.*

Again, how far it is the word *and* that is generating this causal connection is questionable given that in the next example the word *and* seems to imply that a temporal relationship holds between the two actions that are described:

(29) I picked up my hot water bottle and went to bed.

The range of meanings that can be attributed to the word *and* indicates that even where apparently straightforward words are concerned, where the meaning appears to be quite obvious, we, as readers or hearers, are inevitably required to disambiguate what the word means within a given context of use. How far linguistic cues lead us to see strings of propositions as linked becomes even more questionable when the following examples are considered. What this indicates is that readers and hearers are so ready to see contiguous propositions as linked, that even where the word *and* is omitted it is still possible to see the discrete propositions implied in uses of each of these as having the same additive, causal or temporal relationship as (27), (28) and (29)

(30) I was tired. The cat was tired.

(31) I was tired. I went to bed.

(32) I picked up my hot water bottle. I went to bed.

The first point to note in relation to textual connectedness, then, is that even where the connections are not overt (that is, even where words like *and, therefore* and *then* are not included in a text), readers appear to have no difficulty in supplying appropriate connections.

A second point to note is that readers appear to have no difficulty in seeing two or more referring expressions as indexing the same object in the world even where this calls on a great deal more than linguistic knowledge. For example, if the sentences at (33) are seen to be generating two propositions that have either a temporal or a causal relationship, it requires the reader to see the phrases *the spaniel* and *the dog* as co-indexical.

(33) I picked up the spaniel. The dog licked my face.

There could of course be semantic explanations for our ability to see *the spaniel* and *the dog* as referring to the same object in the world. The relationship between the word *spaniel* and the word *dog* can be seen as semantic to the extent that *spaniel* is a hyponym of *dog*. Further evidence that might be cited is that the sentence *this is a spaniel* would semantically entail *this is a dog*. But while the specific link across the sentences in (33) appear to be generated by the linguistic meanings of the words used, the following example does not appear to be explicable in those terms. Sentence (34) is an extract from a newspaper report of an incident in which the former Chancellor of the Exchequer, Kenneth Clarke, was fined for failing to pay for a ticket on the London Underground:

> (34) Former chancellor Ken Clarke has been fined £10 for failing to pay his proper Tube fare. The Tory bruiser had to fork out the on-the-spot penalty . . . (*Sun* 26 July 1999 p. 1)

Although in the second sentence, there is no overt reference to 'Ken Clarke', as readers we are quite ready to make sense of such reports by assuming that both sentences are being used to refer to actions of the same person.

But how and why do we come to do this? Although it is possible to justify the links between the two sentences at (33) in linguistic terms by saying that since *spaniel* is a hyponym of *dog* there are sufficient linguistic grounds for perceiving the two referring expressions as indexing the same object in the world, can this be said of (34)? Is it feasible to say that it is part of our linguistic knowledge that the referring expression *Kenneth Clarke* is a hyponym of the semantic category *Tory Bruisers*? Given the unlikelihood of this, it would seem that readers are prepared to see referring expressions as co-indexical even in the absence of conventional linguistic links between those expressions. But what this also appears to indicate is that it is our expectation that a text will consist of connected units that leads us to find these connections even when those connections cannot be attributed to the language system. So although our knowledge of the language system plays a part in our ability to see links across sentences, it would seem that readers and hearers are also willing and able to make additions and generate meanings with or without recourse to the links that system makes available. And since readers and hearers make sense of a text by inferring connections based on extra-linguistic evidence, the ability to do so appears to depend on communicative as much as linguistic competence.

The pragmatics literature contains much evidence that our communicative skills lead us to expect that contiguous propositions in a text will be linked. As competent readers or interlocutors, it seems that we are content to provide whatever information is necessary in order to be able to construct the appropriate connections. *Why* we do this is outlined in a number of texts including Blakemore (1988, 1992), Enkvist (1985), Green (1989) and Sperber and Wilson (1995). The question will also be addressed in the next chapter. One account of how we do it will be considered below.

3.3.2 Textual coherence

Within the pragmatics literature, the type of interpretative behaviour described above has been explained as the expectation of readers and hearers that texts or contiguous utterances will have the quality of co-herence. Talbot (1997) proposes that we construct a text as coherent on the basis of both (1) the linguistic cues manifest in the text and (2) the knowledge and expectations that we bring to that text. She illustrates this point in her analysis of two sentences which, at a surface level, appear to have little to indicate how they are connected. The sentences she focuses on are from the problem page of a magazine and constitute part of the magazine's response to a reader's letter which is expressing concern about his sexuality. The response states:

> Many heterosexual men have a passing curiosity about homosexuality and that isn't a bad thing. It compels you to make choices. (Gough and Talbot cited in Talbot 1997: 175)

As Talbot points out, in order to see this piece of text as meaningful, it is necessary to see a connection between these two sentences. She suggests that the missing link that readers are likely to provide in producing such a connection is 'an assumption that homosexuality serves the useful function of confirming people's heterosexual identities' (175–6). Talbot makes the point that this assumption is, of course, highly contentious, and that it would be open to challenge if it was explicitly stated. However, since it is a piece of information that the reader has to supply, it is unlikely to be contested, especially she suggests, by an 'unreflective heterosexual' reader, even though (or indeed perhaps *because*) the reader is complicit in its creation (176). In this section I briefly illustrate how a feminist engage-ment with linguistic material can build on the insight that readers play a significant role in constructing a text as coherent. In particular my aim is to show that this insight provides a way of interrogating the questionable assumptions about gender that underlie many mainstream texts.

The study I focus on is Talbot's (1997) analysis of a report on a sexual harassment case that appeared in the *Sun* newspaper. She uses the notion of coherence to support her overall argument which is that the particular report she focuses on combines a number of contradictory messages about 'the challenge to hegemonic masculinity' that is implied by sexual harass-ment cases and that the report resolves these contractions by requiring the reader to draw on specific ideologies of gender and class. Her claim is that, on the one hand, the textual choices evident in the report seem to be indicating disapproval of the defendant's behaviour, but on the other hand, the report leaves intact traditional assumptions about masculinity and sexual relations between men and women. In arguing this, Talbot relates the notion of coherence to the Foucauldian notion of discourse discussed in Chapter 2, where a discourse is seen as a body of knowledge and set of practices that are associated with a particular social institution or group of institutions. Her point in drawing together these two approaches is to show that in the act of making sense of a text readers draw on their expectations about which linguistic factors are likely to recur in the specific discourses that the text employs. Her argument is that where readers are required to provide information in order to connect the propositions their readings generate, they draw on the types of statement that they expect to occur in the discourses typically employed in such texts. She cites Fowler's account of the discourses associated with the *Sun* as illustration of this:

> The newspaper and its readers share a common 'discursive competence', know the permissible statements, permissions and prohibitions . . . (blondes are busty, work is a duty, play is a thrill, strikes are unpatriotic, and so on). (Fowler cited in Talbot 1997: 175)

Talbot illustrates this when she points out that although the newspaper report she analyses draws on the language of the industrial tribunal in its outline of the case, and appears to accept the validity of its ruling, the voice of the tribunal is mediated in that it is 'translated in to a version of vernacular speech' characteristic of the tabloid press. One example is the lead paragraph which states 'A randy fish boss . . . was branded a stinker by an industrial tribunal yesterday' (1997: 179). Talbot suggests that the reporting verb 'branded' is typical of *Sun* discourse and that it almost invariably accompanies accusations and convictions in these stories. She also shows that the report is full of verbal play, and uses as one example 'Mike Always tried every way to go all the way' (179).

Talbot's point here is that the discourse of the *Sun* works to portray the case as primarily a source of entertainment, and that this has implications for the way in which the issues are projected:

> Such intense focus on playfulness (combined with the framing of the whole news item (not least its placement next to the topless 'Page Three Girl'), strongly cues an interpretation of the information content as non-serious and undermines the legal discourse articulated by the tribunal. (180)

This would seem to indicate that the *Sun* is portraying the case as essentially frivolous. In support of this, Talbot points to the way in which references to the women involved in the case draw on the use of 'the dominant, sexist discourse that traditionally permeates "Page Three" (182) in that they are described as *young*, *lovely* and *buxom*. However, Talbot also makes the point that in the course of the article, the defendant is ridiculed and vilified to such an extent that in spite of addressing the case in a frivolous way it would appear that the *Sun* is reporting 'a successful conviction of a sexual harasser with wholehearted approval' (183). Talbot suggests that in supporting the claims of the women, it would appear, therefore, that the *Sun* is taking a feminist stance. She states the issue thus:

> In a social world in which feminism has gained some institutional power in the legal system to bring to bear on perpetrators of sexist practices,

hegemonic masculinity is having to make some adjustments. For one thing, it is no longer invisible; that is, hidden from view as the unproblematic norm, or accounted for as 'just human nature'. (Talbot 1997: 184)

Talbot argues, however, that in spite of the presence of a feminist discourse, the dominant sexist discourse on gender remains unquestioned within the report. This apparently contradictory position is negotiated by the *Sun* report in that it deflects the potential threat to hegemonic masculinity by positing the 'fish boss' as a scapegoat.

Talbot suggests that the vilification of the defendant constructs him as 'an outsider', and that this is achieved by cueing the reader to fill in gaps between propositions by drawing on discourses of class antagonism: the defendant is referred to as a 'boss'; he is reported as offering the claimants money and expensive gifts. Moreover, his attempts at 'chat-up lines' are ridiculed and he is described as a 'balding'.

In this way, the blameworthy practice of sexual harassment is deflected onto a sexually ineffectual, middle-class scapegoat, providing male readers with an easy solution to the dilemma facing their masculinity: Mike Alway is clearly 'not one of us'. All of this means that male readers can condemn Always's behaviour but without having to go through the uncomfortable business of actually changing their own ways. (1997: 185)

Talbot's point then is that the reader has to link the propositions generated by the text by calling on stereotypical notions of masculinity and class relations that are not so much retrievable from the text itself but are drawn from other cultural texts that use these discourse.

While Talbot's account is a useful illustration of the way that readers construct coherence, she does not explicitly locate her methodology within a pragmatic paradigm. As a result when she argues that 'readers must construct coherence' when they are confronted with a text (175), her framework cannot indicate why they must or how they know what would constitute an appropriate link that would render a text coherent. The approach implies, but does not make explicit a model of reading that would explain her findings. In the following two chapters, I will consider the way in which pragmatic theories make such a framework explicit and are able to justify Talbot's claims about the need to construct coherence.

3.4 CONCLUSION

Throughout this book I am arguing that a pragmatic perspective on language use is essential to any engagement with linguistic material, and in this chapter have begun to indicate that this is because there is much evidence to suggest that the meanings generated by language use, whether it is through the use of words, sentences or complete texts, are always the product of some inferential work on the part of the reader or hearer. I have suggested that this inferential work is necessary because the conventional meanings associated with words are never sufficiently stable for a given example of language use to be approached as though it had an immanent meaning. Although the indeterminacy of linguistic meaning has long been recognised, there is evidence that in spite of this, even within critical linguistics and critical discourse analysis, it is rare that its implication are fully taken into account (Widdowson 1995). I have also introduced some of the analytical tools that pragmatics has drawn on in order to address the critical question that arises from the recognition that meaning is underdetermined by language: that is, how do interlocutors get from linguistic string X to meaning Y? Although, in its earlier manifestations, and particularly when the notions of entailment and presupposition were developed, pragmatics tended to address this question by abstracting from actual situations of language use, current pragmatic approaches tend to be concerned with the way in which language users as socio-culturally situated subjects come to use language. This move within pragmatics from a tendency to use invented examples in order to propose universal principles to an attempt to investigate actual uses of language is captured by Verschueren's (1995: 14) argument that pragmatics is now best seen as a functional perspective on language use. He argues that the most basic question that pragmatics asks is: What is it to use language? He goes on to make the following point about the way in which pragmatics has developed:

> When viewing pragmatics as a general functional perspective on language and language use, an additional question should be: *What does language do for human beings, or what do human beings do for themselves by means of using language?* (Verschueren 1995: 14)

In the next chapter I will consider these questions in relation to speech act theory.

4

LANGUAGE AND PERFORMANCE

4.1 LANGUAGE USE AS ACTION

In the previous chapter I indicated some of the ways in which pragmatics distinguishes between different types of implied meaning. So far, the types of meaning I have discussed have related primarily to the representational capacity of language use where meaningfulness is dependent upon the degree of fit between the world and what is asserted or implied about it. For example, when I considered Murray's (1992) argument I did so by questioning what he was, through his use of language, expecting his readers to take for granted about the nature of language, the nature of gender and the nature of the relationship between the two. And in questioning the validity of what he was presupposing about the world, the meaningfulness of his utterance was brought into question. I also suggested that one way of understanding what was being argued in the televised debate on the procedures for selecting government advisers was to consider the way in which the debate centred on the truth of what would necessarily follow (be entailed) if a given assertion was true. As I indicated, by denying the truth of the entailment, the participant was attempting to deny the truth, and therefore the meaningfulness, of what his opponent was asserting. I suggested earlier that this relationship between truth and meaningfulness has been premised on the idea that part of knowing the meaning of a sentence means knowing the conditions under which the propositions expressed by that sentence for a given hearer would be true. Explaining utterance meaning by addressing deixis, entailment and presupposition in terms of truth conditions is a matter of judging how far what is said or implied is a valid representation of a (real or imagined) world. This chapter focuses on an aspect of utterance meaning that is not related to the representational capacity of language, and which is not, therefore, captured by addressing truth conditions. This chapter will address ways in which the idea that language has a performative capacity has been theorised and applied.

The notion that language has a performative capacity is essentially the idea that all utterances perform acts, and that part of being able to understand the meaning of a given utterance is being able to understand the act or acts that the speaker is performing through the use of language. So for example, on the one hand the following assertion can be seen as meaningful if, as English speakers, we know what the string of words can signify and, where it is used in a given context (for example in talk between two people at a party), the proposition it expresses for a hearer can be judged in terms of its truth conditions:

(1) It's late.

On the other hand, however, it is also possible for this utterance to be seen as meaningful by a hearer to the extent that he sees it as implying that what the speaker means by it is:

(2) Let's go home.

This is a different type of implied meaning to that which is captured in the analysis of entailment and presupposition. In order to understanding that (2) is what the speaker is implying, the hearer must recognise that the speaker is not simply using language to describe the world (to report on the lateness of the hour), but is also performing an act in that this utterance might also function as a request, a plea or a command. The claim of speech act theory is that all utterances, no matter how they are formulated, do not just 'say' something. All utterances also 'do' something. In this chapter I provide a brief summary of this aspect of pragmatics and then consider how this notion has been applied in studies of gender and language use. Since the summary is of necessity brief, I introduce only those concepts that are relevant to the subsequent discussion of feminist applications, but in suggesting further reading I point to texts that both offer an introduction to and a critique of speech act theory.

4.1.1   Austin's account of performativity

The notion that language has a performative capacity, one of the central axioms of pragmatics, was initially formulated by J. L. Austin in the early 1950s, and has subsequently been developed into a theory of speech acts by J. R. Searle and others over a number of years. The originality of Austin's account tends to be seen as arising from the fact that approaches to utterance meaning at the time he developed his theory were primarily informed by logical positivism, where the study of utterance meaning is essentially a study of the extent to which a statement has the capacity to describe 'some state or affairs or to "state some fact" which it must do either truly or falsely' (Austin 1975: 1). Austin questions this orthodox approach by pointing out that there is an aspect of utterance meaning that cannot be captured by considering the relationship between what is said and what is being represented. In suggesting this, he makes the point that, as well as describing the world, utterances perform acts. Although the insight that speech has a performative capacity has, over the years, taken on a range of different significances, because in his own account Austin takes the limitations of truth conditional meaning as his point of departure, the performative capacity of language still tends to be introduced in these terms in the pragmatics literature. In summarising his account, therefore, I also pick up on this aspect of the significance of his original formulation, but as the trajectories taken by later applications of the theory indicate, its significance has now extended far beyond this.

4.1.1.1 Performatives

Austin's account of the performative functions of language (first published in the 1962 text *How to Do Things with Words*) was constructed just after his death on the basis of a series of lectures he gave in 1955. The published account retains that form, charting an extended argument about language as action which involves the setting up of claims and distinctions that are subsequently questioned and modified. Most significantly, Austin begins by arguing that the type of utterance that preoccupied philosophers at the time he is writing are what he calls 'constatives', which are a type of utterance that tends to report on the world in some way. Initially he suggests that it is necessary to distinguish constatives from another type of utterance: performatives. His point is that these latter utterances do not have this same relationship to the world in that, while the former are primarily reports about the world, the latter constitute acts that have material effects upon the world. He illustrates this different type of relationship by pointing out 'When I say, before the registrar or altar, etc., "I do", I am not reporting on a marriage: I am indulging in it' (6). By the end of his account however, he suggests that even constatives have a performative function.

Initially the point Austin makes about an utterance such as *I do* is that when it is uttered as part of a marriage vow, it is irrelevant to consider whether it is truthful or not in that the very act of uttering it under the above conditions makes it true. This idea of the irrelevance of truth conditions in relation to performatives is also indicated in a claim Austin makes that there is a distinct type of verb that can be classed as performative. He suggests that the use of this type of verb in an utterance serves to indicate which act a given utterance is carrying out. Performative verbs include words like *deny, suggest, declare, bet* and any other that can be prefixed with the phrase *I hereby*. One of the characteristics of this type of verb is that the very act of uttering it (given an appropriate context) makes what is said true. Therefore utterances that use these verbs cannot be subjected to the same truth conditional analyses as other utterance forms.

The relevance of this to our understanding of everyday uses of speech is indicated by Jenny Thomas (1995: 34) when she points out that to say in a court of law *I plead guilty* is not the same as saying *I am innocent*. If you use the former phrase you are simply saying something about what you are (simultaneously) saying, while if you use the latter you are making a claim about your innocence. She goes on to comment on the implications of using performative verbs:

> I often wonder about the declaration made by Judge Clarence Thomas before a committee of the United States Senate, established to approve his nomination to the Supreme court: 'I deny that I had conversations of a sexual nature or about pornographic material with Anita Hill, that I ever attempted to date her . . .' (Thomas 1995: 34–5)

That he is denying these things is automatically true. What is questionable, Thomas suggests, is whether he is also claiming that he did not do them.

4.1.1.2 Locutions and illocutions

In developing the notion of performativity, Austin coins the terms locution, illocution and perlocution to refer respectively to the act of saying, the act that is carried out in the act of saying and the consequences or effects of these acts. His point is that when we use a language to produce meaningful sounds or inscriptions, we perform locutionary acts. It is a focus on this level of meaning that characterises orthodox approaches to the study of utterance meaning at the time Austin is writing. He adds to the study of locutions by pointing out that in carrying out a locutionary act, we are also always doing something else as well. So for example, when we say certain strings of words such as *Can you pass the salt?* what we are also doing is making a request. His claim is that we use locutionary acts to ask and answer questions, warn people, reassure people, make bets, and perform many other acts that go beyond the act of simply 'saying'. In his terminology, what he is suggesting then is that in performing the locutionary act of saying we also perform a separate illocutionary act. Nicholson's anecdote illustrates this in that, on the one hand, to point out that her relations' utterance of the words *Get out* can be seen as a meaningful sequence of words in English is to point out that a locutionary act is being carried out by these speakers. On the other hand this utterance also performs an illocutionary act. By saying *Get out* Nicholson's relations are ordering her, or commanding her, or possibly warning her to leave. It is in this sense that their words have an illocutionary force.

It is worth pointing out that although speech acts are discussed as though simply using a term like *I deny* will constitute 'a denial by the speaker', in characterising speech acts, Austin is by no means suggesting that the simple act of locution will in every case produce the act of illocution that the speaker is attempting. Indeed he makes the point that: 'We must systematically be prepared to distinguish between 'the act of doing *x*', i.e. achieving *x*, and 'the act of attempting to do *x*' (1975: 105). He explains this as follows:

> [I]t is always possible, for example, to try to thank or inform somebody yet in different ways to fail, because he doesn't listen, or takes it as ironical, or wasn't responsible for whatever it was, and so on. This distinction will arise, as over any act, over locutionary acts too; but failures here will not be unhappiness as there, but rather failures to get the words out, to express ourselves clearly, etc. (Austin 1975: 106)

His point is that illocutionary acts are, essentially, conventional acts, and their success is dependent upon the hearer's understanding and uptake of the force of the utterance. This indicates something about the function of performative verbs in that they may be best seen as a resource the speaker calls on that helps to indicate the intended illocutionary force of an utterance.

An illustration of the way in which language users exploit their tacit knowledge of the conventional nature of linguistic performativity is given in Jenny Thomas's (1985) paper on the language of power in which she describes an incident at a theatre. During a performance of *Richard III* a member of the audience, incensed by the fact that her neighbour kept rustling chocolate wrappers, turned to her and asked whether she could eat more quietly. At the interval the following exchange took place:

A: How dare you tell me to eat more quietly!

B: I didn't tell you to, I asked if you could. If you can't, there's nothing more to be said. (Thomas 1985: 772)

Speaker B's selection of the performative verb *ask* rather than *tell* as a way of indicating the intended illocutionary force of the original utterance illustrates the extent to which speakers are aware that illocutionary acts need to be carried out in an appropriate context if they are to be successful. Thomas's point in citing the above incident is to argue that it tends to be only where there is an overt and substantive power differential between interlocutors that the force of a command or a direct criticism is likely to be openly indicated by the speaker. Because a stranger does not, in normal circumstances, have the authority to command another to be silent, in this case the illocutionary act indicated by the verb *tell* would have been, in Austin's terms, 'infelicitous' on the part of speaker B, and therefore unlikely to be successful.

4.1.1.3   Felicity conditions
The failure to achieve an illocutionary act is described in the previous quote from Austin (1975: 106) in terms of 'unhappiness'. Again he initially explains this term by pointing to the distinction between performatives and constatives and taking the logical positivist approach to meaning as his

starting point. Austin suggests for example that although some aspects of utterance meaning can be explained by pointing to the ways in which one statement implies the truth of certain other statements, this cannot explain all aspects of utterance meaning. He illustrates this by acknowledging that truth conditions are appropriate in explaining the meanings of locutions in that one could reasonably claim that, since the assertion *All men blush* entails *some men blush*, the assertion *all men blush but not any men blush* would be contradictory and therefore meaningless (Austin 1975: 47–8). Equally, he argues that stating *All Jack's children are bald* is to presuppose that *Jack has some children*. Therefore to say *All Jack's children are bald but Jack has no children* is again to utter a contradictory, and therefore meaningless statement. He goes on to comment in relation to the above examples, and an example such as saying *I do* in a marriage ceremony when one is already married:

> There is a common feeling of outrage in all these cases. But we must not use some blanket term, 'implies' or 'contradiction', because there are very great differences. . . . there are more ways of outraging speech than contradiction merely. The major questions are: how many ways, and why they outrage speech, and wherein the outrage lies. (48)

His point is that meaning in relation to performatives needs to be accounted for in a different way to the meaning of constatives. What makes performatives go wrong is not captured by analysing their truth conditions. Performatives go wrong when their felicity conditions are not met.

In explaining this, Austin argues that the locution *I now pronounce you husband and wife* is only ever felicitous to the extent that it performs the illocutionary act of 'marrying' if the speaker is someone who is legally authorised to carry out that act and if the people who are being married are consenting adults, not already married and so on. Equally, the locution *I hereby name this ship Titanic* will only perform the illocutionary act of ship naming where the speaker is the authorised namer, if it is in a naming ceremony and so long as any other formal requirements are fulfilled. While these examples indicate the institutional nature of some speech acts, Thomas's example of the speaker who asks *Can you eat more quietly?* illustrates how an everyday utterance can only perform an illocutionary act where certain felicity conditions are met: the act *command* is only achieved if the speaker has sufficient authority in relation to the hearer for the utterance to have that force.

The successful production of an illocutionary act involves a range of effects. Austin (1975: 116–17) outlines these as (1) securing uptake, (2) taking effect and (3) inviting a response. The securing of uptake is explained as an effect that involves the bringing about of an understanding of the meaning and force of a locution (117). Unless it is achieved, the illocutionary act is not actually carried out. The production of a conventional effect is illustrated by Austin's point that an utterance such as 'I name this ship *Queen Elizabeth*' will produce a consequence. If, through the utterance, the speaker has named the ship, the consequences are that 'certain subsequent acts such as referring to it as the *Generalissimo Stalin* will be out of order' (117). The third effect, the inviting of a response or sequel, is explained in terms of the way that an illocutionary act invites a certain kind of subsequent behaviour: 'an order invites the response of obedience and a promise that of fulfilment' (117).

4.1.1.4   Perlocutions

To the extent it is possible to claim that the speaker has carried out an illocutionary act, it is possible to say that she has performed a further kind of act: for example, she may have convinced or persuaded her hearer about something. Austin terms this the perlocutionary effect. Although perlocutionary effects constitute a change of some sort that takes place in the hearer, and appear to be something that is brought about by the speaker's use of language, how that effect can be described is far from obvious. Austin observes for example that:

> It is characteristic of perlocutionary acts that the response achieved, or the sequel, can be achieved additionally or entirely by non-locutionary means: thus intimidation may be achieved by waving a stick or pointing a gun. Even in the case of convincing, persuading, getting to obey and getting to believe, we may achieve the response non-verbally; but if there is no illocutionary act, it is doubtful whether this language characteristic of perlocutionary objects should be used. Compare the use of 'got him to' with that of 'got him to obey'. (1975: 119)

Moreover, as Austin points out, a speaker's illocutionary act will not necessarily produce the desired perlocutionary effect and he makes a distinction between the perlocutionary object of 'alerting' that would follow from the illocutionary act of 'warning' and the perlocutionary sequel of 'alarming' which may also result.

Austin's ideas have been developed and critiqued by a range of theorists since they were first published. I indicate below further reading where these can be followed up. Here I focus on the most influential theorisation of speech acts, that of John Searle, before going on to show how the initial conceptualisation of speech acts and the formalisation of the process of speech act performance has been applied in studies of gender and language use.

4.1.2   Speech act theory

In developing Austin's notion that utterances have a performative capacity, Searle, in a wide ranging body of work, has addressed the processes by which utterances come to constitute speech acts. As Urmson has pointed out (1998: 504), Austin had indicated an awareness that no simple form/ function link obtains between locutions and illocutions: locutions such as *Don't do that* and *I'm warning you not to do that* can both be seen as having the illocutionary force of 'warning' even though the concept is only articulated in the latter. How a given utterance comes to perform a particular act in both cases is left unexplained by Austin however. A further problem in relation to performatives is pointed to by Searle (1971a: 48–9), who amongst others has made the point that the use of a performative verb in an utterance may actually indicate an illocutionary force that is quite distinct from that which the speaker intended. An example, would be an utterance of the words *I promise I will kill you if you do that again*. How a given utterance comes to have a particular illocutionary force, when it includes a performative verb that indicates a different illocution is also left unexplained by Austin's account. Indeed Searle comments in relation to this aspect of speech act theory: 'The notion of a performative is one that philosophers and linguists are so comfortable with that one gets the impression that somebody must have a satisfactory theory. But I have not seen such a theory. . .' (1998: 519). His aim in much of his work has been to formulate a model of speech acts that can explain the processes by which speakers come to perform acts through their use of language, and it has been argued (see, for example, Geiss 1995: 1) that although Austin introduced the notion of speech acts it is Searle who is responsible for speech act theory.

In spite of the amount of scholarship that has been invested in developing a satisfactory theory of speech acts, current pragmaticians tend to agree that there is still no workable theory of speech acts (for example, Thomas 1995: 93, Verschueren 1999: 132). As Sbisa (1995) points out:

> Speech act theory is tenable in so far as it is possible, and sensible, to view utterances as acts. An utterance is the production (oral or in writing) of a token of a linguistic structure which may or may not correspond to a complete sentence. An act, generally speaking, is something that we 'do': a piece of active (vs passive) behaviour by an agent. In speech act theory, by viewing utterances as acts, we consider the production of words or of sentences as the performance of speech acts, and we posit the speech act as the unit of linguistic communication. It is a task of speech act theory to explain in which senses and under which conditions uttering something can be doing something, thus providing a conceptual framework for describing and understanding the various kinds of linguistic action. (497)

One of the major weakness attributed to Searle's approach has been the tendency to approach speech act phenomena as though the assignment of speech token to speech act types could be explained as a semantic rather than a pragmatic issue. Although Verschueren argues that as a result of this 'there has been a tendency to approach speech act theory as a dead body rather than to use its insights' (1999: 132), I will briefly summarise Searle's approach in order to indicate something of his approach. My aim is to show why it is seen as problematic, but also to show why, in spite of these problems, the notion of speech acts, as well as the issues raised by Searle, continue to influence pragmatics scholarship and work in other disciplines.

4.1.2.1 Intention and convention

In formalising a theory of speech acts Searle approaches the meanings generated by speakers as an issue of intention. He makes the point for example that if a sound or a mark on a piece of paper is taken to be an instance of linguistic communication, it is on the basis that the sound or mark has been produced by a being with certain intentions. Searle expands on this with the following comment:

> It is a logical presupposition, for example, of current attempts to decipher the Mayan hieroglyphs that we at least hypothesize that the marks we see on the stones were produced by beings more or less like ourselves and produced with certain kinds of intentions. If we were certain the marks were a consequence of, say, water erosion, then the question of deciphering them or even calling them hieroglyphs could not arise. To construe them under the category of linguistic communication necessarily involves construing their production as speech acts. (1971a: 40)

Beginning with the premise that the language used in acts of communication is used intentionally in order to generate meaning, Searle's concern is to explain how the intentions of the communicator come to be realised in language use. I consider the notion of speaker intention in more detail in the following chapter. Here I want to make the point that the particular way in which Searle addresses the performance of speech acts is based on the assumption that in conversation hearers arrive at what a speaker intends to communicate through the use of speech by applying a set of rules.

For example Searle makes the point that illocutionary acts have to be understood by hearers, and therefore there must be ways for speakers to make the illocutionary force of their utterances accessible. Although one way of doing this is to utter an explicit performative such as *I promise* simply including the phrase in an utterance cannot determine the illocution. Searle therefore sets out to formulate the process by which a given act comes to instantiate a speaker's intended meaning. He does so by analysing the necessary and sufficient conditions for the 'successful and non-defective' performance of a given act (1969: 54). He sets out his aims and methods thus:

> If we get such a set of conditions we can extract from them a set of rules for the use of the illocutionary force indicating device. The method here

is analogous to discovering the rules of chess by asking oneself what are the necessary and sufficient conditions under which one can be said to have correctly moved a knight or castled or checkmated a player, etc. We are in the position of someone who has learned to play chess without ever having the rules formulated and who wants a formulation. (54–5)

Searle's formulation of those rules has involved an engagement with both the intentional and the conventional aspects of illocutionary acts. In this he takes Grice's theory of speaker meaning (which I discuss in the next chapter) as a point of departure but focuses primarily on the conventionality of linguistic meaning. His point is that, although the performance of speech acts is dependent on extra-linguistic phenomena, 'one's meaning something when one says something is more than just contingently related to what the sentence means in the language one is speaking' (1971a: 46). As he points out:

At one point in the *Philosophical Investigations* Wittgenstein says 'Say "It's cold here" and mean "It's warm here".' The reason we are unable to do this is that what we can mean is a function of what we are saying. Meaning is more than a matter of intention, it is also a matter of convention. (46)

As Sbisa (1995: 499) points out, the focus on conventionality indicates a major difference between Austin and Searle in that while the former sets out to distinguish force from meaning, the latter addresses force as an aspect of meaning.

4.1.3 Developments and applications of speech act theory

Although Searle's work has sparked off a great deal of debate within pragmatics, I will not detail here the way in which he explains the process by which speakers come to perform acts. In part this is because, as a number of writers have pointed out, although the questions Searle asks about how speech acts are performed are entirely valid, his attempt to address performance in terms of the conventional meanings of words is misguided. Sbisa suggests for example that his approach 'stems from a tendency to consider social and relational features as marginal with respect to the speech act's core structure' (1995: 504). Recanati (1987) provides a clearly argued account of why Searle's marginalisation of the context of speech acts is untenable. He illustrates his point by distinguishing between using a hammer to carry out an act, and using language to carry out an act:

A hammer serves to drive nails, and I can use it to this end even if no one understands what I am doing. The imperative mood serves to perform a certain kind of communicative act, but I cannot perform the act if no one understands that this is my intention in using this mood. I cannot

give an order to someone if he does not understand my intention to give
him an order. (16)

Cicourel (1991) also sees the marginalisation of context as a weakness in
Searle's account, and describes his theory of speech acts being too oriented
towards the speaker. He argues that from a Searlean perspective the
addressee of a speech act is passive: 'either "getting" the illocutionary force
of an utterance or failing to "get it" (93). He points out that this account
does not therefore take into consideration the motivations of interlocutors,
and it treats speech acts as 'isolated events, whose meaning is not affected
by the surrounding discourse' (93).

What the arguments cited above indicate is a movement in pragmatics
scholarship away from the language-focused approach taken by Searle,
when he tries to pin speech acts down to semantics, to an awareness that
the force of an utterance is an effect of the interaction in which it occurs.
In practice this has been realised as a movement towards the empirical
and a focus on participants' own perceptions of linguistic interactions. In
developing a modified speech act theory, Connor-Linton for example cites
a range of evidence which suggests that 'the "vertical construction" of
utterances across speakers' conversational turns show how the preceding
talk influences, and even determines to a great extent, the content and
construction of a speaker's utterances' (1991: 93). He also points out that
empirical studies have shown that in the course of its production 'an utterance may change from being one type of speech act at its inception to
another at its conclusion' (94). Moreover, he foregrounds the relationship
between the social identity of the hearer in relation to the speaker and argues
that this can impact on 'the felicitous performance of a particular speech
act' (94) On the basis of such evidence, Mey has argued, that one cannot
take the process proposed by Searle and then simply 'add on' the user:

> Rather, we should use an interactive perspective, in which the role of the
> user is no longer added on, but is an integrated part of our theorizing.
> Applied to the case of promising, this means that we cannot, in all decency,
> talk about promising in the abstract: every promise is a promiser's promise,
> promised to a real-life promisee. The conditions of use for promises should,
> therefore, include these users, promisers as well as promisees, and their
> conditions of interaction. (Mey 1993: 125)

Studies that have engaged with speech acts in ways that consider the
impact of the socio-cultural context, and which take on board the
relationship between interlocutors, include Thomas's (1985) account which
focuses on the institutional use of 'illocutionary force indicating devices'
as a means of enacting power. In addition, Duranti has shown how the
pragmatic force of speech acts is realised across utterances by different
interlocutors 'thus creating larger discourse frames within which speech

and social action can draw upon one another while building (or proposing) a certain version of the world' (1991: 134). What such studies indicate is that although the solutions offered by Searle's formulation of speech act theory may be problematic, the issues he raises about how the performance of speech acts can be described and explained remain pertinent and insightful, as do the original insights about performativity outlined by Austin. As Duranti (citing Mary Louise Pratt) points out:

> The acceptance of the notion of a speech act does not necessary imply the acceptance of the epistemological foundations or underlying ideology of speech act theory. (1988: 221)

Although explanations of speech acts are dogged by problems surrounding the theorisation of intention, the theorisation of the mechanisms for assigning speech acts to utterances, and how best to approach the relationship between the user, the language used and the act, as Duranti (1988) argues, the concept of speech act captures a useful fact about language. Because of this, theories of performativity continue to evolve: a recent example being Verschueren's (1999) reformulation of Austin and Searle's accounts.

4.2   SPEECH ACT THEORY AND GENDER

Although it remains the case that describing and explaining how a speech act is achieved is by no means straightforward, the concept of linguistic performativity has been applied across a range of empirical studies of language use. And these include a variety of studies that address gender. In spite of the difficulties of theorising this process, the idea that we perform acts through our language use has been seen as providing a useful framework for exploring how utterances function at an interactive level and for addressing questions about the impact of gender in relation to interaction, including questions about whether, and why, men and women use language differently. For example, the theory has been used to address questions about whether men and women carry out speech acts differently, whether they have the same force when they are carried out by either gender, and to address questions about the relationship between power and speech acts. The notion of linguistic performativity has also been developed as a means of explaining the process whereby language is implicated in the construction of gender.

4.2.1   Speech acts as a framework for addressing gendered differences in language use

The studies that address gendered differences in language use by invoking the notion of speech acts are not based on one particular model of gender.

For some, gender is taken as a given, as is the premise that men and women have different speech styles (for example Holmes's 1986, 1993, 1995 work, and Troemel-Ploetz 1994). In such cases an essentialist view of gender tends to be adopted, and evidence of the differential use of speech acts tends to be addressed as an effect of *a priori* gender differences. For others, gender as a concept is subject to scrutiny, as is the idea that males and females have distinct speech styles (for example Crawford 1995 and West et al. 1997). In such cases the notion of performativity provides a framework for interrogating the evidence for claims that males and females speak differently. I will begin with a summary of two approaches that adopt an essentialist model of gender difference, and then discuss an example of a study that problematises gendered differences in language use.

4.2.1.1 'Let me put it this way, John': Conversational strategies of women in leadership positions

In her 1994 article of the above title, Senta Troemel-Ploetz begins from the premise that women have their own style of speaking. She states the case thus in her abstract of the article:

> As we are pursuing the question of women's own style, we are finding out what it is that women do differently when they teach or when they interview, when they heal or when they joke. I would like to look at recent results on women's strategies when they lead . . . I want to use these results in order to identify and examine new conversational strategies that account for women's success in leadership positions. (Troemel-Ploetz 1994: 199)

A brief analysis of what is being presupposed by Troemel-Ploetz in the above statement would indicate that she is asking the reader to accept a number of somewhat contentious premises as a basis for her argument. I will pick up on some of these later in my discussion. Here I want to show that what her article indicates is that some interesting issues can be foregrounded when speech styles are addressed in terms of speech acts, even if one may want to question some of the premises of the argument.

Troemel-Ploetz's main argument is based on a claim in an edition of the *Harvard Business Review* that male managers traditionally adopt a 'command and control style' of leadership and that women in management positions are currently succeeding 'because of – not in spite of – certain characteristics generally considered to be "feminine" and inappropriate in leaders' (Rosener cited in Troemel-Ploetz 1994: 199). Troemel-Ploetz extends this argument by suggesting that the 'male style' is not necessarily the best in any organisational context and that it is perceived as successful only because there has been no real competition from other, notably 'female', styles. She points out that this is because in the past it is only those women who adopted the male style who were likely to achieve high positions in large organisations. What she is attempting to argue is that these women and men in leadership roles have succeeded in spite of rather than because of the effectiveness of the 'command and control style' (200).

Her claim is that there is now evidence from a range of studies that there are women in management who adopt a 'female style', and who are more effective in that they characteristically have skills that encourage participation, enable the sharing of power and information, enhance other people's self-worth and 'energise followers by producing enthusiasm' (200). As she points out these skills are performed through language, and she focuses on one linguistic strategy in particular in order to show how they are realised in verbal interaction: through what she calls 'camouflaging a dominant speech act' (200). Troemel-Ploetz provides an analysis of talk between Nancy Badore, an executive director of the Ford Motor Company Executive Development Centre and a subordinate male colleague that exemplifies this style. In the extract that I cite below, the male interlocutor has just indicated that he is not enthusiastic about attending a conference that Badore requires him to attend. I will focus on just one part of an utterance that she analyses in order to illustrate her approach. The clauses are numbered B0–4 in the original.

> But this is something we have to get involved in (B0)
> Let me put it this way, John (B1)
> I INVITE you to go (B2)
> But feel free to leave at any time (B3). (200)

Troemel-Ploetz makes that point that because the employee has objected to going to the conference just before this, Badore is faced with a number of choices. She may contradict the reason he gives for not going or she could give an unqualified order such as *You have to go.* As she points out, the outcome of either alternative could be compliance or open conflict. In choosing B0–4, Troemel-Ploetz argues, Badore selects not to use overt markers of authority but to take time to convince and persuade. She goes on to argue: 'By camouflaging the dominant speech act *order* or *request* Badore is empowering her subordinate and thus constructing more equality with him' (204). However, what is also being argued here is that this strategy involves a great deal of communicative skill on Badore's part in that she maintains her own authority while at the same time empowering her subordinate, and that her ability to apply this skill is related to her gender.

The case Troemel-Ploetz puts in support of her claims is as follows. She suggests that in saying *Let me put it this way, John* Badore is using a speech act that has a range of distinct functions. Firstly, it may be introducing or preparing for an unpleasant or unwanted utterance. She supports this claim by proposing that to use this phrase in an alternative linguistic context would be deviant, and cites the example *Let me put it this way, you won the first prize* as evidence of an utterance that would be unlikely to occur. Secondly, Badore is also establishing authority in using this phrase. This is also supported by pointing out the deviancy that would result if this were not the case. She illustrates this by suggesting that it would be odd if a subordinate speaker were to use such a phrase, which is why something like *Let me put it this way, father, I need your signature on my report card* would be unlikely to occur. The phrase also, Troemel-Ploetz argues, tones down the negative impact of what is to follow by conceding that the speaker is aware that it has this potential. Badore's utterance is therefore seen as indicating something like *I don't like it, but I have to tell you this*. Again, the notion of deviance is invoked in order to justify this claim in that it is suggested that *Let me put it this way, I love to tell you this* indicates that the phrase would be misplaced in such a context. Overall Troemel-Ploetz makes the point that, on the basis of this evidence

> B1, then, functions as an introduction to unpleasant information for the hearer, points to the authority of the speaker and her dislike for the task which, however, is outweighed by the necessity of the utterance to come: B2: I INVITE you to go. (202)

Troemel-Ploetz goes on, using 'deviancy' as the primary criterion against which to judge Badore's linguistic choices, to argue that B2 is also a very skilful set of choices on Badore's part. She argues that an invitation is usually a request to participate with the speaker in a pleasant event or experience, and this is evident from the deviance of utterances such as *I invite you to clean my car* or (the less deviant) *I invite you to clean my car with me*. What would not be deviant in such a context, Troemel-Ploetz argues, are utterances such as: *I order you to go* or *I invite you to go with me*. Badore's utterance is taken to be unusual then in that an invitation implies some kind of generosity on the part of the speaker, and more significantly, unlike an order, it is a speech act that can be followed by a refusal or an acceptance. At this stage, as Troemel-Ploetz points out, it is difficult to uncover the order under the camouflage of the invitation: 'The functions of B1 and the emphatic stress on *invite* are the only indicators that Badore is serious and that *invite* has little to do with invitation' (203). However, B3: *But feel free to leave at any time* is, Troemel-Ploetz argues, a clear indicator that B2 was not an invitation: 'B3 assumes in fact that the action of B2 will be performed' (203).

What is being argued here then is that Badore phrases her utterance so that the acts that are being performed by it are somewhat fuzzy, and the dominant speech act 'order' is, as a result, camouflaged by a more benign speech act such as 'invite'. Troemel-Ploetz suggests that this strategy enables authority to be enacted without loss of self-esteem on the part of the subordinate, and is therefore a very skilful use of speech acts on the part of Badore. Troemel-Ploetz's use of the notion of linguistic performativity is careful in that she foregrounds the conventionality of speech act performance, and therefore takes care to make explicit the criteria she is applying when she is making claims about the possible illocutionary force of the locutions she is addressing. While I feel her claims about Badore's linguistic choices are well supported, what is less well supported is the claim that simply evoking 'gender' explains this difference. But having said that, on the basis of this careful analysis of one aspect of a manager's style, this does then raise general questions about such interactions that could usefully be explored further in relation to gender.

Addressing the impact of speech in this way can therefore provide a way of pointing to differences in speech styles, and the effects of these differences on what is achieved in a given interaction. On the basis of what such an analysis can show, speech acts may also therefore provide a useful framework for interrogating differences between the way that men and women talk in specific situations and how their talk can function in these situations. An example of such an approach can be found in a number of works by Holmes (particularly those surveyed in Holmes 1995), who has argued that there are differences in the way that men and women perform and perceive speech acts such as 'apology', 'compliment' and 'insult'. I will consider these in more detail in Chapter 6 in relation to gender and politeness. Here, I want to point to these works as examples of feminist scholarship which, like that of Troemel-Ploetz, begin from essentialist notions of gender, and which go on to argue that it is the fundamental differences implied by these notions that lead men and women to use language differently. Here I want to distinguish this approach from one where gendered differences in speech are addressed from a non-essentialist perspective. In particular I want to show that while studies based on essentialist notions of gender may indicate that there are differences in the talk of men and women, the question of why those differences exist remains unanswered by studies that adopt that model of gender.

4.2.1.2   Assertiveness and gender
In her (1995) account of gendered differences in language use, Crawford, who writes from the perspective of social psychology, addresses the notion of speech acts in relation to assertiveness. Her account illustrates why it is that although analysing the speech acts carried out in talk by men and women can capture a distinction between gendered styles of talk, attempting to account for these in essentialist terms, tends in practice to lead to the avoidance of an explanation. She shows this by bringing speech act theory to bear on findings in social psychology on gender and assertiveness, and in particular focusing on the assertiveness training industry that flourished in the 1980s. By addressing the relationship between the acts that speakers perform through language, and the extent to which the success of these acts is contingent upon the expectations we have about

'appropriate' male and female behaviour, Crawford shows that differences in speech style are better explained in terms of adaptivity rather than essentialist notions of gender. Her claim is that differences in behaviour can be explained by women's awareness of the consequences of their linguistic choices.

Crawford makes her case by analysing the development of the assertiveness training movement that occurred in the 1970s and 1980s, and by exploring its roots in linguistic and psychological scholarship at that time. She points out that in the 1970s, scholarship on gender and language in both linguistics and social psychology came to view women's linguistic behaviour as fundamentally nonassertive. She cites Lakoff's claim that women's speech is characteristically 'deferential' and 'uncertain' because as girls, they had been socialised to be 'docile, well-mannered, and passive' (Lakoff cited in Crawford 1995: 25–6). Crawford shows how this explanation overlaps with the tendency in psychology at this time to invoke the notion of 'learned helplessness' as an explanation of women's putative lack of assertiveness. Crawford describes this notion as an extrapolation of the findings of laboratory research in which animals are exposed to repeated painful electric shocks from which they cannot escape. The results of such experiments showed that when the animals were then put in similar painful situations from which it was quite easy for them to escape, they failed to carry out simple acts that would have allowed them to avoid the pain (52). She makes the point that linguists and psychologists appear to have come to the same essentialist explanation of women's unassertive behaviour at around the same time, and these explanations can be seen as giving rise to the assertiveness training movement.

> Psychologists relied on social learning theory and on learned helplessness. They assumed that women as a group are deficient in communication skills and that psychology had the answer to that deficiency. The deficiency is a relic of the past, of our misguided 'conditioning'. The implication, and the promise, is that if we do get help and are trained to speak up for ourselves, good things will happen: we will be respected, and admired by others, we will get our own way more often, we will have greater personal and social power. (52)

As Crawford points out, there were a number of problems with the arguments and proposals of the assertiveness movement. For example, the research at this time was not premised on empirical evidence that women's linguistic behaviour was actually different to men's, but on intuitions about male and female behaviour, and, most significantly, on an implicit male norm that constructed women's speech as 'deficient and problematical' (56). Moreover, Crawford argues, in spite of the 'empiricist rhetoric' of the assertiveness movement, there was no actual evidence that the linguistic behaviour that they were proposing women should adopt would actually have any social value. A third problem was that assertive speech 'deviated from natural language in important ways that were not acknowledged' (56). It is in relation to these latter problems that Crawford calls on the notion of speech acts as a way of explaining a fundamental flaw in the assertiveness training paradigm. In particular she shows that the techniques advised by assertiveness training can require the asserter to ignore the conventional means by which speakers perform illocutionary acts. As a result the linguistic behaviour they are being asked to carry out is likely to be read as odd, and because of that it is unlikely to achieve the desired effects.

Crawford adopts Searles's approach to the extent that she suggests that the legacy of what she calls 'the general theory of speech acts' is that it foregrounds the way in which sentences do things as well as describe the world, and that for speech acts to be carried out certain rules and conventions must be met (79). She points out however that assertiveness techniques are flawed because they fail to take on board this fundamental feature of communication. She illustrates this by focusing on a technique termed *clipping* which is described as the provision of a minimal response to an indirect speech act such as that implied by the mother's utterance in the following example:

(1) Mother: The dishes aren't washed
Daughter: That's right. (Crawford 1995: 74)

Here the daughter is supposedly being assertive by refusing to take up the implied illocution (request), and instead responding to the utterance as though the mother was simply making an observation about the dishes. Crawford goes on to argue that while this may have the desired effect to the extent that the daughter's response may indeed serve as an indication that she is refusing to recognise that her mother's utterance is intended as a request to wash the dishes, such a response is not part of 'normal' conversational behaviour.

The notion of 'normality' in relation to conversation is a contentious one, and I address it in more depth in subsequent chapters, here the point that is being made is that Crawford takes on board this aspect of speech act theory to argue that because the daughter is not engaging with the conventional means by which illocutionary acts are carried out, her response is more likely to be heard as aggressive than assertive. She goes on to argue that it is this that indicates the fundamental flaw in assertiveness training: that simply carrying out assertiveness techniques does not work because it does not take into account how linguistic inter-actions work. She argues for example that: 'Research on the social evalua-tion of assertion tells us that formulaic assertive speech is not wholly acceptable as a conversational norm. It is not considered likeable or sensitive' (74). In considering the way in which utterances are received by interlocutors, and the extent to which this is an issue of gender, Crawford goes beyond the usual concerns of speech act theory, and relates illocutionary force to wider social issues. In particular she shows that assertiveness training is flawed because it does not take into account how speech acts come to be performed, and she also shows that this is an issue of gender that can be explained without recourse to essentialist notions of difference.

Crawford's account picks up on the pragmatic argument which posits that speech acts are conventional in that the illocutionary force of an utterance is a function of the expectations that interlocutors have about who should say what to whom in a given situation of use. That people are aware that certain speech acts can only be achieved if the speaker has a position of authority for example is illustrated by Thomas's previously discussed (1985) example. The theatre-goer's explication of the illocutionary force of her earlier utterance as one of *asking* her interlocutor if she was able to eat more quietly during the performance rather than *telling* her she should eat more quietly, indicates that the speaker is aware that the felicity conditions of the latter would not be met. This is an issue that has been addressed extensively in pragmatics, and will be considered further in subsequent chapters, here I want to briefly summarise how this insight enables Crawford to account for women's apparent nonassertive behaviour without recourse to simply saying that it is because they are (essentially) women.

On the basis of her own study of women's assertiveness behaviour, and an analysis of the literature, Crawford argues that part of the expectations we have about which speech acts can be performed by whom arise from the sets of stereotypes we have about gender. As she point out, such stereotypes have changed surprisingly little over the past thirty years. She argues that studies ranging from the late 1960s have shown that women are stereotypically 'easily influenced, submissive, sneaky, tactful, very aware of others' feelings, passive, lacking in self-confidence, dependent, unlikely to act as a leader, unaggressive, and uncomfortable about the possibility of behaving aggressively' (1995: 61). She also refers to a 1974 application of the Bem Sex Role Inventory (a measure developed by Sandra Bem in the early 1970s that indicates perceptions of gender) which, as Crawford argues, gives a window onto expectations about gendered behaviour at the time that the assertiveness training movement was gaining momentum. Three 'feminine traits' indicated by the application of the inventory in 1974 are particularly pertinent to the issue of assertion: femininity is equated with being shy, soft-spoken and not using harsh language. The study also indicates that femininity involves being yielding and sympathetic (62). Crawford also shows that the BSRI indicated that traits considered by both sexes to be more desirable for men than women included the items: assertive, defends his own beliefs, willing to take a stand, forceful, and dominant (62). As she points out a trait such as 'willing to take a stand' implies that being masculine involves a use of speech that is quite distinct from that implied by a use consistent with the feminine traits of 'yielding', 'sympathetic' and 'soft-spoken'. Crawford goes on to argue that 'the proto-type of an assertive person is virtually synonymous with the stereotype of masculinity' (62). Getting women to speak assertively then, appears to be a case of getting women to speak like men.

Crawford then goes on to consider the above findings in the light of her own study of the social consequences of assertive speech. Her study indicated that where the same assertive behaviour was carried out by males and by females, it was judged differently by male and female participants in the study. The findings showed that the behaviour was judged by participants along 'dimensions of social competence and likeability' (65). In particular the women asserters received the lowest likeability ratings from all the older male judges and the highest from the older female judges. On the basis of this, Crawford argues:

> The results strongly suggest that the meaning of assertion is at least partly in the eye of the recipient. Assertive women were perceived as competent, but less likeable, a distinction not made for assertive men. (Crawford 1995: 65)

She explains this by referring to the stereotype indicators discussed above and arguing that it would appear that assertive women may be judged less favourably because their language is considered 'out-of-role'. She sup-ports this by drawing on the findings of a range of studies in social psy-chology which indicate that 'in addition to being less liked, women who use out-of-role behaviour may incur other costs: verbal attack, pointed silence, joking, satire, sexual and off-task remarks, and inattention' (67). Crawford also argues that there is, however, some evidence to suggest that women are willing and able to act assertively when they feel that the conditions are appropriate. On the basis of this range of evidence, Crawford concludes:

> 'Unassertive' speech, rather than being a (female) deficiency in social skills, may reflect a sensitivity to the social impact of one's behavior. Tentative and indirect speech may be a pragmatic choice for women. It is more persuasive, at least when the recipient is male, less likely to lead to negative attributions about personality traits and likeability, and less likely to provoke verbal attack. (68)

In asking how the force and consequences of a given speech act come to be understood by others, and by taking into account what a given speech act implies about the speaker's intentions, Crawford provides a useful illustration of one way in which speech act theory can clarify the issues surrounding apparent gender differences in speech style. This study also indicates that the notion of felicity conditions might usefully be expanded in pragmatic accounts to draw on wider social issues including stereo- typical assumptions about who is sanctioned to carry out which type of speech act. She also indicates the need for speech act theory to engage in the historical conditions that underpin the performance of illocutions.

4.2.2. Identity as performance

Crawford's work is useful in that it indicates that gendered differences in language use do not have to be explained in terms of a fixed gender identity. To that extent it is consonant with much current work in feminism that is centred on the poststructuralist notion of identity as neither unitary nor stable. As Hennessy (1993: 12) argues, it is the emergence of gender as 'a category of analysis' that has led to the general concept 'identity' being 'denaturalised'. One effect of this denaturalisation is that gender identity is increasingly being seen not as a fixed entity but as an effect of the ongoing linguistic choices we all make in everyday life. To that extent being 'masculine' or 'feminine' is something we perform rather than something that we are. West et al. state the issue thus:

> Our thesis is that gender is accomplished *in* discourse. As many feminist researchers have shown, that which we think of as 'womanly' or manly' behaviour is not dictated by biology, but rather is socially constructed. And a fundamental domain in which gender is constructed is language use. Social constructions of gender are not neutral, however; they are implicated in the institutionalised power relations of societies. In known contemporary societies, power relations are asymmetrical, such that women's interests are systematically subordinated to men's. (1997: 119–20)

In this section I want to point to the way in which studies that focus on the linguistic construction of identity illustrate the applicability of the idea of language as action.

4.2.2.1 The linguistic performance of gender identity

Citing Butler's (1990) influential argument in her book *Gender Trouble*, Cameron (1997: 49) makes the point that postmodern conceptualisations of gender draw on this work to argue that 'feminine' or 'masculine' are neither what we are nor traits that we have, but that they are 'effects we produce by way of particular things we *do*'. She goes on to quote one of Butler's more famous comments:

> Gender is the repeated stylization of the body, a set of repeated acts within a rigid regulatory frame which congeal over time to produce the appear- ance of substance, or a 'natural' kind of being. (Butler cited in Cameron 1997: 49)

According to this perspective then, gender is 'performative'. As Cameron points out, what Butler means by this is that 'becoming a woman' or 'becoming a man' is not something that one achieves through 'socialisation' or something that is determined by biology. She suggests that what Butler is arguing is that: 'Gender has constantly to be reaffirmed and publicly displayed by repeatedly performing particular acts in accordance with the cultural norms . . . which define 'masculinity' and 'femininity' (Cameron 1997: 49).

In recent years, there has been a range of feminist research that has addressed the performance of gender through linguistic acts, and this work has focused on both the construction of masculinity and the construction of femininity (see for example Eckert and McConnell-Ginet and other articles in Hall and Bucholtz's 1995 edited collection, Johnson and Meinhof 1997 and Simpson 1997). When gender is seen as performed through language use there is a tendency to focus on the significance of formal, or stylistic aspects of language. An example of this is Cos's (1997) research which shows how masculinity is performed by a group of working-class male speakers in Barcelona by electing to use Spanish rather than Catalan in certain situations. He argues that his data indicate that 'Catalan was being used to invoke dry, serious voices, and was not considered amenable to the expression of ambivalence (a function accorded to Spanish); second Catalan was used to convey what were clearly the voices of *others* – ingenuous, posh and *unmasculine*' (101). Cos is not suggesting that the use of Spanish or Catalan will inevitably symbolise masculinity or lack of masculinity, but that within the linguistic community in which these choices were being made, there is an association between the linguistic form and a set of qualities that is exploited by male speakers as a means of performing gender.

The final point is significant in that as Johnson comments in an essay on masculinity and language: 'the important point regarding gendered meanings which become associated with certain linguistic resources over time is that they are *not* inherent in the structures of language themselves' (Johnson 1997: 23–4). What this indicates, and what such studies do not tend to acknowledge, is a need for a pragmatic approach to the issue. In their introduction to the collection that contains Johnson's article, Meinhof and Johnson summarise her approach as deliberately avoiding generalities about the construction of masculinity and argue: 'Instead she advocates studying the disparate ways in which masculinities express themselves, with conclusions drawn in terms of the content and purpose, rather than the form, of language' (Meinhof and Johnson 1997: 2). However, there is no account of how one bridges the gap between content or purpose and the conclusions about masculinity that are being argued. If the link between a speech token and the act of gender identity it performs is not fixed, then it must be inferred. It would seem therefore that developing a model of interaction that can account for how gender is performed through linguistic choices raises the same problems as developing a model that explains how a speech act comes to be performed by a given speech token. If the link is conventional, what are the conditions that lead a token to signify something about 'femininity' or 'masculinity'?

In the following two chapters I consider the way in which pragmatics has theorised the mechanisms that link the token to the act, and in the final chapter I consider what this has to say about issues of language and gender performance. Here I want to conclude this chapter by showing how Cameron's account of the linguistic performance of heterosexual masculinity addresses the issue by focusing on what is said rather than how it is said.

4.2.2.2 Cameron (1997): Performing heterosexual masculinity

In her study, Cameron focuses on the transcription of an informal interaction between a group of five young men, that appears to include many linguistic features that have been conventionally characterised as 'feminine' in sociolinguistic literature. For example, for much of the transcription the talk is not primarily the competitive 'exchange of information' that Tannen (1992) amongst others has associated with male interactions, but, Cameron points out, instead appears to be serving one of the most common purposes of 'gossip': 'namely affirming the solidarity of an in-group by constructing absent others as an out-group, whose behaviour is minutely examined and found wanting' (1997: 54). Cameron points out that there are many formal features that an analyst could point to in the transcription if one wanted to argue that the men were interacting in what would traditionally be described as a 'feminine' style. Many of their turns begin with 'you know', there is a great deal of simultaneous speech, and evidence of 'latching' (when a speaker takes over her turn at speaking without there being a pause or an overlap of speech). As Cameron points out, this has been seen as characteristic of feminine speech in that 'in order to latch a turn so precisely onto the preceding turn, the speaker has to attend closely to others' contributions' (56).

However, in pointing to these features, Cameron is suggesting that their significance should not be simply 'read off' from the data as indicating something about gender. She argues that when analysts claim that certain styles are masculine or feminine, they are assuming that genders are monolithic constructs that automatically give rise to predictable and distinct speech patterns (62). In contrast to this, Cameron adopts Butler's conceptualisation of gender as performance, and sets out to argue that different contexts of use will lead to gender being enacted in different ways, and it may be enacted using styles traditionally associated with the opposite sex. She suggests for example that since, in the interaction she analyses the men are using the content of their 'gossip' to enact heterosexual masculinity, it would seem that gossip as a speech style should not be seen as automatically indicative of gender. She also makes the point that seeing the interlocutors from Butler's perspective, leads one to see them as 'conscious agents' who actively produce gendered behaviour rather than as automata who passively reproduce it. The way in which Cameron illustrates this is by showing that the interlocutors, in their discussion, actively construct those people that they want to be disassociated from as 'gay', and that this same term can imply that the person is being perceived as homosexual, or that the person does not fit into the interlocutors' own conceptualisation of what it is to be 'masculine'. As she points out there are a number of turns devoted to establishing a shared view of homosexuality amongst the interlocutors. One such example is:

```
Al: Gays =
Ed:        =gays w [hy? that's what it should read [gays why?
Bryan:           [gays]                           [I know]. (Cameron
                                                              1997: 51)
```

Here the symbol = indicates latching, an opening square bracket indicates that the turn onset overlaps the previous turn, and items enclosed in square brackets are where one turn is contained within another speaker's turn. Cameron points out that each of these features has been seen as characteristic of women's speech. But while the form may be perceived as 'unmasculine' if such views are accepted, the content is, she argues establishing a shared view of 'gays as alien' which constructs the speakers as masculine in that: 'the group defines itself as heterosexual and puzzled by homosexuality'(51).

However, as Cameron points out, the speakers do not just construct themselves as masculine by opposing themselves to homosexuality. The term 'gay' can also be used to describe any behaviour that does not fit into the group members' conceptualisation of appropriate masculine behaviour. For example, they ridicule the tendency of a particular student to wear shorts to class in all weathers:

```
Bryan: he's either got some condition that he's got to like have his legs
       exposed all the time or else he's got really good legs =
Ed:                                                     =he's probably
       he' [s like
Carl:     [he really likes his legs=
Bryan:                      =he
Ed:                         =he's like at home combing his
                                        leg hairs=
Bryan:                                        =he doesn't
       have any  leg hair though =
Ed:                          =he real[ly likes his legs =
```

Byran   [yes and oh

Al: = very long

very white and very skinny

Bryan: those ridiculous Reeboks that are always (indeciph) and goofy
white socks always striped=   [tube socks

Ed: =that's [right he's the antithesis of man

(1997: 54)

As Cameron points out: in order to demonstrate that certain individuals are 'the antithesis of man' the group engages in a kind of conversation that might well strike us as the antithesis of 'men's talk' (54).

Cameron's point then is that there are many ways of performing gender, and in enacting 'masculinity' or 'femininity', people have a range of linguistic behaviours to draw on. As she goes on to argue:

> Performing masculinity or femininity 'appropriately' cannot mean giving exactly the same performance regardless of the circumstances. It may involve different strategies in mixed and single-sex company, in private and in public settings, in the various social positions (parent, lover, professional, friend) that someone might regularly occupy in the course of everyday life. (60)

Cameron's argument therefore is an argument about methodology. Her point is that her analysis indicates why linguists should not use rigid models of gendered speech in explaining their data. But what her argument also indicates is that this model of linguistic performance faces the same problems that speech act theory has been faced with: what is the basis of any claim that a given act is performed by a given speech token? What it also indicates is that theories of gender performance may well have something to learn from the pragmatics literature which has shown: (1) that speech acts can be collaboratively performed; (2) that there is a need to develop a model of 'felicity conditions' that can account for differential perceptions of what act is being carried out; and (3) that there is evidence to suggest that which act is being performed depends on what has gone before in a given interaction and what comes after.

In this chapter I have discussed the performative capacity of language. In the final chapter I consider further, on the basis of the scholarship in pragmatics and gender that I discuss in the next two chapters, what feminist accounts of language and the performance of gender can take from pragmatics. I also consider what pragmatics has to learn from feminist accounts of gender and performance. For example, as Mey has argued, a basic assumption of speech act theory is that, while semantic meaning may be shared by speaker and hearer, a logical process leads to primary speech acts being inferred on the basis of secondary speech acts, and a precondition of this process is that interlocutors have a shared understanding of the rules and the meanings involved (1993: 124–7). If it is the case (as some of the feminist scholarship I address in the next two chapters suggests) males and females have different assumptions about the goals and norms of conversation, then speech act theory needs to be able to accommodate this. It also needs to be able to accommodate the issues raised by Crawford's account of the impact of gender stereotypes on the performance of speech acts.

5

GRICEAN PRAGMATICS

5.1 MEANING AND CO-OPERATION

In this chapter, I summarise the work of the philosopher Paul Grice, and indicate something of his contribution to pragmatics. I begin by exploring the implications of his theory of meaning, first published in the late 1940s, which argued that in order to understand how meanings are generated through language use, it is necessary to distinguish between the type of meaning that is generated in acts of linguistic communication from other types of meaning. In arguing this, Grice makes a distinction between 'natural' and 'non-natural' meaning, arguing that the second type (non-natural meaning) is the type of meaning that is of specific interest to the study of linguistic communication. After summarising Grice's theory of meaning, I illustrate one way in which it has informed a feminist approach to gender and language-use before going on to describe, illustrate and evaluate his even more influential theory of conversational implicature which was first published in 1967.

5.1.1 Grice's theory of meaning

According the Gricean characterisation of meaning, *natural* meaning would include instances where a link between two phenomena is inferred on the basis of a causal relationship or where one is a symptom of the other. It is the type of meaning implied by phrases such as *inflation means higher interest rates* or *a hangover means I've drunk too much wine*. Non-natural meaning is where two phenomena are linked but where there is no *necessary* connection: where the relationship is based on convention. And this is, of course, the relationship which holds between things in the world and the linguistic signs we use to refer to them. Jacob Mey illustrates the distinction in the following comment:

Meanings can be natural, as expressed in the old Scholastic saying *Urina est signum sanitatis* ('Urine is a sign of health'); that is, from a person's urine it is possible to conclude about the person's health; and this conclusion is immediate, natural and, in most cases, uncontroversial . . . But it is not the case that we can 'read off' the meaning of an utterance in the same way, and as directly, as a physician is able to interpret the colour and other significant properties of a person's urine. (Mey 1993: 59)

The reason we cannot 'read off' the meaning of an utterance is because, in Mey's terms, the 'invisible workings of the mind' cannot be immediately expressed in a 'natural' way: they become accessible primarily by using 'non-natural' carriers (59).

To address meaning in this way is to take as axiomatic that the 'carriers' of the ideas that a speaker is attempting to express (whether these carriers are words or non-verbal expressions) are not inherently meaningful. The carriers do not, in themselves, 'contain' meaning in the sense that urine 'contains' evidence about a person's state of health: linguistic 'carriers' acquire meaning through convention. From this perspective, to characterise meaning in communication one would therefore need to ask what *speakers* mean or intend by their use of this resource rather than to ask what a particular string of *words* mean. Grice characterised this (non-natural) type of meaning in the following way:

> 'A meant (nn) something by x' is (roughly) equivalent to 'A intended the utterance of x to produce some effect in an audience by means of the recognition of this intention.' And we may add that to ask what A meant is to ask for a specification of that intended effect (though, of course, it may not always be possible to get a straight answer involving a 'that' clause, for example 'a belief that . . .'). (Grice 1989: 220)

Levinson offers the following, more technical, reformulation of Grice's characterisation of meaning-nn, where S is the speaker, H is the hearer, z is the intended meaning of an utterance and U is the string of words used in the utterance.

S *meant-nn* z by uttering U if and only if:
  (i)   S intended U to cause some effect z in recipient H
  (ii) S intended (i) to be achieved simply by H recognizing that intention (i). (Levinson 1983: 16)

Levinson glosses this as indicating that communication involves the sender intending to cause the receiver to think or do something, just by getting the receiver to recognise that the sender is trying to *cause* that thought or action. What is being suggested then is that to say (1) that a speaker means 'I can't come to the phone' by uttering the words *I'm in the bath* is the same as saying (2) that the speaker intended the words *I'm in the bath* to cause the hearer to generate the meaning 'I can't come to the phone' and that, moreover, the speaker intended the hearer to be able to generate that meaning by recognising that this is indeed the speaker's intention. Levinson argues that what this characterisation of meaning indicates is that 'communication is a complex kind of intention that is achieved or satisfied just by being recognised' (16).

At this level of abstraction, Grice's claims about meaning may well appear to be either extremely obscure or else a statement of something so obvious that the point of making those claims seems obscure. In order to give some indication of what this theory can tell us about meaning generation, and particularly what it can tell us about gender and language use, I briefly summarise the argument of an article by Sally McConnell-Ginet in which she suggests that Grice's theory can provide an insight into the production and reproduction of sexist language use both at the level of word meaning (for example the sexualisation of words denoting 'women') and at the more subtle level of 'the relative absence of a woman's-eye view in the most readily accessible linguistic resources' (1998: 198).

McConnell-Ginet acknowledges that macro-political structures play a significant role in 'genderising' discourse in that issues such as who writes what, who preaches sermons to large congregations or whose speeches are broadcast around the world are determined at that level. However, as she points out, understanding the micropolitics of 'daily discourse between ordinary individuals' (199) is essential to an understanding of how language use works to produce and reproduce inequalities of gender. She begins by taking Grice's claim that speaker meaning involves an attribution of an intention by the hearer to the speaker, and shows that this is so intrinsic to communication that it is evident in the interactions that form the earliest moments in a child's acquisition of language. Notwithstanding theories of language acquisition that propose that humans are predisposed to acquire the grammar of a language and to tag certain basic concepts, at a communicative level, McConnell-Ginet argues, it is through the attribution of intention that a child's initially meaningless sounds come to acquire meaning. An example would be where a sound such as *mmmmm* made by a child is taken to mean 'mum' by a caregiver who 'recognises' the utterance as a child's attempt to name its environment. The relevance of a Gricean approach is indicated in McConnell-Ginet's comment:

> The main point here . . . is that endowing linguistic forms with meaning is a socially situated process. The statement applies not just to children learning to communicate but also to more mature speakers struggling to convey increasingly complex thoughts. A major insight of the Gricean perspective is that we can manage to mean much more than what we literally say. How? By relying on what we take to be shared or readily accessible beliefs and attitudes in a particular context. (202)

It is the degree to which these beliefs are shared, are readily accessible and are co-ordinated in acts of linguistic communication that McConnell-Ginet focuses on in her argument. She makes the point that the words

127

used in an utterance are able to provide evidence of a speaker's intention in that one type of shared belief is the set of beliefs we have about what language items can mean at a given moment in a given community.

However, although the conventional links between words and concepts make language a particularly effective communicative resource, she argues that the 'literal meanings' of words are best seen as 'defaults', operative unless something special in the discourse triggers alternative interpretations (206). Moreover, as she goes on to assert, these 'literal' meanings hold only because of the co-ordinated nature of communication in that it is only while there is a consensus about what a word signifies that it can continue to generate a given meaning. She uses the previously stable relationship between the word *he* in its generic sense to mean 'he or she' to illustrate the extent to which meaning generation is dependent upon co-ordination between communicators:

> As we probably all realize, for example, it is becoming harder and harder to make *he* mean 'she or he', because only incredibly isolated speakers can have missed the controversy over the so-called generic masculine, the dispute over whether users of *he* in sex-indefinite contexts indeed intend to refer to both sexes and, if they do, how well they succeed in getting their hearers to recognize that intention. Given the doubts raised, one cannot say *he* and mean 'she or he' because one cannot generally expect hearers to make this identification. (205–6)

McConnell-Ginet's point is that for language items to generate the meanings that we want them to generate, we must get others to co-operate with us: 'At the very least, our listeners must recognize our intention and help us by acknowledging that recognition' (207).

The implications of this for an understanding of sexism in language use are illustrated by McConnell-Ginet's argument that a man who wishes to insult her by saying *you think like a woman* can succeed in that intention. However, the reason that the use of this phrase can succeed as an insult is not founded on a shared belief that there is something inferior about women's thinking. Rather, she argues, it is because:

> I understand that he is likely to have such a belief, and that his intention is not just to identify my thinking as an objectively characterizable sort but to suggest that it is flawed in a way endemic to women's thought. The crucial point is that I need not know his particular beliefs: I need only refer to what I recognize (and can suppose he intends me to recognize) as a common belief in the community. (205)

For these same reasons, she points out, it would be much more difficult for her to insult a man using the phrase *you think like a man*. That is because to recognise that the use of these words was intended as an insult, the man would not only have to know that her opinion of men's thinking is low, he would also have to believe that she knows that he is aware of this. As McConnell-Ginet points out, although such an understanding is imaginable in a conversation between old acquaintances, it would not be likely in other communicative contexts. Moreover, she makes the point:

> even where the intended insult works, it is construed as something of a joke or as a special usage, unless the stereotype disparaging women's thought (or at least elevating men's) is not familiar to both interlocutors ... No matter how much I might wish to insult someone by saying that *she* or *he* thinks like a man, I could not so intend without relying on more than general linguistic and cultural knowledge. (206)

Her point is that sexist uses of language have the power to insult simply *because* speakers are able to assume that hearers have ready access to shared linguistic and cultural knowledges about stereotypes of gender. It is the relative ease with which a speaker's intentions can be recognized that render an attempt to communicate that intention successful or not.

McConnell-Ginet develops her argument by addressing the implications of this insight. She draws on the findings of empirical studies of gender and language use which indicate that men and women have tendencies to develop distinct speech styles, and on claims about macropolitical structures, to argue that there is much evidence to suggest that men are more likely than women to have an opportunity to express their perspective on situations, and also that men are more likely to be attended to when they speak than are women. As a result of these factors, she argues, where men's and women's perspectives on a situation are different the man's view is more likely to be known to the woman than hers to him. A corollary of this is that the man's communicative intent is more likely to be recognised than the woman's. She suggests that this disparity can have important consequences for what men and women are able to 'mean' when engaging in linguistic communication:

> Why? Because what is meant depends not just on the joint beliefs about the language system and its conventional – that is, standard or established – interpretations but also on what interlocutors take to be prevalent beliefs in the speech community about everything else beside language. (204)

For McConnell-Ginet then, Grice's theory of meaning allows her to explain why it is that the English language, as a communicative resource, appears to serve male users more effectively than it does women users.

In showing why women can find it difficult to generate the meanings they wish to generate using linguistic resources, and to challenge the meanings that conventionally hold within that system, she sums up her argument thus:

> Language matters so much precisely because so little matter is attached to it: meanings are not given but must be produced and reproduced,

negotiated in situated contexts of communication. Negotiation is always problematic if an equality of resources enables one negotiator to coerce the other. (209)

By using it to explain how some meanings come to be more easily generated than others and by showing how this relates to gender inequalities, McConnell-Ginet's discussion offers a well-argued illustration of one way in which Grice's theory of meaning is relevant to feminist research. She points out, however, that the theory is useful not only in explaining the problems, it also indicates possibilities for the solution of those problems. If Grice's account is accepted as an accurate model of how meaning is generated, then it is also indicates something about how new meanings might be generated. As she points out, new meanings are dependent upon acts of co-ordination that require co-operation between interlocutors, which indicates how feminists as a group might promote meanings that are oriented to women's empowerment. It also indicates where the problems lie in making those meanings generally accessible across a given culture.

To summarise: Grice's theory of meaning postulates that in order to understand a speaker's meaning, it is necessary to 'recognise' the speaker's intention. The issue of how far intentions can precede their articulation, and to what extent it is ever possible to recognise such phenomena has been taken up in a range of pragmatic debates. While, as a result, both the term *recognise* and the term *intention* have been extensively problematised over time, both within and outside of pragmatics scholarship, Grice's basic insight that non-natural meaning is a distinct type, and that it is generated in part through interlocutors' inferences about what each 'means' by what they 'say', has remained a useful framework for analysing speech and writing. McConnell-Ginet picks up on one implication of Grice's by showing how it provides a model for understanding why it is much easier to generate sexist meanings through language use than to generate meanings that problematise or run against stereotypical notions of gender. By arguing that a speaker's meaning is more easily accessed when it draws on ideas and perspectives that are generally accepted across a community than when it draws on less accepted ways of seeing the world, McConnell-Ginet is able to offer a level of explanation that simply would not be available at the level of content analysis. Explanations of sexist language that draw on the idea that meanings are an effect of content, are simply unable to explain the why it is that *you think like a woman* is, across a range of contexts of use, more capable of being seen as an insult than *you think like a man*.

Although Grice's claims about speaker intention have triggered a great deal of debate, and although his work has been used as a framework for understanding linguistic communication across a range of studies, what his account does not provide, is an explanation of *how* a speaker's intended meaning is communicated by what is said. His later formulation of the way in which such meanings are generated by the expectations we have about communicative behaviour provides the basis for such an explanation.

5.1.2 Grice's theory of conversation

Although Grice's model of the way in which speaker meanings are generated is initially formulated as a model of conversation, over time it has been extended to cover all forms of communication (see, for example, Burt 1992, Sarangi and Slembrouk 1992). It should also be noted that, as with his earlier theory of meaning, the terms within which Grice initially formulated his argument have been extensively problematised by later pragmaticians. However, Grice's original framework remains highly influential, even if it is often referred to in ways that sometimes obscure its contribution to current work. And because there is much work that does apply Grice's initial terms, I retain them in the following summary. I also keep my evaluative comments to a minimum at this stage. After showing how his theory has been applied in research on gender and language use, I will provide an overview of how Gricean pragmatics has been critiqued, and what aspects might remain significant to feminist scholarship.

5.1.2.1 The co-operative principle

Grice's theory of conversation was formulated as a way of explaining the type of meaning that is generated by the following example:

> (1) Suppose that A and B are talking about a mutual friend, C, who is now working in a bank. A asks B how C is getting on in his job, and B replies *Oh quite well, I think: he likes his colleagues, and he hasn't been to prison yet.* (Grice 1989: 24)

As Grice comments, whatever B means, implies or suggests in the final clause of his reply, it is quite distinct from what B has actually said, which is, simply, that C has not yet been to prison. In pointing to this specific distinction between what is 'said' and what is 'meant' Grice sets out to argue that this type of implied meaning is an effect of conversational norms rather than an effect of conventional linguistic meaning. To that extent, it is a type of implied meaning that is quite distinct from entailment or presupposition. Both of these, as I showed in Chapter 3, are 'unstated' or implied meanings that are strongly linked to the conventional meanings of language items. Entailment is explained in terms of word meaning (if I say *I have a spaniel*, it implies *I have a dog* because part of the meaning of the term *spaniel* is that it is a type of dog), while presuppositions are triggered by specific terms such as *realise* or *regret* or by specific

131

constructions such as assertions (If I say *I realise you were right* I am implying, but not actually stating *you were right*). The type of indirect meaning that Grice points to in the above example, and which he terms conversational implicature, is different to either of these in that this type of implied meaning is determined less by language choices and more by the expectations that interlocutors have about conversational behaviour.

Grice formulated these expectations as a set of maxims and argued that underlying these maxims is a basic principle. He begins his formulation of this principle with the following observations:

> Our talk exchanges do not normally consist of a succession of disconnected remarks, and would not be rational if they did. They are characteristically, to some degree at least, cooperative efforts; and each participant recognizes in them, to some extent, a common purpose or set of purposes, or at least a mutually accepted direction. This purpose or direction may be fixed from the start . . . Or it may be so indefinite as to leave very considerable latitude to the participants . . . But at each stage some possible conversational moves would be excluded as conversationally unsuitable. We might therefore formulate a rough general principle which participants will be expected, other things being equal, to observe, namely: make your conversational contribution such as is required, at the stage at which it occurs, by the accepted purpose or direction of the talk exchange in which you are engaged. One might label this the Cooperative Principle. (Grice 1989: 26)

Grice's point in arguing that conversational behaviour is constrained by the expectations he outlines above is that such expectations can explain how it is that interlocutors get from what is said to what is meant, that is, they can explain how implicatures are generated.

Schiffrin provides a useful overview of the Gricean approach and argues that what it suggests is that 'human beings work with very minimal assumptions about one another and their conduct, and that they use those assumptions as the basis from which to draw highly specific inferences about one another's intended meanings' (1994: 9). These minimal assumptions include the assumption that one's interlocutors are rational, and that conversations are essentially co-operative efforts. What marks conversations as co-operative is not, it should be stressed, an issue of style. It is not the type of 'co-operation' that Coates (1989: 95) for example points to when she says that women's speech tends towards group needs more than their own desire to speak. In contrast to this, co-operation from a Gricean perspective is a basic premise about the nature of communicative behaviour that interlocutors share and which enables implicatures to be generated. An example might clarify this distinction.

Grice provides the following exchange as an illustration of the co-operative principle (CP) in action.

(2) A: I am out of petrol.
    B: There is a garage round the corner. (1989: 32)

As he points out, the unstated connection between B's remark and A's remark is, at one level, quite obvious. However, if we take B's meaning to be that A can get petrol from the nearby garage, given that what B means is not actually retrievable from the words she uses, the connection can only be explained in terms of how the utterance functions as a contribution to the conversation. If A is able to perceive B's remarks as meaningful, it is because he is assuming that B believes, or at least hopes that the garage is open and that it has petrol to sell. That is to say, the remark is meaningful to the extent that A perceives that B is fulfilling the expectations A has about the co-operative nature of conversation.

What Grice is suggesting when he argues that interlocutors have expectations about the co-operative nature of conversational behaviour is that in conversation speakers are expected to adhere to a principle that can be expressed through the following set of maxims (see Grice 1989: 26–7).

The Maxim of Quantity: Make your contribution as informative as is required (for the current purposes of the exchange); do not make your contribution more informative than is required.

The Maxim of Quality: Try to make your contribution one that is true: do not say what you believe to be false; do not say that for which you lack adequate evidence.

The Maxim of Relation: Be relevant.

The Maxim of Manner: Be perspicuous; avoid obscurity of expression; avoid ambiguity; be brief (avoid unnecessary prolixity); be orderly.

Although he formulates them as though they were prescriptive, Grice's point is that the maxims are not indicating what people *should* do or even what they *actually* do in framing their utterances. Rather he is suggesting that these are expectations about rational conversational behaviour that interlocutors assume are shared, and to that extent they are a set of premises that interlocutors are able to *exploit* in order to generate conversational implicatures (that is, to be able to mean more than is said).

Grice argues for example that a speaker can select to 'flout' the maxims blatantly in order to generate meaning indirectly. He illustrates this with the ironic statement *X is a fine friend* made by A in a context where X, who had previously been on close terms with A, has now betrayed a secret of A's to a business rival. Grice argues that this constitutes a flouting of the first maxim of Quality (do not say what you believe to be false) to the extent that it is a clearly recognisable failure to fulfil the maxim. Where addressees are able to recognise that such a failure is deliberate, and where they also assume that the speaker is still adhering overall to the CP, they will, Grice argues, look for an alternative meaning to the 'literal'. He glosses the process thus:

> It is perfectly obvious to A and his audience that what A has said or has made as if to say is something he does not believe, and the audience knows that A knows that this is obvious to the audience. So, unless A's utterance is entirely pointless, A must be trying to get across some other proposition than the one he purports to be putting forward. This must be some obviously related proposition; the most obvious related proposition is the contradictory of the one he purports to be putting forward. (1989: 34)

Grice's point then is not that the maxims that express the CP are adhered to by speakers, but that they are shared premises about conversational behaviour that can be exploited as a means of generating indirect meanings.

Grice argues that a speaker may fail to fulfil the maxims in a number of ways: she may (1) quietly and unostentatiously violate a maxim and in doing so mislead the audience; (2) opt out from the operation of the maxim and the CP by making it plain that she is unwilling or unable to co-operate (for example, by saying something like *my lips are sealed*); (3) be faced with a clash whereby if one maxim is to be fulfilled, another cannot be and (4) flout a maxim, such as in the above example. An example of a clash is given in Thomas (1995), where she shows how it can be resolved by exploiting a maxim and thereby generating an implicature rather than violating a maxim. The speaker here is Rupert Allason, who is a British member of parliament, an author and an expert on the British intelligence services. He is discussing the identity of a hitherto unnamed member of an espionage ring, the so-called 'Fifth Man':

> (4) It was either Graham Mitchell or Roger Hollis and I don't believe it was Roger Hollis. (Thomas 1995: 65)

Thomas points out that Allason has given more information than is required here since he could have just said 'The Fifth Man is Graham Mitchell' and to that extent he appears to have breached the maxim of Quantity. She goes on to suggest that if a reader has no reason to believe that Allason is deliberately being unco-operative (and therefore uncommunicative) then the non-adherence to the maxim of Quantity would be seen as a flout and would therefore trigger the generation of an implicature. She sees the implicature here to be that Allason is communicating that he strongly believes that Mitchell was the spy, but he is also indicating that he does not have sufficient evidence to assert this as a fact. She argues that Allason's reply might be seen as a compromise in that he is confronted with a clash between his ability to observe both the maxims of Quality and the maxims of Quantity. He has flouted the second maxim of Quantity, therefore, in order to observe the second maxim of Quality: Do not say that for which you do not have adequate evidence. What is at issue here is that in flouting a maxim at one level, Allason is observing the co-operative principle at a deeper level. This is quite distinct from the violation of a maxim where the speaker is *not* attempting to generate implicatures on the basis of a non-observance of a maxim, for example when a speaker is lying.

Before discussing how this theory can be applied in feminist research, it is worth pointing out that Grice distinguishes between conventional implicatures and conversational implicatures. Conventional implicatures are meanings that are implied by the conventional meanings of words. Again, Thomas provides a good example of such an implicature, here in relation to the word *but*:

> The American actress, Kathleen Turner, was discussing perceptions of women in the film industry: 'I get breakdowns from the studios of the scripts that they're developing . . . and I got one that I sent back furious to the studio that said "The main character was thirty-seven but still attractive." I circled the *but* in red ink and I sent it back and said 'Try again!' (Thomas 1995: 57)

Grice's example is that if he states *He is an Englishman; he is therefore, brave*, he is conventionally implicating, through the use of the word *therefore* that it is because he is an Englishman that he is brave. He argues that he has not however, in the strict meaning of the word, *said* this. While the implicatures generated by such usage will tend to occur in *every* usage of those terms, conversational implicatures are always context specific. To be able to argue that a conversational implicature is being generated, it is necessary to show that it can be calculated on the basis of the contextual evidence that gave rise to it. It will only count as a conversational implicature if it is replaceable by an argument, and can be shown to be a meaning that is context specific.

In the following section I will briefly illustrate how Grice's approach has been applied before concluding this chapter with a summary of the developments that have attempted to accommodate his approach to current models of communication.

5.2 THE ROLE OF PRAGMATICS IN CRITICAL THINKING

In an article entitled 'Teaching conscientious resistance to co-operation with text: The role of pragmatics in critical thinking', Burt (1992) critiques the methodology employed by American teachers of essay writing in classes that are designed to teach students to recognise and unravel flaws in the logic of the texts that they read and produce. Her claim is that the teaching of critical thinking is better served by a familiarity with Grice than through the traditional engagement with logic and the learning of lists of logical fallacies. Her point is that Grice's theory provides both a descriptive base and an explanatory framework that allows a student to recognise and critique a flawed argument. Although Burt's account is not explicitly feminist, and does not set out to foreground issues of gender, it does have a pertinence here in that her point is that being able to apply a Gricean analysis in the critique of language use is empowering for readers. And if, as much feminist scholarship has argued, language use is implicated in gendered power relations, it has an obvious application in this area. I provide an illustration of this application at the end of the following overview of Burt's argument.

5.2.1 TEACHING CONSCIENTIOUS RESISTANCE TO CO-OPERATION WITH TEXT

Burt points out that, as part of composition teaching, students in the US are traditionally taught to critique arguments through the learning and application of 'fallacy lists' which categorise and describe the range of logical flaws that can occur in argument. One example of such a fallacy is the circular reasoning demonstrated in the following student text which Burt glosses as intended as a discussion about whether abortion ought to be legal:

> It is my opinion that since it is the woman's right to have an abortion, the decision must be entirely up to her. Even if everyone does not agree with the woman's choice, it is illegal to prohibit any woman from exercising her rights. The government must protect these rights because they are guaranteed to everyone by law. (Burt 1992: 401)

Burt indicates that what the student is actually arguing here is that abortion is lawful because it is legal. She suggests moreover that when a student is taught to recognise that this form of argument is problematic it would normally be dependent upon the student having learned about and memorised up to seventeen distinct and unconnected logical fallacies. She makes the point that, while this is difficult in itself, the student is also faced with the added problem of recognising when an argument that he or she encounters or produces falls into one of these seventeen categories. Burt argues that this is a far from straightforward activity, and that as a result students are rarely wholly successful in either recognising or critiquing fallacious arguments. For example, although in the above case the traditional fallacy name is descriptive and it is therefore not too difficult to recognise that the argument falls within the category of 'circular reasoning', Burt points out that this is not always the case. The names of some fallacies are less descriptive (for example, the 'slippery slope' or the 'distraction' fallacy) and therefore recognising their occurrence in a text is not easy. Burt also points out that although they raise awareness that circular reasoning is an inappropriate way of arguing, and although they make it possible to recognise that circular reasoning is being employed, fallacy lists do not sufficiently account for *why* it is inappropriate to argue in this way, and they are therefore of limited effectiveness on a number of counts.

Burt suggests that adopting a Gricean framework allows students to do all that the fallacy lists allow them to do, but that the Gricean approach is more straightforward and therefore more likely to be applied effectively. Her point is that when critically evaluating a text from a Gricean approach there are just four sets of connected maxims that need to be kept in mind, and looking for violations of this small number of maxims is a more manageable exercise than looking for examples of seventeen different types of flawed argument. Burt also points out that an awareness of the maxims would enable readers to recognise other problematic aspects of argument not covered by the lists. She goes on to suggest that applying a Gricean model also provides an explanatory framework: it shows *why* fallacious arguments are problematic thereby indicating how and why they might critiqued. Finally the Gricean framework provides a descriptive vocabulary that allows the critique to be clearly articulated. Burt illustrates these advantages in relation to the above textual example by pointing out that failing to address the question of whether abortion *ought* to be legal can be seen as a failure of Quantity on two counts. The two sub-maxims of quantity are (1) Make your contribution as informative as is required (for the current purposes of the exchange), and (2) Do not make your contribution more informative than is required. The use of circular reasoning means that the student is not being sufficiently informative about the issue she *should* be addressing, and, moreover, in repeating herself (abortion is lawful because it is legal) is violating the second maxim of Quantity. As well as being relatively easy to spot, what the Gricean framework also adds is the awareness that since such violations can be pinned down to the maxim of Quantity, and given that this maxim relates to the *amount* of information provided, then the flaw can be explained and rectified by considering how the argument might be made more effective in this specific area.

Burt also argues that since a Gricean framework is predicated on the assumption that for communication to work, there needs to be a form of co-operation between participants (in this case between a reader and a writer), students who approach a text with this in mind are conscious of both the extent and the appropriateness of their compliance with the writer's communicative strategies. Burt argues for example that a reader's engagement with a text is predicated on his or her expectation that the writer will comply with the CP. And while co-operation between the writer and reader facilitates communication to the extent that it enables the generation of implicatures when a writer flouts a maxim, given that this approach foregrounds the need for the reader to be complicit in this process, it also alerts the reader to the possibility, and appropriateness, of withholding that co-operation when maxims are being violated rather than flouted. This is particularly useful when a text is promoting an ideological perspective that a reader might want to question. For example, Burt makes the point that although in the case of student essays such as the above, maxim violations can be attributed to a student's inexperience in putting together an effective argument, writers can of course deliberately violate a maxim in order to mislead a reader, or to promote a particular point of view without making their agenda explicit. She cites the following example of an argument that occurred in a text on nuclear disarmament by Edward Teller published in the early 1980s where the 'we' is presumably the United States and the 'totalitarian empire' is the then Soviet Union:

> We have negotiated for 25 years, and the results are readily visible. Why would a totalitarian empire that depends on military force to maintain its power voluntarily disarm itself? (Teller in Burt 1992: 407)

As Burt points out, the reader here is invited to infer that the totalitarian empire in question would not disarm itself, but that this proposition is generated indirectly by a rhetorical question rather than explicitly articulated by Teller. She suggests therefore that the writer overtly commits the fallacy named 'many questions' here, describing it as an instance where the writer 'presupposes a proposition that ought to be argued for' (1992: 407). However, the use of a rhetorical question to achieve this effect is not addressed in the fallacy lists, and Burt argues that for this reason a Gricean approach would allow a more explanatory account of the problem. In Gricean terms the above would be seen as a maxim violation in that by substituting a rhetorical question for an argument that would establish the main proposition, Teller fails to be 'as informative as required and also fails to give adequate evidence for what he intends to lead readers to believe' (408). As such, Burt remarks, Teller is violating the first sub-maxim of Quantity in that he is not being adequately informative and is also violating the second sub-maxim of Quality in that he is, through the use of a rhetorical question, implying that a proposition is true without adequate evidence that it is true. In summing up her discussion of the extract Burt comments:

> The example illustrates that a clever writer can use maxim violations – which are usually innocent – as well as traditional fallacies to mislead

readers. Alerting readers to the possibility of manipulative non-fallacy violations of maxims in a text will further encourage their resistance to co-operation with manipulative texts. (Burt 1992: 409)

A familiarity with Grice that alerts readers to the extent of their own co-operation can therefore heighten readers' awareness of the possibility of being manipulated, and this in turn encourages the development of critical thinking.

5.2.2 Applying Grice in feminist textual criticism

The following analysis of a lead article from *the Daily Mail* illustrates how Burt's argument might be applied in a feminist analysis. The text is typical of the large number of *Mail* articles that focus on compensation awards in sexual harassment cases during 1996. I discuss this issue further in my account of relevance theory below. Here the article is of interest to the extent that it uses the same type of strategy Burt points to in the above discussion of the Teller extract, to imply that a proposition is true when there is insufficient evidence.

UNDUE HARASSMENT OF THE TAXPAYERS

So distressed was Detective Constable Libby Ashurst by the treatment to which she was subjected that she resigned from the North Yorkshire police. She should be somewhat consoled now that she has been paid at least £100,000 to drop her sex discrimination claim and say nothing more about it. In all too many forces, the canteen culture can still be loutishly sexist. It should be confronted. Women officers must have legal redress.

But by any standards, £100,000 is a vast sum of money for injured feelings. It is four times what a policeman, who had been criminally assaulted, would receive in compensation for the loss of an eye; twice what he could expect for the loss of a leg.

Is this political correctness gone mad or has Libby Ashurst been subject to sexual harassment so appalling as to be worse than the loss of a limb? We just don't know. Under the terms of the settlement we are kept in the dark. What taxpayers do know is that they must pay the bill. They have every right to be told the facts. (*Daily Mail* 1991)

At one level the article can be read as pointing out that the primary issue here is the fact that the North Yorkshire Police have failed to be sufficiently accountable to the British taxpayer. For example, the question that begins the final paragraph: *Is this political correctness gone mad or has Libby Ashurst been subject to sexual harassment so appalling as to be worse than the loss of a limb* is followed by the observation that this information is not available: *We just don't know.* It would seem then that the point is being made that British taxpayers (and, of course, the *Mail*) lack adequate information to be able to judge whether the level of compensation Ashurst received is justified. Since the compensation settlement requires Ashurst to remain silent about her experiences, the stated lack of knowledge here seems to function, given the other claims made in the remainder of the third paragraph, as a means of illustrating how inadequately informed the taxpayer is, and that this is what is so unacceptable: it is the taxpayer who will have to pay for this award, without ever knowing whether it was justified.

However, although, on the evidence of the meanings generated by the final paragraph, the question that opens that paragraph appears to be rhetorical, I would want to argue that the text is designed to generate an interpretation of the situation that would lead the reader *not* to see the question as one which cannot be answered. I would also want to argue that, without making this explicit, the article questions the validity of sexual harassment compensation generally and of this award in particular. Indeed what I am proposing is that the text is constructed in such a way that it is likely to generate the interpretation that Ashurst's treatment could not possibly have been appalling enough to warrant the compensation she was awarded and therefore the award must be an example of political correctness gone mad. As such, I see the text as implying that the police are to blame on two counts: for not recognising that they are accountable to the taxpayer *and* for being such poor judges of sexual harassment claims that they allow an example of *political correctness gone mad* to cost so much money. But given that this is not actually stated, how can I justify this? What evidence might be called on to substantiate this claim? If the claims made by the Gricean framework are posited, it is possible to argue it in the following ways.

One way would be to consider the meanings *conventionally* implicated by the text. As I indicated above, Grice argued that certain words generate similar implied meanings no matter where they are used, and *but* is one such word, in that it conventionally implicates that the proposition that follows the use of the word will go against the expectations generated by the proposition that preceded its use. Therefore when *Women officers must have legal redress* is followed by *but by any standards, £100,000 is a vast sum of money for injured feelings w*hat is conventionally implicated here is that the payment of £100,000 goes against reasonable expectations about what legal redress for women officers might consist of. Further evidence that an analyst adopting a Gricean approach might point to would be based on the premise that readers of the article expect that the writer is adhering to the CP. If this is what readers expect, then they would anticipate, for example, that the propositions generated either through explicit or implicit means in the article will be, amongst other things, true and relevant. To take the sentence which follows that just discussed: if the writer is adhering to the CP and not violating the maxim of relevance then it should be immediately evident to the reader why it is that the *Mail* is informing us that the sum of money awarded to Ashurst is more than a policeman might expect if he is physically injured. However, the relation between the previous sentence and the comparison of awards for physical and non-physical injuries is not made explicit. For example the comparison between the awards might be there in order to emphasise the *severity* of Ashurst's injuries (for example, if the loss of a leg gets £50,000 and injured feelings get £100,000 then Ashurst must have suffered a great deal) or it could be there to support the conventional implicature I pointed to previously: that the award is excessive.

Given that the relevance is not actually stated (the writer does not for example include a clause saying 'The award is clearly excessive given that it is four times . . .'), it could be argued that the writer does not seem to be observing the maxim of relevance here. However, the Gricean approach would assume that if the reader has no reason to think that the writer is opting out of the CP (that is, no reason to think that the writer is deliberately *not* being relevant) then this would be interpreted by a reader as a flout designed to generate an implicature. Therefore, if the reader has already interpreted the previous sentence as conventionally implicating that *the award is excessive* it is possible to see that the comparison is flouting the maxim of relevance in order to avoid failing to fulfil the third sub-maxim of Manner: be brief. If this is the case, it is possible to read the comparison as pointing, in a concise way, to evidence that would support the conventionally implicated proposition that the compensation award is excessive.

Note however, that at no point does the *Mail* writer explicitly *say* any of this. And indeed how could it be stated explicitly? As I have pointed out, the writer indicates in the next but one sentence *we just don't know* whether Ashurst's injuries are comparable to the physical injuries the article compares the harassment to. To that extent, I would want to argue that the overall impression created by the text is achieved through violating rather than flouting the maxims that express the CP. It is implying a proposition that is not substantiated by the argument or the evidence, and this is achieved specifically through the use of what is ostensibly a rhetorical question in the final paragraph. This is evident in that if, by co-operating with the text so far, the reader has already generated the implicature that the payment is excessive, it would be somewhat inconsistent (and irrelevant) to do other than answer *no* to the second part of the question (*has Libby Ashurst been subject to sexual harassment so appalling as to be worse than the loss of a limb?*). And given that the question poses an either/or option, if we answer *no* to the second part, it would imply that the answer to the first part should be: *yes this is political*

141

correctness gone mad. To this extent then, the writer appears to be violating the CP by implying that a state of affairs holds when there is no evidence for this state of affairs.

What I have used a Gricean approach to argue here, then, is that this framework allows an analyst to critique a version of events when that perspective is being implied but not made explicit in a text. In this case a basic employment right that has been identified and defined by feminists, and which today is legislated for in employment law, is projected as 'political correctness' and is significant primarily for the amount it costs the taxpayer, and for what it indicates about police departments who are unable to discriminate between 'real injuries' and 'injured feelings'. My own research on the reporting of sexual harassment (Christie 1998b) has indicated that *Mail* texts consistently equate sexual harassment claims with the notion of political correctness and that this act of association works to discredit the idea that *any* sexual harassment claims are justified. However, no newspaper could make this point explicitly since it would leave them vulnerable to legal action given that in this context the maxim of Quality is actually reinforced by libel laws. And because this point of view is inevitably implicated rather than stated, critiquing such a view is problematic. The application of a Gricean framework provides one way of accessing and critiquing the unsaid therefore. And although it is inferred meaning that is being discussed here, and to that extent the focus is on a type of meaning whose very existence is open to question, Gricean pragmatics can make explicit the route by which an implicature is generated, and allows a way of being able to frame such questions. To that extent, this type of analysis provides material that can be used as the basis for argument. You may not agree with my reading, but adopting this approach provides a means for it to be articulated and supported, and if it is disputed, it also provides the grounds on which that dispute can take place.

5.3   A GRICEAN APPROACH TO GENDERED DIFFERENCES IN LANGUAGE USE

Suellen Rundquist's article 'Indirectness: A gender study of flouting Grice's maxims' provides an illustration of the way in which a Gricean framework can inform empirical studies of naturally occurring linguistic behaviour. The study focuses on the way in which a group of men and women engaged in informal conversation with their own children and with other adults, and the results showed that the men who took part tended to exploit the CP by flouting the maxims much more frequently than the women did. Her study also indicates a range of different forms that indirectness can take, and some of the distinct functions indirectness can have. On the basis of her analysis Rundquist concludes that the men's use of indirectness is predicated on, and works to perpetuate their relative power within the interactions she records. I briefly summarise the study in order to show how Grice's account can be used in such a context, and then go on to consider the validity of Rundquist's claim, and how it relates to other studies that have addressed the CP in other contexts.

5.3.1   Indirectness and gender

Rundquist's study examines men's and women's speech recorded in two informal situations (1) mothers and fathers talking to their children over a family meal and (2) those same males and females engaging in conversation with the other adults in the study over a series of dinner parties. The study focused on what Rundquist refers to as 'a very small part of one socio-economic group' (1992: 433) in that the participants were seven couples, all of whom were (American) college graduates aged between thirty-five and forty-five all of whom were professionals, working outside the home (ethnicity is not made explicit). Each of the couples had between one and three children who were aged between five and fourteen. In all cases the participants were aware they were being recorded, but Rundquist asserts that although the participants initially tended to indicate a consciousness of the tape recorder, in each case 'as the meal progressed the recorder was usually forgotten and conversation became more spontaneous' (433).

Rundquist analysed the data by indicating how many turns each adult participant took in the conversations and how many of those turns involved some sort of maxim flouting. She then calculated the percentage of flouts in relation to turns and compared the mean for males with the mean for females. She found that the results indicated that statistically the difference between the male and female linguistic behaviour was significant. In the condition where the adults were in conversation with children, the mean score for the men was 16.79 per cent flouts per conversation, while for the women it was 5.73 per cent. In the condition where there were no children present the mean for the men was 16.3 per cent and for the women it was 5.0 per cent. While Rundquist acknowledges that, because of the size and specificity of the sample, generalisations would be inappropriate, given the extent of the difference, there is some indication here that the use of indirection is in some way related to the gender of the participants, and is worth exploring further. In particular, because her approach draws on Grice, and this gives her a descriptive vocabulary that enables her to distinguish between distinct types of indirectness, she can also point to differences in function that might shed light on gender roles in these contexts. It is worth noting, however, that in this particular study, because the female use of indirection was so limited, it is primarily the male data that provides evidence of trends in the range of forms and functions of indirectness. Although, therefore, an extensive comparison of male and female uses of flouting is not possible here, the following examples of the male uses gives some indication of the range of issues raised by being able to point out differential uses of flouting mechanisms.

The distinct functions that Rundquist points to in relation to male use of flouting are: regulating children's behaviour, superficial self-criticism, putting others down, and humour. An example of the former can be seen in this comment by the father (D) in couple 1:

> (Child has been refusing to speak because she is angry with her father. Now she is making exaggerated motions to indicate that she is having trouble cutting her piece of pizza.)

> D1: Would you like a hatchet? (Rundquist 1992: 439)

Rundquist comments that in this example the father is flouting the maxim of Quality in that he is not being sincere 'since a hatchet is an unlikely tool for a child to use on a piece of pizza' (439). She suggests therefore that he is implicating that the child's behaviour is inappropriate. However, Rundquist makes the additional point that on the basis of other evidence from the conversation, the father here is not only criticising her behaviour, he is also attempting to get his daughter to speak to him since she has earlier become angry with him for shouting at her and is now refusing to talk. She suggests that the above comment by the father is therefore acting on two levels: on the one hand he is criticising the way she is using her cutlery, but on the other hand is also trying to get her to stop ignoring him. Both of these actions are being attempted indirectly: the father doesn't explicitly say *Stop ignoring me* or *Stop using your knife like that.*

Rundquist draws on work by Deborah Tannen in which she develops the distinction between power and solidarity to argue that a father in her own study of informal talk is attempting to control the child without making that control explicit. Rundquist cites Tannen's following comments:

> The father who lets his daughter know what he thinks she should do without actually telling her wants to get his way. But he'd rather feel that he's getting his way because his daughter wants the same thing (solidarity) than because he's twisting her arm (power). (Tannen cited in Rundquist 1992: 440)

Although there is clearly a power differential here, Rundquist's point is that the use of indirection indicates that the father has elected to avoid an overt display of power. Rundquist comments that there is little evidence of this type of behaviour in the speech of the mothers in the study. I will pick up on this after illustrating one more function that indirection has for the men in the study: superficial self-criticism. In the following example, the parents have been discussing the children's teachers and one of the fathers comments:

D8: I'm really up on the kids. I don't even know for sure who they have. (1992: 441)

The first part of the comment is ironic which, in Gricean terms, in this case involves flouting the maxim of Quality (saying what you do not believe to be true). Rundquist asserts that this is one of many examples from the males' speech where the aim of the speaker appears to be to make fun of his own shortcomings.

Rundquist comments that none of the women used either of the above types of strategy, and in her discussion of the general infrequency of the women's use of indirectness, argues that the paucity of the data makes it difficult to discern clear trends in the women's use of this type of linguistic behaviour. One tendency that Rundquist's study does indicate however is that the men often initiated a sequence of flouting, and that the women, where they did flout, often did so as a response to this trigger. The following is such an example.

M5: I used to spend a lot of time playing field hockey, good sport.

D5: Yeah, Mummy was probably playing field hockey when Herbert Hoover took office

M5: Yeah

D5: Woodrow Wilson and Teddy Roosevelt.

M5: Mhm

D5: George Washington

Child: Abraham Lincoln

D5: Aristotle and..

Child: Thomas Jefferson

M5: Yeah, . . . even when they bombed Pearl Harbor I was. (1992: 437–8)

Rundquist's point here is that since much of the women's flouting was triggered by the men's flouts, without this trigger, they may have flouted even less than they did. Moreover, it is also worth noting that if this is the case, the *type* and *function* of the flouting (in this case with the function presumably being self-deprecatory humour) in such instances would have been determined by the men since they initiated it.

While the scope of Rundquist's study is small, her application of Grice in the analysis of her data offers some interesting insights into the relationship between gender and the use of implicatures. In particular, as I shall show in the discussion of politeness theory in the following chapter, in the past there has been a tendency to take as axiomatic that indirect speech is more likely to be used by women than by men. This has, however, tended to refer to the type of linguistic behaviour whereby speakers use indirect forms in order to avoid asking directly for some service or to avoid giving explicit orders. By bringing into the issue of gender and speech the type of indirectness that Grice's theory of implicature captures, Rundquist shows that the notion of indirectness may have been addressed in a somewhat over-general way in the past. She also argues that while indirectness, when it is addressed by politeness studies, tends to be seen as the form of speech that is most likely to be used by less powerful speakers, in this case, it is, she argues, used by the more powerful speakers. For example, her conclusion states that the men 'appear to be more indirect than the women are' (447); but more significantly she states that the results show that men appear to use flouting as 'attention-getting strategies' (446) and she argues 'flouting the maxims of conversation fits more into a hierarchical way of viewing conversation than it does as a way to connect with others' (446). Rundquist's conclusion, then, is that the men use flouting as a strategy for maintaining power.

5.3.2 Implicature and power

While Rundquist's study is an interesting indication of how a Gricean framework can inform an empirical study, the link between the data and explanation is questionable and it is worth considering why. One of the problems is that Rundquist appears to have an *a priori* set of assumptions about gender relations that she bases her explanation on. Evidence of this can be seen in this extract from her discussion of the men's use of indirection:

> Besides flouting more frequently than the women, they tended to initiate flouting. They use it in directives as well as in criticism when speaking to their children. People in a position of power can be confident in expressing their dominance through humour and teasing, or more severely through sarcasm. (1992: 445)

The link between the second and third sentence here is not self evident: the relevance of moving from a description of the men's behaviour in the study to a general comment about 'people in a position of power' con-stitutes, for me, a problematic leap in logic that needs at least some attempt at justification. Without an explicit link, it must be assumed that the reference to *people in a position of power* after discussing the men's use of indirectness indicates that *men* and *people in a position of power* are co-referential. This easy, and highly questionable slippage between gender relations and power relations is a weakness in Rundquist's discussion: the discursive data are seen as expressing power *because* it is a male speaking. Although Rundquist does draw on existing scholarship to support her claims, she tends to take at face value stereotypical generalisations about the nature of masculinity or femininity. For example, in her discussion of the use of indirectness in humour, she draws on a study that claims that men's humour affirms their place in society in that it appears to be 'reinforcing their competitiveness' (446) while women's humour supports 'their goal of greater intimacy in its supportive and healing nature' (446). Rundquist then relates this to her own study by suggesting that the examples of flouting 'could be interpreted as men's attention-getting strategies' (446). There is no indication that the humour might be women's 'attention-getting' strategies since it is already assumed that women are not interested in such things. Clearly they are too preoccupied with being supportive and healing.

In all forms of empirical work, when it comes to explaining data, there is always a danger of drawing on unexamined, folklinguistic assumptions about what men and women are like and how this is observable through, or explained by their use of language. Such assumptions tend to presuppose a static and monolithic notion of gender, which is particularly unfortunate in this instance in that it does not allow Rundquist to do justice to the richness of her data. For example, when assumptions about gender relations are taken as self-evident, the data are often not interpreted according to what they show but according to how far they reinforce the stereotype. But having said that, there is research that, although critical of some aspects of the Gricean approach, does provide evidence that analysing the generation and uptake of implicatures is a useful way of addressing power relations, and these lend support to what Rundquist is arguing.

For example, a number of theorists have argued that one of the problems with Grice's notion of the CP is that it is predicated on the assumption that conversation occurs between equal participants who have shared communicative goals. This has been pointed to in Fairclough (1989), Harris (1995) and Sarangi and Slembrouk (1992). One point that is made in such critiques is that these assumptions tend to lead analysts to address implicatures as though they are inferred effortlessly and automatically by hearers. Sarangi and Slembrouk's (1992) critique of Grice is based on an empirical study of interactions where there is an asymmetrical power relation between interlocutors. Their analysis demonstrates that where interlocutors are involved in an unequal exchange, there is a strong likelihood that the participants will have distinct communicative goals, and that there is less likelihood that implicatures that are generated by the linguistic choices of either speaker will be taken up by the hearer. Not only is this an issue of differential goals, Sarangi and Slembrouk argue, but an imbalance of knowledge, and, as they point out, this failure to generate or infer implicatures is likely to have worse consequences for the less powerful interlocutor. They demonstrate this in their analysis of an exchange between a man who has applied for financial assistance from the Department of Health and Social Security (DHSS) and a social worker with that institution. Sarangi and Slembrouk show that where the more powerful participant (here, the social worker) speaks in ways that require the less powerful participant (the applicant) to access his implicatures, this can be particularly problematic for the latter. In this case, the applicant lacks vital information (for example, the meaning of specific terms) and the more powerful party makes no effort to provide that information. As a result the applicant is unable to make the appropriate inferences about the social worker's meaning, and he leaves without being able to resolve the problem he is having over non-payment of benefits. What Sarangi and Slembrouk show is that, where implicatures are not taken up, it is the more powerful participant's perception of the exchange that matters. In this case, whether or not the implicatures were picked up by the applicant is irrelevant to the outcome of the talk as far as the social worker is concerned, since the decision about benefits is based on his, rather than the applicant's assessment of the information that was exchanged. Sarangi and Slembrouk also show that where the less powerful participant attempts to generate implicatures through their language choice, the more powerful party can simply decline to do the inferential work that would enable those implicatures to be accessed. Here, then, the more powerful party appears to be refusing to do the necessary inferential work required to understand his interlocutor's implicatures, while the less powerful party is simply unable to do the necessary inferential work, and doesn't know the questions to ask that would make the social worker's meaning accessible to him.

This idea that inferencing is 'work' carried out by the hearer is also addressed by Ochs (1992) in an article that makes the point that Samoan mothers are considered by their interlocutors to be more powerful than American mothers are considered to be by theirs. She argues that these differential perceptions of power are strongly related to the linguistic behaviour of the two sets of mothers. She shows for example that American mothers simplify their utterances and make great efforts to make their meaning as accessible as possible for their children. Moreover, American mothers, she argues, work hard to infer the meanings generated by their children's language choices. Ochs contrasts this with the linguistic behaviour of Samoan mothers who, she suggests, make no effort to understand their children's language unless it is straightforward, and do not, moreover, simplify their own language when they speak to their children. On the basis of this and the argument that women are held in more respect in Samoan society, Ochs suggests that there is a link between power and the work that is required of interlocutors in the generation of meaning. Her point, in Gricean terms, is that expecting other people to pick up on your implicatures is a way of doing power, as is refusing to do the inferential work that is required to pick up on your interlocutor's implied meaning.

If Rundquist's conclusions are seen with the above as a backdrop, her claims are more tenable. And that the above claim about inferential work is an underlying premise of her work is evident in that she points out that where women do generate implicatures, they are often implicatures that she describes as 'conventional'. It should be noted that these implicatures are not conventional in the sense that Grice uses the term to explain the implicatures generated by words such as *but* and *therefore*. The point she is making is that women use flouts that require less inferencing work, such as a mother's ironic response *Wow! What a happy thought* to her child's comment about the possibility of a plane crash. Although Rundquist's study does not of itself provide sufficient evidence for the claims that men use indirect forms more because they are the more powerful interlocutors, when these claims are considered in the context of Och's and Sarangi and Slembrouk's arguments about inferencing and power, it seems to be a feasible one. And it does indicate that this would repay further investigation.

5.4 CONCLUSION

In this chapter I have demonstrated how a Gricean approach can inform empirical work and textual analysis while indicating some of the problems scholars have pointed to (see Davis 1998 for an overview). However it is worth unpacking what is retrievable from Grice's account. Clearly the type of meaning that he terms *implicature* seems to be a particular type of meaning that is linguistically generated, while not actually being derived from the language system alone. As such it is distinct from other forms of implicit meaning. Where Grice has been critiqued is in terms of his assumption that conversation is regulated by the CP and that this CP can be characterised in terms of a set of maxims which appear to represent a set of norms shared by conversationalists with a common goal. However, although he assumes that interlocutors have shared goals, in fairness to Grice what he is proposing is a way of explaining acts of communication that *work*. What Sarangi and Slembrouk's analysis points to is what happens when interlocutors do not have shared goals, and it is clear from their analysis that what went on in the DHSS interaction is not an example of successful communication. And it is precisely the lack of a shared goal, and the asymmetries of power that accompanied this lack that they point to in order to account for the breakdown: which is exactly what would be predicted by Grice's account.

Although Grice's notion of a CP is somewhat problematic, therefore, it does not necessarily indicate that his theory of how implicatures are generated is invalid. For example, it may be that the maxims that Grice isolates are norms for particular genres of speech rather than norms for a whole community of practice. And it is worth considering this in relation to the *Daily Mail* article I analysed above. Clearly, the goal of the article is not to be as communicative as possible. Indeed it could be argued that the primary goal of the newspaper is to be financially viable. Since the cover price of newspapers is never sufficient to defray production costs and newspaper firms are as a result financially dependent upon being able provide advertisers with access to potential customers, then it is more likely that the goal of the paper is to sell to a wide and appropriate audience rather than simply to communicate 'the truth'. Given this context, it could be argued that editorial decisions about what to write and how to write it are not determined by a need to provide the truth in a relevant, unambiguous and efficient manner. However, this does not necessarily refute the notion that a CP is in force here. It is still the case that newspapers cannot simply lie since that would leave them open to prosecution. Moreover, as Grice argues, the notion of relevance is not an absolute. A contribution is judged as relevant given the aims of the particular communicative event. It is also possible to argue that what newspapers are faced with is a clash whereby they cannot, if they are to be relevant in the sense of producing what are 'newsworthy' utterances, also be entirely truthful, or unambiguous. So for any given newspaper article, it may be that the goal is not to communicate everything there is to know about an event, it is to communicate what is newsworthy about that event while at the same time avoiding saying anything that is actually untrue for fear of libel laws. The conceptualisation of newsworthiness may go against maxims of Quantity and Quality, and may indicate that Relevance and Manner are more important than Quality and Quantity in this context. This is not to suggest that the maxims are not valid, but that what was proposed as a universal may be particular to specific communicative situations. The point is that newspapers can not overtly and entirely opt out of the CP any more than the social worker can in the exchange analysed by Sarangi and Slembrouk. If they did, they would fail to communicate anything to their addressees.

There is much current work in pragmatics that takes Grice as a point of departure. For example, speech act theory in the form that it has developed is triggered by Searle's dialogue with Gricean theory. And politeness theory as it has been developed by Brown and Levinson ([1978], 1987) argues that if, as Grice proposes, speakers are rational, and if it is the case that they regularly express themselves indirectly, this raises questions about why they should do this. The response offered by politeness theorists is that indirectness is a function of the need to consider one's interlocutor's 'face'. Moreover, as I show in the next chapter, relevance theory takes Grice's initial theory of meaning and his notion of implicature as points of departure, in that they argue that it is not the case, as Grice proposes, that *some* forms of communication are dependent upon inferencing. Their argument is that *all* communication is inferential. In the following chapter I will briefly introduce the latter two theories and then show how they have been used in the study of language and gender.

6

POST-GRICEAN PRAGMATICS: POLITENESS THEORY AND RELEVANCE THEORY

6.1 POLITENESS THEORY: AN INTRODUCTION

Taking Grice's account of the relationship between implicature and conversational norms as a general model of how human beings communicate with one another, Brown and Levinson ([1978],1987) develop a theory that, they propose, adds a necessary level of explanation to the Gricean account. They take Grice's claim that it is because interlocutors are 'rational' that they are able to generate implicatures as their point of departure, in that it begs the question: why, if this is the case, do speakers not simply say what they mean? Why do speakers only orient their speech towards the norms of conversation that Grice points to with his maxims, when the most rational course would be to actually adhere to them? That speakers consistently flout rather than adhere to the maxims, and often appear to avoid 'saying' what they 'mean' is indicated not just in work that explores implicature, but also in scholarship on indirect speech acts and in ethnographic studies of language use across cultures (Brown and Levinson 1987: 55). Brown and Levinson's response to such evidence is to suggest that if indirect ways of communicating are so common, and this behaviour is found across so many different contexts of use, then it must occur for a reason. Their proposal is that choices about directness are strategic and are motivated by a speaker's orientation to a specific set of her own and her addressee's needs. They premise their argument on their conceptualisation of interlocutors as social beings who have a need to be allowed to go about their business unimpeded but who also have a need to be approved of. They term these needs 'face wants', and argue that their existence explains what would otherwise be irrational linguistic behaviour.

Brown and Levinson describe their theory as an attempt to illustrate 'in considerable detail how certain parallels in language usage in many different languages can be shown to derive from certain assumptions about "face" – individuals' self-esteem' (1987: 2). Their theory builds on these parallels in language behaviour to argue that there is a single set of 'politeness' principles, related to the notion of face, that can explain both the motives that underlie a range of linguistic strategies, and the impact of such strategies. They describe the need for politeness strategies in the following terms:

> From a gross ethological perspective, perhaps we can generalize somewhat: the problem for any social group is to control its internal aggression while retaining the potential for aggression both in internal social control and, especially, in external competitive relations with other groups. (1)

They draw on Goffman's work to argue that like formal diplomatic protocol, politeness behaviour 'presupposes that potential for aggression as it seeks to disarm it and makes possible communication between potentially aggressive parties' (1). Based on this conceptualisation of society as founded on the containment of aggression, their premise is that linguistic interaction always has the potential to threaten the face wants of either speaker or hearer, and they therefore propose that speakers use strategies that either express solidarity or else express restraint in order to minimise these potential threats. Blum Kulka succinctly summarises their account in the following terms:

> [F]or Brown and Levinson *politeness* is the intentional, strategic behaviour of an individual meant to satisfy self and other face wants in case of threat, enacted via positive and negative styles of redress. (Blum-Kulka 1997: 50)

Brown and Levinson's account has been highly influential in pragmatics and has generated a large number of empirical studies of interactive behaviour, many of which are centred on the claims to universality made by the theory. An indication of the interest the theory has generated can be seen in the opening chapters of the 1987 edition of *Politeness: Some Universals in Language Use* which consists of an engagement with and a summary of the wide range of academic responses to their original (1978) edition. Useful introductions to the theory can be found in Blum-Kulka (1997), Mey (1993), Thomas (1995) and Verschueren (1999). Each of these indicate some of the implications and applications of the theory, and in particular stress that Brown and Levinson's model provides a useful set of analytical tools for exploring culturally specific behaviour, and for carrying out cross cultural comparisons (see Blum-Kulka 1997 for a recent survey of such studies). In this section, I limit my outline of Brown and Levinson's account to those key points that will allow me to go on and show how it has been applied, and critiqued, in studies of gender and language use.

6.1.1 Key points of politeness theory

In order to make their case that there is a universal set of principles that appear to regulate language behaviour, Brown and Levinson base their account on a 'Model Person' (MP). They describe their project thus:

> All our Model Person (MP) consists in is a wilful fluent speaker of a natural language, further endowed with two special properties – rationality and face. By rationality we mean something very specific – the availability to our MP of a precisely definable mode of reasoning from ends to the means that will achieve those ends. By 'face' we mean something quite specific again: our MP is endowed with two particular wants – roughly, the want to be unimpeded and the want to be approved of in certain respects. (Brown and Levinson 1987: 58)

In positing this MP, Brown and Levinson are deliberately abstracting (from actual, socially situated, users of language) these two characteristics which they see as common to all human beings, irrespective of their culture, class or gender. Their point is that the existence of these characteristics alone can explain a great many regularities in linguistic behaviour across a range of cultures and contexts of use. Although they begin with an abstraction, their point is that the way in which politeness behaviour will manifest itself and the impact it will have in any given context will be influenced by cultural factors. The politeness principle they propose is seen to hold across cultures, however, as is the notion of 'face'.

6.1.1.1 Face

Face is characterised as a 'set of wants' by Brown and Levinson, and they argue that these wants are only satisfied by the actions of others. The face wants of MPs that need to be oriented to in interactions are divided into two types: negative face wants and positive face wants. Negative face wants are related to a person's desire for freedom of action and freedom from imposition, while positive face wants are related to a person's desire that their self image is appreciated and approved of by their interlocutors. Face wants are maintained, they argue, because it is in the mutual interest of two MPs to maintain the other's face. The assumption is that if you don't maintain my face in a given interaction, I'm not going to maintain yours. Of course issues of power are implicated in the maintenance of face in that in certain circumstances one interlocutor can afford not to maintain the other's face without there being a risk that their own will not be maintained by the subordinate interlocutor. Indeed where there is a power differential that is institutionally sanctioned, there may be of course be a range of overt or implicit constraints on the less powerful interactant threatening the face of her superior: examples would include interactions between teacher and pupil or boss and subordinate. Significantly, however, Brown and Levinson (1987: 29–33) propose that gender is not implicated in the mutual maintenance of face, a point that is disputed by studies such as those reported in Deuchar (1988), Holmes (1995), and Johnstone et al. (1992) that I discuss in section 6.1.2.1 below.

Although they argue that it is in the interests of interlocutors to maintain each other's face, Brown and Levinson also suggest that this is not straightforward in that there are a large number of linguistic acts that will inevitably pose a threat to the speaker's own or her interlocutor's face. Face-threatening acts (FTAs) that threaten negative face include (1) acts that impede the hearer's freedom of action such as orders, requests, suggestions, threats and warnings; (2) acts that have the potential to put the hearer in the speaker's debt such as offers or promises; and (3) acts that predicate some desire of the speaker towards the hearer or the hearer's goods such as compliments or expressions of strong emotions such as hatred or lust (1987: 66). FTAs that threaten positive face include (1) those that show the speaker has a negative attitude towards the hearer's positive face such as criticism, ridicule or challenges; and (2) those that indicate that the speaker does not care about the hearer's face wants such as bringing bad news about the hearer, boasting, irreverence, mentioning taboo topics, interrupting, making non-sequitors or showing non-attention to the hearer. Again, Brown and Levinson do not propose that the gender of interlocutors will lead to these acts being perceived differentially in terms of how face-threatening they are. Their point in citing these acts is to argue that because there are so many ways by which speakers might threaten their addressee's face, and because it is in the interest of speakers that they maintain their own and their hearer's face, speakers, irrespective of their own or addressee's gender, are constantly called on in interactions to weigh up the impact of their linguistic choices, and to consider strategies that may mitigate potential threats.

6.1.1.2 Face-saving strategies

One route available to speakers when they find it necessary to carry out a potentially face-threatening act would be simply not to carry out that act at all. So for example if a speaker one day finds that she has not brought any money with her to work, a way of dealing with the problem would be to ask a colleague to lend her some. Because such a request for another's goods is what Brown and Levinson consider an intrinsically face-threatening act in that it is an imposition on the addressee, the speaker may elect simply not to carry out this threat to her colleague's negative face. If however she does decide to go ahead with it, she is faced with a choice of how to carry out the act. Brown and Levinson suggest that if the speaker decides to carry out the FTA she needs to decide whether to go 'off or on record'. If the decision is to go 'off record', this would mean that rather than make the request the speaker may elect to say within earshot of a colleague: *Damn, I'm out of cash, I forgot to go the bank.* Brown and Levinson indicate that such an utterance would imply:

I may be intending to get you to lend me some cash, but I cannot be held to have committed myself to that intent (as you would discover were you to challenge me with 'This is the seventeenth time you've asked me to lend you money'). (1987: 69)

If the speaker decides to go on record, she has the choice of making the request 'baldly' (for example, *Lend me some cash*) or making the request with 'redressive action' (69). If the decision is to go for the latter, the speaker has to decide whether she should attempt to counteract the potential damage to the hearer's face by using positive politeness or by using negative politeness.

'Positive politeness' strategies are those that are oriented to maintaining the hearer's positive face. These might be acts that treat the hearer as 'a member of an ingroup, a friend, a person whose wants and personality traits are known and liked' (Brown and Levinson 1987: 70). Negative politeness strategies that are oriented towards the speaker's negative face and are usually 'avoidance based', characterised by 'self-effacement, formality and restraint', and centring on the hearer's want to be unimpeded. In such cases, the speaker might include apologies for interfering or transgressing, or use hedges that would temper the illocutionary force of the act. Brown and Levinson describe these strategies as often achieved by the use of:

impersonalizing mechanisms (such as passives) that distance S and H from the act, and with other softening mechanisms that give the addressee an 'out', a face-saving line of escape, permitting him to feel that his response is not coerced. (70)

An example of such a strategy would be something like *You haven't got a fiver have you?* which would allow the hearer to refuse the speaker's request on the grounds that he cannot lend her any money, rather than on the grounds that he does not want to.

6.1.1.3 The politeness principle

Brown and Levinson argue that their model is predictive in that the five strategic options represent a scale of politeness beginning from (1) do not do the FTA, (2) do the FTA off record, (3) do the FTA using positive politeness, (4) do the FTA using negative politeness and (5) do the FTA without redressive action (baldly). What this would predict is that if one were particularly concerned not to threaten the face of one's addressee, (1) would be the most likely choice, while it would be predicted that (5) would most likely be chosen where the speaker is unconcerned about whether or not she threatens her addressee's face. Extreme examples of this latter choice would be where the speaker has absolute power over the addressee or where there is such urgency about the act that face is not taken into account. Giving the order *Run!* in order to save someone from being flattened by a falling tree would be such an instance. Brown and Levinson argue that 'any rational agent will tend to choose the same genus of strategy under the same conditions' (71), and they go on to suggest that factors that would affect this choice would include variables such as power, social distance and the culture-specific ranking of impositions. Their claim that their account is both universal and predictive is justified, they argue, 'by virtue of the fact that the particular strategies intrinsically afford certain payoffs or advantages, and the relevant circumstances are those in which one of these payoffs would be more advantageous than the other' (71). Their claim is then that the politeness principle underlies linguistic choices and explains why a speaker produces utterance forms, in that politeness is a premise that is called into play when determining the function of a given piece of linguistic behaviour.

The theory has been critiqued from a number of perspectives. Roman Kopytko (1995), for example, argues that the assumptions Brown and Levinson make about the deductive reasoning involved in an interaction are untenable, and he asserts that their notion of face is under-theorised. In particular he argues that Brown and Levinson's model is deterministic in the sense that it assumes that a speaker with face and rationality will react automatically to factors such as power, distance and rank of imposition, and that the strength of each of these factors will correlate closely with that which the addressee would attach to them. He argues therefore that a speaker is seen as 'a deterministic device, or an abstract concept devoid of attitudes, personality' (Kopytko 1995: 487). He goes on to point out that in reality linguistic interaction is not so predictable:

> Irrespective of the intention of the speaker, it is the hearer who assigns politeness to any utterance within the situation it was heard. Thus politeness is a property of utterances and not of sentences, so that politeness cannot be assigned out of context to any particular structure. (487)

Applications of politeness theory in studies of gender and language use, as I show in the following section, often provide evidence that would support Kopytko's claim in that they suggest that a single strategy can be understood in quite distinct ways, and that the gender of the interlocutors appears to have an impact on which strategies are selected and how they function. In this sense these scholars, like those who have carried out cross-cultural studies of language use (see Brown and Levinson 1987: 16–17) challenge claims about the universality of the politeness principle. I will address these issues after the following summary of some applications of politeness theory in research on gender and language use.

6.1.2   Applications of politeness theory

As I discussed in Chapter 3, although the Gricean model aims to account for *how* indirect communication works, it cannot explain *why* speakers should choose not to 'say' what they 'mean'. In response to this, Brown and Levinson's account postulates that a principle that underlies acts of communication is the need to accommodate interlocutors' face wants: choices about degrees of explicitness are thus explained by this motive. The politeness scale I detail above indicates that, contrary to Rundquist's claim (discussed in Section 5.3.1 of the previous chapter), Brown and Levinson's theory would predict that in asymmetrical interactions a less powerful interlocutor is more likely to employ strategies that involve indirection, for example, strategy (2): going off record. As Brown and Levinson (1987: 69) point out, if a request is articulated in sufficiently indirect terms, it is possible to deny it actually is a request, and this, therefore, is likely to be a strategy that is employed by a speaker who is concerned not to threaten her hearer's face. I will consider the implications of this apparent contradiction between Rundquist's and Brown and Levinson's positions towards the end of this section. At this point, it should be noted that indirection is just one of a number of strategies that Brown and Levinson suggest are oriented towards saving the hearer's face. There are other negative politeness strategies such as the speaker's use of self-effacement, formality, restraint and acts that generally take into account the hearer's want to be unimpeded (Brown and Levinson 1987: 70). There are also strategies oriented towards the hearer's positive face which are aimed at indicating that the speaker wants at least some of the hearer's wants (70) and include making the hearer feel that his or her values are shared or making the hearer feel valued by the speaker.

As Eckert and McConnell-Ginet (1994) point out in their survey of approaches to gender and language use, politeness strategies have been strongly associated with female speech. They also indicate that this has tended to be seen negatively by feminist scholars who have argued that women's use of such strategies constitutes either 'passive enforced deference' or 'wilful "prissy" avoidance of real social engagement'. However, the point that Eckert and McConnell-Ginet make is that what is significant about work that engages with issues of politeness in relation to gender is that it addresses women as agents who are actively using available linguistic resources for specific ends. They argue moreover that although politeness strategies can be interpreted as 'coping' practices which 'ultimately help maintain existing inequalities (simply making them more "bearable" for the oppressed)' more recently they have tended to be seen as 'partial strategic solutions to the problems posed for women by their social oppression' (1994: 448). One example they give of such an interpretation of politeness behaviour is that proposed by Deuchar (1988) who asserts that where women's language orients more towards prestige forms than men's, this can be seen as a motivated choice.

6.1.2.1 Politeness as an explanation of gendered differences in pronunciation patterns

Deuchar begins by pointing to the finding prevalent in sociolinguistic studies that women tend to use 'standard' pronunciations more than do men of the same class. She points out that these studies have been mainly carried out in the UK and the USA and other western industrialised countries where there is a recognised standard pronunciation. In Britain, for example, the standard would be a version of Received Pronunciation. Deuchar uses Trudgill's (1974) study of Norwich English as an early and very influential example of such scholarship. She points out for example that Trudgill found that the pronunciation of verbs ending in *ing* tended to vary according to the class and sex of the speaker and the degree of formality in the speech style the speaker was required to use (whether speakers were engaging in casual speech or reading from a word list). His results, in common with many subsequent studies, showed that on average women tend to use pronunciations closer to the prestige form, and less close to the local accent than do men when variables of class and speech style are held constant. Her point in invoking Trudgill's research is to demonstrate the type of explanation that studies following his work have tended to use to account for their results. She argues that in general the results have been explained in terms of status consciousness or in terms of solidarity. Where status consciousness is invoked, Trudgill, it is argued, 'suggests that as women have lower social status than men they are more aware of the value of linguistic indicators of status' (28). Where solidarity is invoked, it is argued that men use local forms of pronunciation because although these are usually perceived as non-prestigious, they also tend to be associated with masculinity. These forms have therefore acquired a 'covert prestige' for male users: using regional pronunciation norms works to indicate allegiance with other men.

As Deuchar points out however, while they assume that the linguistic choices made by their subjects are goal oriented such explanations do not specify what those goals are, and neither do they address the mechanisms by which such goals might be achieved linguistically. For example, the status explanation does not account for *why* women should use linguistic markers of status which neither reflect nor determine their real status (28). Her argument is that Brown and Levinson's politeness theory does offer an explanation for women's linguistic usage that addresses the issue of goal-oriented linguistic behaviour. To illustrate this, Deuchar builds on Brown and Levinson's notion of face to argue that it can be applied as an explanation of differential uses of standard speech according to gender on the basis of the following premises:

1. participants in an interaction wish to protect their own face;
2. attention to other's face is affected by relative power in relation to other;

3. attention to other's face may involve damage to one's own;
4. women have less relative power than men. (Deuchar 1989: 30)

Although the first three assumptions are intrinsic to Brown and Levinson's politeness theory, the fourth is a postulate added by Deuchar. Her argument is that that if the latter postulate is accepted then this sets up a problem for women:

> Assuming that women are relatively powerless speakers (assumption (4)), then they will receive little attention to their own faces, and will damage their own while paying attention to the face of others. Yet we assume they have face wants like anyone else (assumption (1)). So how can their own faces be protected in ways which do not threaten the face of others? (31)

Deuchar uses the act 'boasting' as an illustration of how strategies for protecting the speaker's face can threaten the hearer's face. She argues that while boasting 'anoints' the speaker's positive face it implicitly threatens that of the addressee by indirectly belittling him. Conversely, strategies that pay attention to the addressee's positive face, such as a promise to perform a service, threaten the speaker's negative face in that they constitute an imposition on her own freedom of action.

Given the prediction that there is a likelihood of damage to one's own face when attending to the face of another, and given the claim that women are less powerful than men, Deuchar argues that this would predict that women's own face wants are unlikely to be addressed by male interlocutors. Her point is that the use of pronunciations that have connotations of prestige offers women a means of protecting their own positive face without engaging in strategies that would threaten the face of a male addressee. Eckert and McConnell-Ginet summarise Deuchar's point thus:

> [W]here women's language is more standard than men's it may serve to defend them against accusations of stupidity or ignorance, thus increasing the likelihood that they will be recognized as agents, capable not only of communicating but also of creating meanings, as not only consumers but also producers of symbols. (Eckert and McConnell-Ginet 1994: 448)

Although Deuchar's argument is premised, like Rundquist's, on the rather over-generalised assumption that all women in all circumstances have less relative power than men, what is useful here is that the employment of prestige forms is posited as one strategy for achieving a specific goal: the maintenance of one's own face in circumstances where it is expected that it will not be maintained by one's interlocutor. Although Deuchar does not specifically indicate this, her account would not therefore predict that all women use prestige pronunciation forms in all situations. Therefore, even though it would appear to be drawing on a rather static model of gender relations, it can help to explain the dynamics of interaction across a range of contexts that would in turn explain variation within women's use of prestige forms, both in the sense that any given woman will, to different degrees, use the local variant on one occasion and the prestige form on another, and in the sense that there are inevitably variations between one and another woman's uses of these forms. However, this would require a model of utterance interpretation that is less deterministic than that posited by Brown and Levinson, in that such a strategy would need to be theorised as a resource that has differential politeness effects according to different contexts of use. I comment on this issue in relation to, and in the light of, Sperber and Wilson's relevance theory later in this chapter.

6.1.2.2 Politeness as a framework for sociolinguistic studies

Although I have questioned Deuchar's somewhat homogeneous view of women's relative power, Janet Holmes's (1995) account of studies of gender and politeness in New Zealand, provides evidence that supports and expands Deuchar's points about face maintenance and gender. Holmes also shares Deuchar's essentialist approach to gender in that she begins her account with the assertion that women are more polite than men (1995: 1) and states that the aim of her book is to explore the evidence for that conclusion. Although her approach to gender is controversial, Holmes's work does provide a useful illustration of the relationship between pragmatics and sociolinguistics in that it demonstrates how a pragmatic theory can inform data collection and provide a framework that explains the significance of the data. What is also interesting about Holmes's account is that it demonstrates that the theoretical framework she employs might require modification in the light of her data. I consider how far her approach is compromised by her conceptualisation of gender towards the end of this section.

Drawing on a broad and highly varied range of linguistic material, Holmes argues that female speakers appear to attend to the face wants of male interlocutors far more than vice versa, and she suggests that there is evidence that it is a mark of masculinity to ignore the face wants of another. One example is her claim that women are more responsive to another's face in the context of academic seminars. Holmes reports on a study she carried out of the types of question that men and women asked in public meetings and seminars which involved a formal presentation followed by a discussion. Her findings indicate a consistent pattern of men dominating the discussion. Although, as she points out, this was not entirely surprising in that there were approximately twice as many men as women attending the 100 sessions that she focused on, the gender imbalance is evident in that on average 17 per cent of the women spoke compared to 30 per cent of the men. Moreover, even in those sessions where there were similar numbers of men and women, the men contributed 62 per cent of all the elicitations following a presentation (1995: 42). Holmes argues that the reasons for this became evident when characteristics of the seminar contributions were considered. She points out that:

> In general women were much more likely to contribute to the discussion when there was a woman speaker, when there were more women in the audience, and when the topic was one on which they could claim expert knowledge. (42)

Holmes argues that there may be many explanations for this including the possibility that women find formal settings uncomfortable, but that where there are more women present the situation may feel less threatening. However, she also looks to politeness theory for an explanation, arguing that it is possible that women feel that in order to take part in a discussion in such a context they need to be particularly well informed: 'ignorant questions can be perceived as insulting to the speaker' (42). By avoiding elicitations that might be perceived as ill-informed, Holmes suggests, women may be attending to the speaker's negative face. Alternatively they may be protecting their own positive face. To support this explanation Holmes points to the fact that the women who did speak were often recognised experts on the topic under discussion.

A further possible explanation that draws on politeness theory is Holmes' argument that it may be that the women in the study assessed the situation in terms of others' positive face wants:

> From the presenter's point of view, it is generally regarded as desirable that there be some discussion at the end of a paper; otherwise the occasion may be regarded as a failure. In most situations there are plenty of men to fill the gap. Women may participate more when they fear no one else will. Moreover, they may feel particularly concerned to protect women presenters in this respect, and so expressing positive politeness in this context will involve women asking questions. (43)

While Holmes acknowledges that it would be difficult to be certain which, if any, of the above explanations account for women's behaviour in formal seminars, she argues that when the types of question asked by men and by women were compared, the results supported the explanation that women are more concerned than men not to threaten the positive face wants of the seminar presenter. In analysing the questions Holmes distinguishes between different forms of elicitation, categorising them as supportive, critical or antagonistic. Of the 500 elicitations she analysed, the majority were supportive in that they implied a generally positive response to the content of the presentation and functioned to provide an opportunity for the presenter to speak more about some aspect of it (43).

Holmes gives as an example of a supportive elicitation: 'I really liked your comments on . . . could you expand a little?' (44). Critical elicitations, which included comments such as 'I can see what you're getting at, but it seems to me the material in your figure 5 could be interpreted somewhat differently' (44) were used less by both males and females. Antagonistic elicitations, exemplified by 'It's not much use having a policy if it's not going to be effective is it?' (45) were more scarce still. However, although they were rarely used (they constituted less than 10 per cent of the total), the variation between male and female uses of this form was significant. Holmes makes the point that where antagonistic elicitations occurred they were twice as likely to come from a man as a woman and argues that since such elicitations are face threatening it would indicate that the men were less concerned with the face wants of the presenter than the women.

Holmes also comments that the study indicates something about a general difference between male and female goals of communication. Throughout the book she develops the claim that men are more oriented towards the referential functions of language use while women orient more towards the affective functions of language use. The referential function is seen by Holmes to be the role of language in conveying information, facts or content, while the affective function refers to the use of language to convey feelings and reflect on social relationships (3). As I have suggested throughout my discussions in this book, and as I have indicated in section 5.3.2 of the previous chapter, the question of whether there are significant differences between male and female communication remains a controversial issue, and has been addressed by a great deal of feminist research on language use in the past. However, if one accepts Holmes's claim that in the context of the seminar data the male subjects, by asking more antagonistic questions, indicated that they were more concerned with referential content than affective or social considerations, her argument has implications for research on politeness. What she is suggesting (and the above is just one example of many she cites to support her claim) is that the men and women in this specific context of use orient towards distinct norms of communication.

While ignoring at this stage the questions this begs about how this state of affairs comes about, if this is the case, then it is possible that Brown and Levinson's account may not be able to accommodate the impact of gender on politeness strategies. Although it is assumed that there will be differences in norms between cultures, as Kopytko's (1995) critique indicates, Brown and Levinson take it as axiomatic that speakers and hearers within a culture will share norms of politeness. Holmes's survey suggests otherwise. She argues for example that her study provides evidence that compliments are employed differently by males and females. She suggests that there are distinct patterns in who carries out compliments, who is complimented and how compliments function across a range of contexts and argues:

> This analysis of a corpus of New Zealand compliments and compliment responses suggests that men and women may operate with different socio-pragmatic rules. It seems possible that women use and perceive compliments more often as solidarity signals, while men may more often experience them as patronising or embarrassing face-threatening speech acts, or in some contexts as more referentially oriented evaluative utterances. (1995: 43)

If the men and women in the studies Holmes surveys were orienting towards different goals then the claim that 'politeness' constitutes a universal set of principles that underlie and explain the motive behind linguistic choices might need to be rethought. For example, Holmes's analysis raises questions about how far a single notion of politeness can explain the linguistic choices of both men and women. Indeed she makes the observation that although what seem to be male ideas of what constitutes face-threatening behaviour appear to match Brown and Levinson's account, some of the women's linguistic behaviour appears to be better explained by Woolfson's 'bulge' theory (Holmes 1995: 167–8). This latter theory argues that speakers tend to use similar (minimal) politeness behaviour with people they hardly know and with people they are close to, whereas people who neither fall into the category of stranger or friend tend to be the recipients of more elaborate politeness. Holmes's evidence suggests that this latter group of people are apologised to more, complimented more and offered more overt invitations: hence the idea of the bulge in the centre of the two extremes of maximum and minimum social distance. That male and female politeness patterns are different appears to be particularly evident in relation to apologies. Holmes points to data that implies that men's apology behaviour tends to conform to Brown and Levinson's model in that the frequency of their apologies tends to increase with social distance and the seriousness of the offence. Women's apology behaviour on the other hand is more frequent between interlocutors who are acquaintances and casual friends, rather than between strangers and intimates (186).

As I have suggested above, the idea that men and women's language use is qualitatively different has been critiqued, and as I discuss in section 4.2.2 of Chapter 4, Cameron (1997) has argued that it is counterproductive to use rigid models of gendered speech styles when analysing linguistic data. In fairness to Holmes however, what she is pointing to is evidence of tendencies in her data rather than categorical differences in language use. Moreover, while her attribution of differences in linguistic behaviour to gender imply that she is working with an essentialist model, this does not invalidate her data. Her use of politeness theory as a framework for exploring gendered differences in linguistic behaviour indicates that there do appear to be distinct patterns in the data. What remains to be explained (and what essentialist accounts tend to elide) is *how* interlocutor gender might relate to patterns of linguistic behaviour. I will address this after a brief discussion of one more study that indicates that politeness theory needs to take gender into account

6.1.2.3 The impact of addressee's gender on politeness behaviour

Johnstone, Ferrara and Bean (1992) carried out a study of public opinion-poll interviews in which female interviewers elicited information from male and female respondents. Their results indicated that not only do women put in a great deal of face work in their interactions but the gender of their addressees appears to be a factor that influences the degree and type of face work they do. Johnstone et al.'s finding was based on data that consisted of forty-eight telephone interviews of between fifteen and forty-five minutes in length, that were carried out by eighteen middle-class American women in their twenties. The interviewers were employed by the Texas Poll, which is described as a non-partisan polling service that conducts quarterly public opinion surveys on behalf of government agencies, non-profit organisations and academic researchers. Johnstone et al. argue that because the interviews are scripted the overall structure of the conversation and the sequence of topics were identical across the interviews. Moreover, since these interviewers are required by their employers not to deviate from the script, it was assumed that any deviations that did occur would be for pressing reasons. Deviations would characteristically include using strategies to keep the respondent from hanging up, and strategies designed to ensure that the respondent hears and understands all the questions, answers them in an appropriate way and enables the interview to be completed. By analysing the type and frequency of the deviations from the script the authors found that there were distinct patterns in the strategies according to the gender of the interviewee. They found what they call 'subtle but interesting differences between talk to men and talk to women by the female interviewers in this highly task oriented type of discourse' (1992: 427). They go on to suggest that the results showed that the interviewers tailored their discourse to fit the gender of their respondents: that the male interviewees had their wants and needs attended to more whereas the women interviewees were managed less and thanked more. The authors argue that there is some evidence that this was because the men in the study tended to subvert the question–answer format of the interview more frequently than the women, using banter and teasing and by playfully providing answers that did not match the categories offered by the interviewer, and which she could not therefore code. In contrast they describe the women respondents as displaying co-operation and a general willingness to operate within the question–answer framework.

While it would be risky to infer from this that women as a group tend towards a more co-operative style than men, this context-specific data does appear to confirm what Holmes found in her New Zealand studies. In a 1993 paper that reports on this research Holmes makes the following point:

> In the data examined New Zealand women respond sensitively to the demands of context with respect to the amount of talk which is appropriate. They encourage others to talk in contexts where their task is to facilitate the interaction, but when their role is that of interviewee they contribute generously themselves. In informal contexts they do not interrupt in order to gain the floor as frequently as men do; rather they provide positive and encouraging feedback, supporting the contributions of their interlocutors. That these behaviour patterns are not evidence of powerlessness, but should rather be seen as positive features of women's speech is suggested by the fact that many of the facilitative patterns which characterise women's speech in general also characterise the speech of those in leadership roles or positions where they are responsible for ensuring the success of an interaction. (Holmes 1993: 112)

She goes on to argue that there is much evidence that women's politeness behaviour is not determined by 'male norms' but that they adhere to 'clearly definable female norms' which put the addressee's interests and needs first. She concludes that in consequence 'both women and men recognise that talking to women is a positive experience. But not everyone realises why' (113).

What these patterns appear to indicate is that on the one hand the notion of politeness may provide a framework for understanding linguistic strategies, but that accounting for how these strategies implicate politeness is more complex than the original theory proposes. This might explain the problems that Brown and Levinson point to in their discussion of politeness and gender where they remark that research at that date had not found patterns of behaviour that relate the two phenomena (Brown and Levinson 1987: 29–33). If, as the above research indicates, acts like compliments or apologies take distinct forms and have distinct functions according to the gender of the interactants and if, moreover, they are oriented towards different communicative goals, then these patterns may not be evident. They only become evident when the specific meanings that they have for the participants are taken into account. Given that Brown and Levinson adopt a Gricean model which presupposes that communicative goals are straightforward, stable and, most significantly, *shared* by interlocutors within a given culture, it is unlikely that such patterns would emerge using their model.

6.1.3   Discussion

Although Holmes's claim that men and woman have different communicative goals is somewhat problematic since it implies an essentialist conceptualisation of gender identity that many feminists would find questionable, her survey of politeness data does raise some useful questions when it demonstrates that a given politeness strategy such as a compliment can have quite distinct functions and meanings. This issue is addressed by other studies that consider the relationship between politeness phenomena and gender (see, for example, Brown 1980, 1994), and is also highlighted by Rundquist's (1992) data which suggests that the concept of 'indirect' linguistic behaviour appears to be too general to be meaningful at present. If Brown and Levinson argue that indirect forms of linguistic behaviour constitute a negative politeness strategy that is motivated by a speaker's lack of relative power, while the studies discussed in relation to Rundquist's account in the previous chapter indicate that it is an effect of a speaker's relative power in relation to her addressee, then this would imply that the behaviour may have a range of functions. It may be, then, that either concepts like 'indirectness' or 'compliment' need unpacking if they are to constitute useful analytical tools. Or it may be that a given 'politeness' strategy simply does not have a unitary function. Either way, it would appear that context of use has more of an impact on how a given strategy will function than politeness theory would predict, and moreover, interlocutor gender may be a significant aspect of that context.

There is also evidence that simply to call on 'gender' as a variable that can explain how these different meanings come to be attributed to politeness behaviour is to propose too rigid a characterisation of the process by which a given form generates one meaning in one context of use and another in a different context of use. As West et al. argue:

> [T]he issue is not so much the particular forms women use (such as tag questions) but the specific pragmatic work these forms can accomplish (such as demonstrating a speaker's stance) *and* the norms associated with the distribution of this work between women and men. (West et al. 1997: 132)

They go on to suggest that 'sex differences' in talk are more likely to result from 'habitual differences between men and women in the pragmatic work they must do' (132). Research reported in Cameron, McAlinden and O'Leary (1988) that builds on the findings of one of Holmes's own earlier studies provides a well-argued illustration of this in that, the report indicates that where a differential use of 'tag questions' had been explained as an effect of gender in Holmes's study, their own analysis enabled a more precise explanation. Their data showed that a particular type of tag question that appeared to function as a way of facilitating conversation and encouraging others to contribute, and which tended across a range of studies to be used primarily by women, was, in one part of the study used extensively by certain male subjects. They suggest that where this occurred, it was because these particular men knew that their conversation was being recorded. The authors explain the men's behaviour thus:

> It may be that their speech reflected a concern to elicit as much talk as possible from other participants, in order to generate as much data as possible for the Survey. In other words, these speakers had either consciously or unconsciously taken on the role of conversational 'facilitator'. (Cameron, McAlinden and O'Leary 1988: 85)

What this indicates, therefore, is that 'gender' as an explanation is not explanatory enough. It also indicates a weakness in studies that focus on tendencies rather than on the relationship between the language use, the language user and the context of use. Cameron et al.'s account opens up the issue of gendered linguistic behaviour in that it raises specific questions about who takes on which conversational roles, and how role might relate to gender.

According to West et al. (1997: 132) such differences are best seen not in essentialist terms (women facilitate speech because they are more co-operative than men) but rather as 'a way of mapping or *indexing* gender'. However, although an essentialist explanation may not be required in accounting for gendered differences in linguistic behaviour, what such evidence does require is a pragmatic explanation. The question an analyst is left with is *how* these different meanings come to be generated, and *how* a given piece of linguistic behaviour comes to be perceived as having distinct functions. The final theory I address provides one of the most comprehensive accounts of how these issues can be addressed.

6.2 SPERBER AND WILSON'S RELEVANCE THEORY

Sperber and Wilson's ([1986], 1995) theory of relevance is premised on a very specific notion of what the scope of a pragmatic theory should be. The authors state that their aim is to construct an explanatory theory of communication 'grounded in a general view of human cognition' (vii), and this approach tends therefore to be represented as one that is not concerned with social or cultural issues. Blakemore (1992: 39–40), for example, suggests that, although relevance theory can help to explain socio-cultural phenomena, these phenomena do not impinge on the theory itself. This is because the theory is concerned with the basic, universal principles that underlie utterance interpretation rather than the content of interpretations. Therefore, although issues of gender might be explored through the application of relevance theory, the principles postulated in that theory are assumed to be sufficiently abstract for them not to actually already be gendered (see Cameron 1998b for a discussion of this issue). I will consider how far this is the case in the final chapter in relation to the authors' (1995) revisions to their original (1986) account of relevance theory. Before this however I provide a brief summary of Sperber and Wilson's theory and then outline a study in which I have applied the insights offered by relevance theory in the analysis of a media representation of feminist politics. It may be that the approach to language use I am outlining here appears familiar. That is because Sperber and Wilson's theory has informed my own approach to pragmatics, and this is evident in much of my argument throughout this book.

6.2.1   A summary of the argument

In developing their theory, Sperber and Wilson take as their point of departure the model of communication that underpinned much current work in pragmatics at the time the first full account of relevance theory was published in 1986. In particular they set out to distinguish their own inferential model from that which informed Gricean and speech act theories of pragmatic phenomena: the code model. They distinguish between these two models by pointing out that decoding is the recovery of a message that is made possible because there is a fixed link between the signal and the message, while inferencing is the process of working from a premise (or evidence) through logic to reach a conclusion. They suggest that while the Gricean approach assumes that utterance interpretation can involve both decoding (recovering what the speaker has 'said') and inferring (recovering what is implicated or 'meant' by the speaker), their own approach is premised on the assumption that all utterance interpretation is inferential, and this includes the process of working out what has been explicitly said. Although, it may not be immediately obvious why it should be, this is a controversial claim to make. Some of the implications of seeing utterance interpretation as primarily inferential should become evident in the outline that follows. It should be noted however, that relevance theory has much wider implications than those indicated here. This summary is structured around, and designed to introduce, the aspects of relevance theory that I feel are the most significant to my subsequent illustration of the way it can be applied in feminist analyses of linguistic data. In this section I begin by pointing briefly to two aspects of relevance theory that I think are particular significant. I then fill in some of the theoretical background.

6.2.1.1 Two significant features of relevance theory

Firstly, what Sperber and Wilson have contributed to pragmatics is a way of distinguishing what is made explicit in an utterance from what is implied by an utterance. The distinction they posit between implicatures and what they term 'explicatures', is not the same as Grice's distinction between what is meant and what is said. Grice's theory of implicature is centred on the insight that there are certain types of utterance (where maxims are being flouted) that require an inferential process of meaning generation, but for the most part he takes as axiomatic that what is 'said' is encoded in the language of an utterance. For Sperber and Wilson, although the language system might be seen as a code, what is 'said' is never simply the product of an encoding process. Therefore what is said cannot be decoded: it has to be inferred by the hearer. So, for example, when interpreting an utterance like *This is men only*, a hearer has to assign a referent to words like *this*, and words like *men* have to be disambiguated (is the speaker using the term to indicate human beings generally or adults of the male sex?). And as I indicated in Chapter 3, words like *and* also have to be disambiguated (is the speaker implying that a causal relation holds between two phenomena, or is there a temporal relationship implied?). Sperber and Wilson's argument is that it is only after a process of enrichment, disambiguation and the filling in of what is elided by an utterance that a hearer can infer the propositions that it is 'expressing'. To argue that the way in which a hearer uncovers what is 'said' is through inferencing rather than decoding has extensive implications for the way that language use is addressed. For example, while Gricean and speech act accounts assume that what is explicitly said is self-evident, Sperber and Wilson's model foregrounds the extent to which a single utterance might be seen as 'saying' a number of different things. This in turn raises questions about how speakers and hearers ever come to communicate anything successfully when even the apparently explicit meaning of an utterance is not fixed by the linguistic code. These questions become more complex in the light of the second aspect of relevance theory I consider.

The second element, and to my mind, one of the most enabling aspects of relevance theory, is Sperber and Wilson's theorisation of 'context' as a psychological construct. I have indicated throughout this work that seeing context as a fixed *a priori* element of an utterance is highly problematic. The different responses to Nicholson's anecdote are an indication of how speculative the process of context selection can be, and how it can involve an engagement with a range of different types of phenomena. As I indicated in Chapter 1, when audience members in my study interpreted Nicholson's report of her relations' utterance *This is men only*, there was evidence that some looked to the visual context to interpret *this* as 'Parliament' while others drew on the linguistic context and cultural knowledge to interpret *this* as 'the Carlton Club'. The problem is, however, that if one were to use such evidence to try to explain how it is that addressees come to an understanding of an utterance, this would leave much of the communication process unaccounted for. For example, the evidence indicates that selecting a context is a necessary part of working out the explicatures of an utterance in that it informs reference assignment and disambiguation. Moreover, Sperber and Wilson's claim is that context also plays a part in working out what a speaker means by what she has said. Context, is therefore a significant element of utterance interpretation. But if it is selected at the moment at which a speaker's meaning is being interpreted, and seems to be drawn from a wide range of sources, on what basis is that selection made? Presumably it is not an entirely random selection process. Evidence such as the interpretations of Nicholson's anecdote indicates the risks involved in linguistic communication, but in general, if context selection always had the potential to be that wide of the mark, the chances are that communication would be so hit and miss, on most days, we wouldn't get as far as finishing breakfast. If ellipses were restored, words disambiguated and references assigned as the result of a random process of context selection the communicative results would be chaotic. Our lives would be interspersed with utterances like

(1) *When I said 'pour my tea out' I meant pour it into my cup not my shoe!*

The fact that (1) isn't a normal feature of breakfast discourse indicates that while context selection may be a dynamic part of the process of working out what a speaker is saying, and may call on a number of different types of evidence, it must also be a highly regulated act. The question is: what regulates it? Sperber and Wilson's account is a sustained attempt to formulate the principles that underlie context selection, and, as a result, the principles that underlie communication generally. Below, I briefly summarise how they argue their case.

6.2.1.2   The ostensive–inferential model of communication

Sperber and Wilson suggest that the process of disambiguation required to understand an utterance such as their example: *Betsy's gift made her very happy* (1986: 10) illustrates the limitations of the code model in that the linguistic meaning here clearly falls short of encoding what the speaker means: it is not encoded whether the referent for *gift* is a particular talent or whether it is a birthday present. Evidence such as this leads to their claim that since a coding–decoding process cannot even account for the way in which a hearer comes to understand basic linguistic stimuli, this would indicate that even if the language system itself can be described as a code, and even if, therefore, communication may involve some degree of linguistic encoding and decoding, that process must be subordinate to an ostensive-inferential process of communication. The authors describe this process as follows:

> Inferential communication and ostension are one and the same process, but seen from two different points of view: that of the communicator who is involved in ostension and that of the audience who is involved in inference. (1986, 1995: 54)

Ostension is posited as 'behaviour that makes manifest the intention to make something manifest' (49). It is, they argue, behaviour which provides two layers of information that must be picked up by an audience if any degree of communication is to take place.

A non-encoded example of ostension which Sperber and Wilson give is of a woman on holiday coming out of a hotel in light summer clothing who is met by a man who grimaces and points to the sky which is full of rain clouds (1986: 51). The two layers of information are (1) the evidence that it is going to rain and (2) the intention to communicate that evidence. Both layers are needed to avoid the first (the evidence) being missed by the addressee. In the case where communication takes the form of language, the encoded elements of syntax and semantics constitute some part of the evidence contained in the first layer. For Sperber and Wilson, a crucial component of their model is that addressees assume that, in claiming their attention through ostensive behaviour, communicators have something of relevance to impart. In the above example of ostension, the reason that the woman coming out of the hotel makes a hypothesis about the man's intended meaning (that it is going to rain) is because she assumes that his intention is to communicate something to her that will be relevant to her. If she had not made that assumption, the argument goes, she would not have set about making sense of his gestures. Sperber and Wilson summarise this process as follows:

> Ostensive behaviour provides evidence of one's thoughts. It succeeds in doing so because it implies a guarantee of relevance. It implies such a guarantee because humans automatically turn their attention to what seems most relevant to them. (1986: 50)

It may seem somewhat odd to claim that all ostensive behaviour (including utterances) implies a 'guarantee' of relevance, since we all know that the point of what we and others say in the course of a day is highly questionable at times. But what is actually being claimed here is that it is the assumption that what is said will be relevant that triggers off the process of utterance interpretation. Without that assumption, utterance interpretation would not happen. Whether the utterance actually fulfils that guarantee is, of course, another issue. In order to understand what is significant about this, it is necessary to consider what, according to Sperber and Wilson, is communicated through language use, and how communication works.

6.2.1.3 What is communicated

Sperber and Wilson distinguish their own theory from pragmatic theories such as speech act theory and Grice's theory of implicature, by pointing out that the latter tend to assume (1) that the goal of communication is to make the speaker's meaning accessible to the hearer and (2) that communication is the successful transfer of this meaning to the hearer. They also suggest that according to the model of communication which informs most pragmatic theories at the time they are writing, the difference between explicit content and implicatures is accounted for only in terms of the *means* by which communication occurs. These earlier accounts also therefore assume (3) that inferencing is the means by which implicatures are accessed and decoding is the means by which explicit content is accessed. In both cases communication is seen to occur either fully or not at all. Sperber and Wilson contest all three of these assumptions.

For example, in arguing that the processing of both explicit and implicit meaning requires the hearer to utilise inferences, Sperber and Wilson suggest that *what* gets communicated depends on the *type* of evidence the communicator uses. This is because within Sperber and Wilson's paradigm communication is a matter of degree: communication occurs in varying strengths and cannot be equated with 'speaker meaning'. This is explained more fully when they propose that what it is to 'communicate' something and what it is to 'mean' something are quite distinct and when they suggest that something can be 'communicated' without strictly having been 'meant'. An example would be the implications of Mary's response in the following exchange.

(2) *Peter*: What do you intend to do today?
    Mary: I have a terrible headache. (56)

As Sperber and Wilson argue, there would be no precise assumption, apart from the one explicitly expressed, which Mary can be said to have intended Peter to share. And yet she clearly intends Peter to draw certain conclusions from her utterance. They argue, therefore, that it is not the case in such an exchange that an assumption is either communicated or not communicated, it would be more appropriate to say that in such an exchange there is a set of assumptions which as a result of communication become manifest or more manifest to the hearer to varying degrees (59). 'Manifest assumptions' are described as facts that individuals are capable of representing mentally and accepting as true or probably true (46). To say an assumption is manifest, therefore, is to say it is 'perceptible or inferable' (Sperber and Wilson 1987: 699). While it is presumably made strongly manifest to Peter as a result of (2) that Mary has a headache, what is less manifest to Peter is what this indicates about what Mary plans to do with her day. What is communicated here then are a number of assumptions that are manifest to the hearer to different degrees.

This notion that communication is a matter of degree is based on Sperber and Wilson's claim that the communicator's informative intention is not to modify the 'thoughts' of the addressee, but to modify his 'cognitive environment' with 'only partly foreseeable effects on the audience's actual thoughts' (700). They describe the cognitive environment of an individual as 'the set of all facts that he can perceive or infer: all the facts that are manifest to him' (Sperber and Wilson 1986: 39). I discuss what Sperber and Wilson mean by the terms *cognitive environment* in more detail below, here it is significant in that what they are arguing is that in aiming to modify the cognitive environment of an addressee the speaker can use a mixture of coded and non-encoded evidence. They suggest that a speaker will choose the degree of inferencing required of the addressee according to how precisely she wants to affect his cognitive environment. 'Weak' communication, where there is little linguistic encoding, is sometimes sufficient or, indeed, preferable in face-saving situations. An example of weak communication would be the type of 'off-record' utterance I cite in Section 6.1.1.2 of this chapter when I suggest that *Damn, I'm out of cash, I forgot to go to the bank* could function as a way of indirectly asking a colleague for a loan.

Before going on to describe how ostensive-inferential communication is seen to work, I outline the main points of Sperber and Wilson's argument so far:

Human beings use two different modes of communication:

1. coded communication (e.g. the English language, morse code, sign language);
2. ostensive-inferential communication

The two modes are used in different ways:

1. ostensive-inferential communication can be used on its own, and sometimes is (for example, grimacing at clouds);
2. coded communication is only used as a means of strengthening ostensive-inferential communication

Communication is a matter of degree:

1. the communicator's behaviour is used as evidence by an addressee in the construction of assumptions about her meaning;
2. the strength of the communication depends on the type of evidence the communicator uses.

A description of the principle of 'relevance' and its role in the communication process is given in the following section, after a brief account of how Sperber and Wilson explain human inferential abilities.

6.2.1.4 How communication works

Sperber and Wilson describe the inferential process as goal-oriented, but as I indicate above, the goal is not, as the Gricean accounts argue, to understand the speaker's meaning. While the goal of the speaker is to modify the hearer's cognitive environment, the goal of the hearer is to improve his own knowledge of the world, by supplementing it with information that has some significance for him. If the modification to his cognitive environment that the speaker intends is indeed relevant to the hearer, he will, through the process of utterance interpretation improve the mental representation of the world that he has, and it is this, they suggest, that therefore motivates utterance interpretation. The notion of a cognitive environment is crucial to Sperber and Wilson's account of how communication works in that it explains both what triggers utterance interpretation (in a way that does not posit that speakers and hearers have shared conversational goals) and also indicates how utterance interpretation is made possible. Since I also pick up on this concept in my discussion of feminist applications of relevance theory, I will briefly summarise Sperber and Wilson's description of this phenomenon.

I suggested above that Sperber and Wilson define a cognitive environment as the set of all facts that are manifest to an individual. As Sperber and Wilson point out this would include both 'truths' and 'beliefs': 'From a cognitive point of view, mistaken assumptions can be indistinguishable from genuine factual knowledge, just as optical illusions can be indistinguishable from true sight' (1986: 39). Moreover, in suggesting that it is the total set of what is 'manifest' to an individual, the cognitive environment does not just include what is immediately perceptible to an individual, plus their stock of assumptions about the world, it also includes all of the inferences that can be derived from an individual's perceptions and their beliefs about the world. They illustrate this by pointing out that without being told, it is already 'manifest' to you that Noam Chomsky never had breakfast with Julius Caesar even though it had probably never actually crossed your mind that you knew this (40). They go on to say that, although it would be impossible for two people to have exactly the same cognitive environment (in the sense that everything that is manifest to one is also manifest to the other person), the cognitive environment of two people can intersect in the sense that there may be some facts and assumptions that are mutually manifest (41). However, as they point out: 'to say that two people share a cognitive environment does not imply that they make the same assumptions: merely that they are capable of doing so' (41). They sum up their discussion of cognitive environments thus:

A cognitive environment is merely a set of assumptions which the individual is capable of mentally representing and accepting as true. The question then is: which of these assumptions will the individual actually make? This question is of interest not only to the psychologist but to every ordinary communicator. We will argue that when you communicate, your intention is to alter the cognitive environment of your addressee; but of course you expect their actual thought processes to be affected as a result ... [and] ... that human cognition is relevance-oriented, and that as a result, someone who knows an individual's cognitive environment can infer which assumptions he is actually likely to entertain. (1986: 46)

In explaining communication then, Sperber and Wilson are arguing that, like other cognitive processes, it is 'relevance-oriented'. Individuals turn their attention to what is relevant in order to improve their representation of the world (where this representation is defined as a stock of 'factual assumptions' with some internal organisation). In acts of communication, new assumptions that result from an act of inferencing are added to this stock (75).

Improvements to an individual's representation of the world are a product, Sperber and Wilson argue, of a 'deductive device' which they posit as part of the central thought-processing system. The device they propose is intended to model the system used by human beings in spontaneous inference. An analysis of the intricacies of this model is outside the scope of this introduction, but the following should indicate how this notion informs their account. Sperber and Wilson assert that inferences are made up of a combination of assumptions. These assumptions have varying strengths depending on their source. Four potential sources are proposed by Sperber and Wilson, three of which are perceptual: visual, auditory or linguistic perception, and the fourth source is the set of assumptions that have been processed by the deductive device. In claiming that inferences are made up of assumptions whose source can be perceptual as well as being the output of the deductive device, Sperber and Wilson distinguish between 'new' and 'old' information: perceptual information constitutes new information while the assumptions which the deductive device has processed and stored in encyclopaedic memory constitute 'old' information. Their point is that these different types of information are synthesised in the act of utterance interpretation: that already processed information acts as a contextual background against which new information is interpreted.

They describe the process in the following terms 'a deduction based on the union of new information {P} with old information {C} is a *contextualisation* of {P} in {C} ' (1986: 108). Where this contextualisation yields new conclusions that would not have been derivable from either the old or the new information in isolation, these new conclusions are termed 'contextual implications'. An example of how such implications are generated, which is based on one provided by Sperber and Wilson (133) would be the meanings that might be derived from the utterance:

(3) Peter: I'm tired.

If the above (new information) that Peter is tired is, in the act of interpretation, contextualised by the following assumption manifest to Mary:

(4) It is Peter's turn to make dinner

and if Mary is aware that assumption (4) is mutually manifest, in that it is an assumption that is manifest within the cognitive environments of both herself and Peter, then interpreting (3) in the context of (4) may lead Mary to draw the contextual implication:

(5) Peter is telling me he doesn't want to make dinner.

In the above case, the contextualisation of the new information (3) in the old information (4) leads to the generation of a third piece of information (5). Sperber and Wilson's argument is that the more contextual implications that are generated by such a process, the more the individual's existing representation of the world will be improved. Another way of describing this process is to say that the more contextual effects the process generates the more relevant the new information is. In their revised version of the theory (1995: 265) they go on to argue that where a cognitive effect contributes to the fulfilment of cognitive functions or goals (for example, if they have improved a hearer's representation of the world) it is a *positive cognitive effect*.

At this point of the argument the significance of Sperber and Wilson's notion of 'relevance' should become more apparent. As the authors suggest in their description of ostensive-inferential communication, human beings automatically turn their attention to what seems most relevant to them and they do this in order to improve their understanding of the world (1987: 697). The concept of relevance is possibly best seen therefore as a function of the individual's overall cognitive goals. A corollary of this is that for a communicator's use of ostensive behaviour to work, she has to be capable of indicating that what she wishes to communicate will have this specific benefit for her hearer. This is necessary because the assumption that a given piece of linguistic evidence is relevant constitutes a basic premise that underlies any inferences he goes on to make. If the speaker does not succeed in indicating that what she has to impart is relevant to the hearer, then, according to this model, the inferential process will not be triggered. This is not to say that the *linguistic* meaning will not be interpreted by the hearer, but that what the speaker means by what she says will not be interpreted. To this extent then, the hearer's belief that what is being said will be relevant is axiomatic to any act of utterance interpretation. The following example of how relevance theory differs from other pragmatic theories which assume a notion of relevance should indicate the significance of this claim.

In other pragmatic theories such as those which follow Grice, it is assumed, Sperber and Wilson (1986: 182) argue, that within an act of communication, first of all the context is determined, then the interpretation process takes place, then relevance is assessed. The problem with the idea that a context somehow pre-exists an interpretation process can be seen in the differential notions of context generated by the audience of the Nicholson anecdote. If context was a fixed *a priori* feature of an utterance, every audience member would automatically have accessed the same set of assumptions. In their own version of the process, Sperber and Wilson claim that the addressee begins with the premise that the utterance he is in the process of interpreting is relevant and, on the basis of this premise, he accesses a context that would justify that premise. A crucial difference between their own and previous theories therefore is that, in the earlier models, relevance is a variable to be assessed in function of a pre-determined context, while in their own model, relevance is a given, and context is a variable (141). This account therefore addresses the question of how, if context is not predetermined, the addressee comes to select a context (from either encyclopaedic memory, previous utterances or from the immediate environment) which will make an utterance fulfil its putative guarantee of relevance.

In accordance with their theoretical framework, Sperber and Wilson explain this by positing a model of cognition which operates according to the principle of producing maximum effects for the minimum effort. When they describe the way in which an individual accesses a context that would justify his premise that what a speaker is saying is relevant, they define the relevance of an assumption to the individual in terms of 'extent conditions' which balance the effect and effort of the process:

(6)   *Extent condition 1:* an assumption is relevant to an individual to the extent that the positive cognitive effects achieved when it is optimally processed are large.

(7)   *Extent condition 2:* an assumption is relevant to an individual to the extent that the effort required to achieve these positive cognitive effects is small. (1995: 266)

The audience's selection of a context which will make an utterance fulfil its guarantee of relevance is therefore accounted for in terms of maximum contextual effects for least processing effort. The ease with which a hearer accesses a context that will produce contextual effects and thereby improve his representation of the world is an indication of the extent to which an utterance is relevant. If I shout *Fire!* and you smell burning, then you would no doubt register that perception as a particular relevant context in which to interpret my utterance, and therefore my use of that word would improve your representation of the world in a very useful way. If a hearer cannot provide a context which will produce any contextual effects then presumably the hearer would deduce that this utterance is not relevant to him (as when one overhears a snatch of conversation on a bus) and the search for a context would cease, which would leave the speaker's meaning uninterpreted.

What Sperber and Wilson are arguing then is that since as human beings we automatically turn our attention to what is most relevant to us, then there must be a mechanism that enables us to select, out of all the available perceptual phenomena, which is the most significant. Their point is that this mechanism also governs our communicative behaviour. When it comes to communication, therefore, although we cannot avoid comprehending the *words* or *sentences* we read or hear any more than we can avoid seeing the colour blue when we look at the sky in summer, we are only motivated to interpret the significance of words if we believe (and this is not necessarily a conscious belief) that they are relevant to us. So, if you are an English speaker, you cannot for example see or hear the word *fire* and not understand that it is a word of English that has a specific set of meanings associated with it. However, hearing somebody shout *Fire!* in a given situation of use requires you to work out its relevance to you if it is to communicate anything to you.

As well as explaining how hearers interpret utterances, Sperber and Wilson's account also explains the behaviour of speakers, in that because human beings share the tacit knowledge that we can only communicate with a hearer if we make him believe that what we are saying has a relevance for him, we have to ensure that when we communicate our intention to communicate (that is to say when we engage in ostension) by speaking or writing, our utterances have to be in a form that will raise this expectation of relevance. One of the things we have to do in order to achieve this is to make hypotheses about our interlocutor's cognitive environment: are the assumptions I need him to access if he is to understand my meaning manifest to him? Have I phrased my utterance in such a way that will lead him to access the appropriate set of contextual assumptions?

Although much of this account of relevance theory may seem somewhat abstract, it does have a range of practical applications that, unfortunately, there is not space to address here (but see for example Blass 1990, Carston and Uchida 1998 and Smith and Wilson 1992). Neither is there space to explore the theoretical implications of adopting this rather than an alternative model of communication, although the authors themselves, as well as Blakemore (1995), Carston (1988) and Jary (1998), have shown how the adoption of the relevance model requires a rethinking of phenomena such as coherence, speech acts, politeness behaviour and implicature. An extremely accessible introduction to relevance theory that covers some of this ground is provided by Blakemore (1992), while a good precis of the theoretical implications of relevance theory can be found in Blakemore (1995). It should also be noted that the overall argument, as well as specific details of relevance theory, have been strongly disputed, and there remains a great deal of controversy over the claims made by Sperber and Wilson (see for example Chametzky 1992 and Gorayska and Lindsay 1993). I would argue however that although the theory remains somewhat controversial and that, to date, it has not been widely applied in studies of gender and language use, it can usefully inform such studies. In what follows therefore, I briefly summarise an example of my own work that has drawn on relevance theory in order to show how, although there may be problematic aspects of the theory, it provides some useful insights into the analysis of language use.

6.2.2   Applying relevance theory

I have, in recent years, carried out two studies that have explored the inferential structures that are mobilised in the process of interpreting media representations of feminist issues (see Christie 1994, 1998a and 1998b). My aim in both was to consider the power of media representations by addressing the type of issue outlined in Section 2.3.1 of Chapter 2. In the study I describe below, I focus on a positive media representation of an aspect of feminism that is not likely to be familiar to all audience members. In the second (reported in Christie 1998b), I focused on a negative media representation of a feminist issue. I draw on the model of communication formulated by Sperber and Wilson (1986) in both studies in that each is informed by the postulate that communicators need to take into account the cognitive environment of their addressees when they phrase their utterances, and that this is (1) because they need to imply that what they are saying is relevant to the addressee and (2) because this maximises the chances that the addressee will access the specific contextual assumptions that will lead him to infer the communicator's intended meaning. Each is also informed by Sperber and Wilson's argument that contextual assumptions are inferred in the process of interpreting utterances and that they play a part in the hearer's assessment of what a communicator has said, and in the assessment of what the communicator means by what she has said. I focus on media texts because, if Sperber and Wilson are correct, the above postulates would predict that there is a great deal of scope for communicative failure in broadcast events in that if one is addressing a mass audience, it is more difficult to construct utterances that would take into account the cognitive environment of all one's addressees. There is, therefore, an increased likelihood that, even if a speaker managed to imply to a given audience member that her utterance was relevant, because there is less chance that the assumptions manifest to the speaker when constructing the utterance will overlap with those manifest to the hearer when the utterance is interpreted, there is also less chance that the contextual assumptions that the hearer accesses will be those that will generate the interpretation intended by the speaker. The responses to the Nicholson anecdote are, of course, an indication of this. What I am particularly interested in is: given what relevance theory suggests about the way in which utterances are interpreted, what can this tell us about media power, and what, in particular, can it tell us about the way that feminism is represented linguistically in the media and the way that these representations are interpreted by audiences?

This latter issue is of particular significance given the range of discourses of feminism that are available to a mass audience, and given the relative obscurity of some of these discourses, since this diversity suggests that when feminist issues are represented by the media, there must be a particularly wide scope for variation in the interpretations of such representations. For example, if you are a feminist whose goals (or sympathies) are oriented primarily towards promoting equal-opportunities legislation in education or the workplace, or changing the law, or the taxation system where they discriminate against women, you are likely to see gender politics as a set of practices that take place in the public arena. As is evident from the survey in Chapter 2, there are of course many other types of feminist approach. To an extent a range of these other feminist approaches crystallise around the shared assumption that the 'personal is political'. As I indicated earlier, whether this position is arrived at from poststructuralist or materialist premises, feminists who believe that our beliefs and behaviour are affected by the way we categorise the world, and the way that we perceive ourselves and others, tend to assume that consciousness and identity are matters of critical importance to gender politics. From this perspective politics is not something that is 'out there', it is what people do in their everyday lives: when a woman is trying to decide whether or not to return to work after childbirth; in disputes over who will take charge of the television remote control. Whether or not one actually subscribes to one of these beliefs about the domain of gender politics as public or personal, everyone has a way of explaining feminism to themselves. In terms of a relevance theoretical approach, what this would suggest is that within an individual's cognitive environment certain assumptions about feminism will be manifest. However, which particular assumptions are manifest to an individual will depend on a number of factors, including the political and educational experiences that individual has had.

As I indicate above, within relevance theory *assumptions* are 'facts that individuals are capable of representing mentally and accepting as true or probably true' and *assumptions that are manifest to an individual* are those assumptions that are 'perceptible or inferable by an individual'. Sperber and Wilson's claim is that when interlocutors interpret each other's utterances, the assumptions that make up their cognitive environment are the pool from which contextual assumptions are drawn. What I am suggesting on the basis of this is that the chances are that not every audience member will have access to the same pool of assumptions about feminism. While one does not need to approach the issue from a relevance-theoretical perspective in order to come to the conclusion that individuals have different understandings of what feminism is, why this should be a significant factor in relation to utterance interpretation is something that only arises when communication is approached in terms of a pragmatic account such as Sperber and Wilson's. It gains its significance from the postulate that utterance interpretation is predicated on one's ability to access relevant contextual information rather than on the language of the utterance itself.

6.2.2.1 Preaching to the converted

Working on the hypothesis that a familiarity with feminist discourses is often acquired through specific institutional or educational experiences, and with the aim of comparing the responses of women with different assumptions about gender politics to a single media representation of feminism, I located two friendship groups, one consisting of post-graduate students, and the other consisting of a group of women who had a range of different occupations, but who had all left school without going on to further education. It was not my intention to establish differences in the women's familiarity with feminist discourses in advance of the study, but rather to set up conditions within an interview that would draw out differences in the assumptions about feminism that were manifest to them. My questions were designed to make explicit the contextual assumptions that the women were accessing when they interpreted a particular media representation of feminism. This method brought out differences both between and within the groups, but there were consistent patterns in their responses that indicated that the members of the post-graduate group were drawing on a set of assumptions about feminism that were not available to the other group. In particular, what this indicated was that the two groups interpreted the meaning of one presentation of feminism in radically distinct ways. Although I have reported on this study in the past (see Christie 1994 and 1998a) I have still to resolve what to call these groups, since what distinguishes them for the purposes of the study is just one of a number of variables that could potentially distinguish them. I have tended to term the post-graduate group the 'radical' group based on the fact that they called on a set of assumptions about 'radical feminism' that the other group did not have access to. I have called the second group the 'mainstream group' since, the members indicated a knowledge of feminist ideas that would, I believe, have been accessible to most audiences of this programme. This is not, of course, to suggest that all of the other factors that distinguish the groups may not have some bearing on their responses, but rather that this study was not designed specifically to address those factors.

The particular presentation of feminism I asked the groups to view consisted of an episode of a 1990 Channel Four Series entitled *Ordinary People*. The specific episode they viewed was entitled 'The Politics of Experience' and it included individual presentations by three women, each of whom spoke about their experience of gender politics. The presentation by one of these women, Eugenia Piza Lopez, was of particular interest in that it provided an account of how she became aware of gender politics through her everyday experiences. The significance lay in her presentation of gender politics as an issue of consciousness, and to that extent she was drawing on a notion of feminism that was clearly only manifest to the radical group. The type of evidence that indicated this can be seen from their understanding of Lopez's meaning when she describes how she first became aware of gender politics. I will briefly summarise Lopez's presentation in order to contextualise the data. Lopez's presentation opens with a statement of her background: she was the daughter of intellectuals, whose questioning of society was wide but did not extend to issues of gender. She gives as an example of this limitation her mother's dedication to the preservation of her daughter's virginity. This obsession with virginity led Lopez to begin to question the assumptions about gender she encountered, which in turn led to her perceiving gender as a political issue. Eventually Lopez began working with women in an (unspecified) area of rural South America, where she filmed the extensive amount of work these women carried out each day with the expressed intention of using the film, and the process of making it, to raise the women's awareness of the value of their labour to the community. The point about this summary is that it is based on my own understanding of what Lopez means by what she is saying. What I wanted to do in the study was to explore what the respondents understood her to mean.

In order to show what scope there was for differential interpretations, I will focus on just one part of her presentation, the point at which Lopez describes her mother's concern that she remain a virgin until she is married:

> And it really alienated my understanding of my own body and my sexuality because it made me feel that there was something wrong with it. There's something wrong with being the owner of your own body. Your body is not yours. It is for somebody else who will eventually indulge it when you get married. And it got to a point where I felt as a woman and not exclusively as a human being, but as a woman, there are a number of things I want to say. There are a number of things I want to struggle for. (Try Again Productions 1990)

In my own understanding of her presentation, Lopez is here referring to her emerging awareness of gender politics, and, moreover, I am assuming that she is stating that this development was at least in part caused by the attitude to virginity which she encountered as a young woman. In order to infer this meaning however, I have, of course, to resolve ambiguities in the language used, and assign referents to deictic words. I want here to indicate just one ambiguity that I am conscious of having had to resolve. Where Lopez states in the above quotation 'and it got to the point where I felt as a woman' the conjunction *and* has a number of possible functions. For example it could be there (1) to list a series of distinct phenomena; (2) to indicate a temporal connection between feeling alienated about her body and her feeling that there were things she wanted to struggle for, in which case it could be alternatively stated as 'and then'; or (3) it could imply a causal connection between these two states which could be alternatively stated as 'and therefore'. My own understanding of the text assumes the latter function: that a causal connection is being made. When I asked the respondents what they thought Lopez meant, neither of the groups exactly matched my own understanding of Lopez's meaning, but what was significant was that the mainstream group tended to see the point of her presentation as an illustration of life in the culture that Lopez was brought up in:

(A) I think she's just basically – just I think she's trying to give you an idea of how – what they think like in that country – well her family are more concerned about that she doesn't sleep with anyone before she gets married instead of being concerned how she's spending the rest of her life in the sense of work or whatever if you know what I mean that's their first priority
(B) Losing her virginity
(A) Yeah like don't lose your virginity sort of thing
(C) And stick to one man
(D) She wanted to be able to do her own/
(A) I don't think she was saying that she wanted to sleep around or anything I think she was just trying to say that's what they thought sort of thing – how bad she thinks their priorities were. (based on Christie 1994: 59)

On the basis of evidence such as this it became clear that although both groups understood what Lopez was saying in similar ways, they varied in terms of their assessment of the relevance of Lopez's point about virginity: why Lopez should talk about it at all in relation to feminism. The radical group produced interpretations that were not the same as my own, but which did indicate that they inferred that Lopez was making a claim about gendered power relations as they are instantiated in everyday life. However, the mainstream group appeared to view Lopez's account of this and other aspects of her life as designed to illustrate what life was like for her growing up and working in South America. For example at the end of the interview I asked each group whether they thought that Lopez's account had anything to do with politics. Again, the radical group did not indicate they were interpreting Lopez's account in exactly the same way as I had, but they talked of it being about 'politics with a small p'. In contrast the mainstream group responded as follows:

(B) To me it's her attitude to their way of life
[CC: So you don't think their way of life has got anything to do with our way of life over here?]
(General) No
(A) No it's not as over the top as what it is over there.

What responses such as these indicate is that the mainstream group did not share the assumptions that I took to be manifest to Lopez when she was describing her experience of gender politics. And because the cognitive environments of these audience members did not overlap with that of Lopez in the same way that those of the radical group appeared to, they did not access the contextual assumptions that this presentation appeared to require if it was to be understood in the way that (based on my own reading) Lopez intended. Although therefore, the explicatures assigned to Lopez's account seem to be the same for the two groups, their understanding of the relevance of what she was saying was quite distinct: the mainstream group saw her presentation as designed to communicate something of the way women live in a culture foreign to their own, the radical group saw her presentation as communicating something about what gender politics meant for Lopez. In my (1994 and 1998a) accounts, I suggest that this finding has implications for the way in which the power of media representations is explored in that my findings indicate that, if an audience does not already have access to a particular way of representing the world, or to a particular discourse, then a media representation cannot simply 'impose' that perspective on them. My findings also indicate something about representations of feminism in the media, in that they suggest that simply presenting positive accounts of feminist politics will not necessarily lead audiences to perceive feminism in a positive light. Such representations will not necessarily be interpreted in the anticipated way by audiences who are not already familiar with the aspects of feminist politics they are premised on. There is always the danger, therefore, that unless feminist ideas can be presented in an accessible way, they can only ever preach to the converted.

6.2.3 Conclusion

What the above application of relevance theory offers is just one limited indication of its usefulness to feminist studies of language use. What I hope to have shown is that a logical consequence of Sperber and Wilson's theory is that it is not possible for an analyst to state categorically what any utterance means by pointing to the language of that utterance alone.

However, the model does provide a descriptive vocabulary and an explanatory framework that would enable an analyst to put together a case in support of his or her own interpretation of a piece of naturally occurring language use and also provides a framework for exploring other people's understanding of linguistic events. Because of this, their model has implications for understanding the sort of issue raised by politeness and indirection that I point to at the end of Section 6.1.3 of this chapter. Sperber and Wilson's model takes as axiomatic that all utterances are, to some degree 'indirect' and that we can *never* 'say' what we 'mean'. However, in providing a descriptive account of how speakers are able to manipulate linguistic resources, the theory shows how degrees of indirection are employed according to the communicative intentions of the speaker, and in providing a model of utterance interpretation that postulates context as a psychological construct, it can explain how linguistic strategies are differentially interpreted.

As such the model of communication they have formulated enables questions to be asked about the way in which one meaning rather than another appears to be generated by a reader or hearer of a given utterance. An example of the form such a study might take is my (1998b) account of readers' interpretations of sexual-harassment reports in the popular press. In this study I apply a relevance-theoretical analysis to data which shows that although readers might potentially have access to a set of assumptions that would lead them to question tabloid accounts of sexual harassment cases, they do not necessarily make these assumptions manifest in the act of interpreting these reports. I argue that this might be explained by Sperber and Wilson's claim that, in interpreting a text, addressees search for contextual assumptions that would justify the premise that what they are reading is relevant. In the case of tabloid representations of sexual-harassment cases, it is often only possible to read a report as relevant if the reader generates contextual assumptions in the act of processing the text that would lead him to infer that the case is spurious in some way.

Evidence of how difficult it is to not make manifest textually directed contextual assumptions, even when they are assumptions whose truth one would normally question, can be seen in the way in which jokes like the following come to be seen as meaningful:

(8) What is mad cow disease?
    PMT.

Understanding this joke requires the reader to make manifest assumptions that are stereotypes of the way that women behave before menstruation. Now whether one believes that this is how women act or not, you cannot help but access the required contextual assumptions if you happen to be part of a culture where it is not unusual for women to be referred to as *cows* and in which women's behaviour is regularly represented as erratic

186

and driven by their hormones. As readers you cannot 'choose' not to understand this joke if those assumptions are available to you. And this is the case even if you would want to question the assumptions that underlie such a joke. What such evidence suggests about the way in which assumptions acquire strength, and what this implies about the way that ideologies come to take hold remains to be explored. My point is that because Sperber and Wilson's model theorises context as a set of available assumptions, it would provide a useful framework for exploring such an issue.

Their notion of context is, I think, a potentially very useful way of approaching gender and language use generally. If, as Sperber and Wilson argue, contextual assumptions are generated in the act (and as part of the process) of interpreting utterances, one could ask in what way might assumptions about gender constitute aspects of context in everyday inter-actions? For example, as I indicated in my discussion of politeness theory, there is a need to explain how a single politeness form comes to be per-ceived as having different functions according to the gender of the interactants. As I suggested, although the evidence supplied by Holmes and other researchers has indicated that gender appears to play a part in the process by which an addressee assigns a given function to a given use of a linguistic form, explaining how gender *per se* plays a part in this is not accounted for by politeness theory. However, if 'gender' is concep-tualised as a set of assumptions that are differentially manifest to indivi-duals according to how they represent the world to themselves (and this is, of course, related to people's life experiences) then this may offer a framework for exploring the relationship between interlocutor gender and the production and impact of politeness and other types of behaviour. It would also open up many of the other issues surrounding the controversy over whether gender should be understood in essentialist or constructivist terms, and indeed might allow an explanation of the way in which gender comes to be perceived as an 'essence'.

7

CONCLUSION

As I stated in the opening chapter, my aim in this book has been to demonstrate what a pragmatic approach to the study of gender and language use would entail, what analytical tools it would generate and what its specific benefits might be for feminist research in this field. Although it would be premature to see pragmatics as providing a ready calibrated tool-kit for exploring language use from a feminist perspective, I hope I have shown that approaching linguistic data from a perspective that asks how language functions in relation to its users brings into view a number of issues that are obscured by other methodologies. I also stated that my aim was to consider what pragmatics has to learn from feminism. My hope is that this survey of work in feminism and pragmatics will open up a productive dialogue between the two fields. Because that dialogue is at such an early stage, I will resist the temptation to pull the various strands together to argue for what a feminist pragmatics would consist of for fear of closing down potential directions that conversation might take. I will limit my comments in this chapter to just two issues therefore: a brief discussion of what pragmatics needs to take from studies of gender and language use, and a brief summary of why I think pragmatics has much to offer feminist research. I therefore return to two questions I raised in the first chapter: why a *feminist* pragmatics? and why a feminist *pragmatics*?

7.1 WHY A *FEMINIST* PRAGMATICS?

The main point I want to make here is that if pragmatics is to provide a productive theoretical framework for empirical research on gender and language use, and I believe that it can, it needs to take into account the questioning of identity that has taken place within feminist scholarship, and it needs to build on the findings of empirical studies of naturally occurring language use, both within and outside of pragmatics that show how gender is implicated in language use. Cameron (1998a: 445) argues that one of the strengths of the pragmatic approach is that it is not premised on the particulars of social engagements but draws on principles that obtain across all uses of language. She describes pragmatics thus:

> Human language-users are envisaged as rational actors who must behave in certain ways if communication is to be possible at all; it follows that the most basic principles of human communication hold at a high level of generality where they are unaffected by social and cultural differences. That does not of course mean that such differences are nonexistent or not worth discussing. (Cameron 1998b: 444)

Her point is that pragmatics postulates that it is not that men and women differ in *how* they reason but that they may differ in the *assumptions* they bring to their reasoning (445). As she points out there are convincing practical and theoretical reasons why it should be that variation is addressed at the 'lowest or most "local" level where it can still account for the observed facts' (445). However, such comparisons are only possible if there are 'global' principles that obtain across uses that explain such differences.

One of the outcomes of empirical studies that have applied pragmatic concepts is the questions they raise about whether some pragmatic principles that have in the past been perceived as universal, or sufficiently abstract to be applicable across all uses, are themselves too 'local'. They may be based on either male norms of language use as Holmes (1995) suggests in relation to politeness theory, or else they may be based on specific types of language use that assume that conversations are inevitably interactions between equals as Sarangi and Slembrouk (1992) and Harris (1995) have suggested in relation to Grice's maxims. Moreover, I wonder if it has been as evident to readers as it has been to me, that in adopting Sperber and Wilson's convention of using *she* to indicate the speaker and *he* to indicate the hearer in abstract discussions of language use, the effect is to gender interlocutors and model persons. For me, once these abstract entities are gendered, issues about the assumptions such theories make about the relationship between language use and language users come into play, not least in relation to that most abstract of concepts: relevance. One question this raises is whether the theorisation of relevance is sufficiently abstract to be able to address notions of gender, or whether the readiness of a hearer to assume that what a speaker has to say is relevant, that their model is premised on, indicates that the abstract entities 'speaker' and 'hearer' are already gendered.

One body of evidence that comes to mind that would raise questions about whether relevance is already gendered is the cross-gender talk analysed by Pamela Fishman in the 1970s. On the basis of her data, which consisted of extensive recordings of conversations between male and female couples, Fishman argued that it was consistently evident that when the men initiated a topic of conversation, the women were prepared to engage with what they said. However, when the women attempted to initiate a topic, it had less chance of being successful. For that reason, Fishman argues, women tend to ask more questions than men. She states her case thus:

> I found that women, using a variety of utterance types to introduce topics, succeeded only 36 per cent of the time in getting their topics to become actual conversations. In contrast, all but one of the men's topic attempts succeeded. However, when we look at the number of topic attempts that women introduced with a question, their success rate jumps considerably. (Fishman 1998: 255)

Fishman's point is that although her study could show that women's and men's linguistic behaviour was quite distinct in terms of the quantity of hedges or questions that occurred, this was not necessarily an issue of gender *per se*. Her argument is that women were using these strategies because they were not being listened to by their male interlocutors. She suggests that if the men found themselves in a situation where they were not listened to, they would use the same strategies as the women had. She also makes the point, however, that gender relations tend to be systematic and this situation is therefore more likely to be faced by women than men in that women's speech tends to be consistently seen as less significant than men's. If this is still characteristic of gender relations, (and Lakoff's 1995 discussion seems to indicate that it is) then possibly the ability to imply relevance is circumscribed by the assumptions that the addressee has about the speaker's gender.

That Sperber and Wilson are already at some level taking into account the idea that speaker identity matters is, I think, evident from one of the revisions they make in their updated (1995) version of the theory. In their original account they describe their 'presumption of optimal relevance' (which is what a hearer has to take as axiomatic if the interpretation process is to be triggered) in the following terms:

(a) The set of assumptions {I} which the communicator intends to make manifest to the addressee is relevant enough to make it worth the addressee's while to process the ostensive stimulus.

(b) The ostensive stimulus is the most relevant one the communicator could have used to communicate {I}. (1986: 158)

In their revised version, the presumption of optimal relevance is described thus:

(a) The ostensive stimulus is relevant enough for it to be worth the addressee's effort to process it.

(b)   The ostensive stimulus is the most relevant one compatible with the communicator's abilities and preferences. (1995: 270)

In writing into their theory the premise that not all interlocutors are equally able to produce linguistic 'stimuli' that their addressee's will perceive as relevant, Sperber and Wilson are accommodating one way in which 'local', and possibly gender-specific contexts impact on a hearer's readiness to search for relevance. As a result, it may be that all speakers are not able to imply to all addressees the same guarantee of relevance. Sperber and Wilson's claim, as I indicate in section 6.2.1 of the previous chapter, is that a hearer is motivated to generate inferences in order to improve his own representation of the world. Presumably therefore the status of the speaker, and her ability to imply to her hearer that what she has to say, will achieve this end, will play a part in whether the hearer will impute to her utterance the presumption of optimal relevance that triggers the interpretation process. How far this is the case, and whether it is an issue of speaker status or speaker gender, or even the status of gender, remains to be explored.

While pragmatics has, I feel, a great deal to offer feminist research, therefore, it is also my belief that the way in which pragmatic principles are formulated might usefully be interrogated in terms of what they assume about the relationship between interactants, about gender identity and about the motivation of interlocutors. This is particularly the case if pragmatics is to be of use in explaining the relationship between gender and language use.

7.2   WHY A FEMINIST *PRAGMATICS*?

The main point I want to make here is that pragmatics is necessary to feminist research on language use primarily because communication is hazardous. Because, as I hope I have shown, we can only ever hypothesise about speaker meanings and utterance meanings, we can never make absolute claims about the function or the meaning of a given example of language use. When analysing language therefore, it is incumbent on the analyst to justify the interpretations she or he attributes to a given utterance. Pragmatics is essential to any engagement with language use, therefore, because:

- a methodological consequence of adopting a pragmatic approach is that interpretations cannot be taken as self evident and therefore need to be supported by argument.
- pragmatics provides a set of analytical tools and a descriptive base that enable arguments about interpretation to be justified and laid open to interrogation.
- pragmatics provides a theoretical framework for explaining interpretations by looking at the relationship between socio-culturally situated language use and language users.

Adopting a pragmatic perspective in feminist studies of language use can help to strengthen an argument, therefore, in that it alerts analysts to the need to avoid making untestable claims about meaning that are premised on unarticulated intuitions.

In claiming that utterance meaning is not determined by either language or context, I am not suggesting that utterances can mean *anything* we want them to mean. As Cameron argues:

> The relativity of linguistic strategies confronts ordinary conversationalists from moment to moment as a practical problem. The utterances they have to process are potentially ambiguous, but for the enterprise of conversation to proceed in the way we know it does, they must in practice narrow down the set of possible interpretations and come to some decision about what utterances actually mean. In most cases it seems they do this to their mutual satisfaction, i.e. they believe they have understood one another. (Cameron 1998b: 439)

That current studies of gender and language use are concerned with what examples of language use mean to their users, is evident in the reasons often given for dismissing the validity of Lakoff's early accounts of language and gender (see, for example, Cameron et al. 1988). As Meinhof and Johnson (1997: 2) argue, because such accounts tend to be premised on 'armchair' theorising there is a perceived need to challenge them through the analysis of 'authentic linguistic data'. Presumably what makes data 'authentic' is that it constitutes language use that has a specific set of functions and meanings for its users. The relevance of adopting a pragmatic perspective in exploring this is particularly evident in Cameron's (1998b) argument in which, as the above quote indicates, she points out that although linguistic strategies can have a range of effects, in actual contexts of use certain meanings are rejected by users and others taken up. However, as she also points out, this should not be taken to imply that all interpretations are equal. Whose meaning counts can, Cameron argues, be an issue of gendered power relations. This is not to say that gender relations have to be seen as inevitably an issue of power in all contexts, that gender relations have to be seen as static and unchanging, or that they have to be explained in terms of men and women having different conversational goals. Indeed, Cameron points out that the 'misunderstanding' of strategies is a communicative resource, used differently in different circumstances and for different ends. It is also likely to be historically specific in that it appears to be an effect of social change:

> One of the most important changes in this regard must be that in some societies and in some contexts, women and men are now in competition for the same kinds of power and status, as opposed to taking up complementary roles. This situation creates fertile terrain for 'strategic'

misunderstanding, where the relativity of linguistic strategies is exploited as a weapon in conflicts between men and women. (1998b: 447)

Cameron's point is that adopting a pragmatic approach to issues of gender and language use that recognises both the relativity of linguistic strategies and the way in which interpretation is a site of conflict, allows issues of power to be addressed in very context-specific ways, at the level of what individuals bring to interactions. As a result gendered power differentials can be taken into account in analyses without assuming that they will always manifest themselves or that they will always manifest themselves in the same ways and have the same effects across all interactions. More-over, from a pragmatic perspective, male and female interlocutors, are addressed as agents who use linguistic strategies for their own ends, not-withstanding that, as Cameron points out in her paraphrase of Marx: 'men and women make their own interactions, but not under conditions of their own choosing' (1998b: 453).

What is significant in studying language use from a pragmatic per-spective, then, is not to point to the endless range of meaning possibilities that utterances might have, even though pragmatics does foreground this potential, but to point to the meanings that utterances actually appear to have for language users, and how linguistic strategies appear to function in relation to the needs and goals of their users. As I hope I have shown, there are many ways of using pragmatics to investigate the factors that would produce a given interpretation. What I also hope I have shown is that this perspective can open up for exploration the relationship between language and its users that feminist research is concerned to address.

BIBLIOGRAPHY

Althusser, L. (1971), 'Ideology and ideological state apparatuses', in *Lenin and Philosophy*, trans. Ben Brewster, London: New Left Books.

Arianrhod, R. (1993), 'Physics and mathematics, reality and language: dilemmas for feminists', in Kramarae and Spender (eds), pp. 41–53.

Ashworth, G. (1995), *A Diplomacy of the Oppressed: New Directions in International Feminism*, London: Zed.

Austin, J. L. (1975), *'How to do things with words': The William James Lectures delivered at Harvard in 1955*, Oxford: Clarendon Press.

Basu, A. (1995), *The Challenge of Local Feminisms: Women's Movements in Global Perspective*, Boulder and Oxford: Westview Press.

Beasley, C. (1999), *What is Feminism: An Introduction*, London: Sage.

Bergvall, V., J. Bing and A. Freed (eds) (1996), *Rethinking Language and Gender Research: Theory and Practice*, London: Longman.

Bing, J., and V. Bergvall (1996), 'The question of questions: beyond binary thinking', in Bergvall et al., pp. 1–30.

Blakemore, D. (1988), 'The organization of discourse', in Newmeyer (ed.), pp. 229–50.

Blakemore, D. (1992), *Understanding Utterances: An Introduction to Pragmatics*, Oxford: Blackwell.

Blakemore, D. (1995), 'Relevance theory', in Verschueren et al. (eds), pp. 443–53.

Blass, R. (1990), *Relevance Relations in Sissala*, Cambridge: Cambridge University Press.

Blum-Kulka, S. (1997), 'Discourse pragmatics', in Dijk (ed.), pp. 38–63.

Blum-Kulka, S., J. House and G. Kasper (eds) (1989), *Cross-Cultural Pragmatics*, Norwood, NJ: Ablex.

Bodine, A. (1998), 'Androcentrism in prescriptive grammar: singular "they", sex-indefinite "he" and "he or she"', in Cameron (ed.), pp. 124–40.

Braun, F. (1997), 'Making men out of people: the MAN principle in translating genderless forms', in Kotthoff and Wodak (eds), pp. 31–50.

Brown, P. (1980), 'How and why women are more polite: some evidence from a Mayan Community', in McConnell-Ginet et al. (eds), pp. 111–36.

Brown, P. (1994), 'Gender, politeness and confrontation in Tenejapa', in Roman et al. (eds), pp. 322–39.

Brown, P., and S. Levinson (1987), *Politeness: Some Universals in Language Use,* Cambridge: Cambridge University Press.

Bryson, V. (1992), *Feminist Political Theory,* London: Macmillan.

Burman, E., and I. Parker (1993), 'Introduction: discourse analysis: the turn to the text', in Burman and Parker (eds), pp. 1–16.

Burman, E., and I. Parker (eds) (1993), *Discourse Analytic Research,* London: Routledge.

Burt, S. M. (1992), 'Teaching conscientious resistance to co-operation with text: The role of pragmatics in critical thinking', in Stein (ed.), pp. 397–416.

Butler, J. (1990), *Gender Trouble: Feminism and the Subversion of Identity,* New York: Routledge.

Butler, J. (1993), *Bodies that Matter: On the Discursive Limits of 'Sex',* London: Routledge.

Butler, J. (1997), *Excitable Speech: A Politics of Performance,* London: Routledge.

Butler, J., and J. W. Scott (eds) (1992), *Feminists Theorise the Political* London: Routledge.

Cameron, D. (1992), *Feminism and Linguistic Theory,* London: Routledge.

Cameron, D. (1995), *Verbal Hygiene,* London: Routledge.

Cameron, D. (1996), 'The language-gender interface: challenging co-option', in Bergvall and Bing (eds), pp. 31–53.

Cameron, D. (1997), 'Performing gender identity: young men's talk and the construction of heterosexual masculinity', in Johnson and Meinhof (eds), pp. 47–64.

Cameron, D. (1998a), 'Is there any ketchup Vera?: gender, Power and pragmatics', *Discourse and Society* 9 (4): 437–55.

Cameron, D. (ed.), (1998b), *The Feminist Critique of Language,* London: Routledge.

Cameron, D., and J. Coates (1988), 'Some problems in the sociolinguistic explanation of sex differences', in Coates and Cameron (eds), pp. 13–26.

Cameron, D., F. McAlinden and K. O'Leary (1988), 'Lakoff in context: the social and linguistic functions of tag questions', in Coates and Cameron (eds), pp. 74–93.

Carston, R. (1988), 'Implicature, explicature and truth-theoretic semantics', in R. Kempson (ed.), *Mental Representations* Cambridge: Cambridge University Press, pp. 155–81.

Carston, R., and S. Uchida (eds) (1998), *Relevance Theory: Applications and Implications* Amsterdam: John Benjamins.

Chametzky, R. (1992), 'Pragmatics, prediction and relevance' *Journal of Pragmatics* V. '17': 63–72.

Christie, C. (1994), 'Theories of textual determination and audience agency: An empirical contribution to the debate', in Mills (ed.), pp. 47–66.

Christie, C. (1998a), 'Preaching to the converted? Media representations of feminist politics and their reception', *Journal of Gender Studies* 7(2): 211–24.

Christie, C. (1998b), 'Rewriting rights: A relevance theoretical analysis of press constructions of sexual harassment and the responses of readers', in *Language and Literature* 7(3): 214–34.

Cicourel, A. V. (1991), 'Semantics, pragmatics and situated meaning', in Verschueren (ed.), pp. 37–66.

Coates, J. (1998), '"Thank God I'm a woman": The construction of differing femininities', in Cameron (ed.), pp. 295–320.

Coates, J. (1988), 'Gossip revisited: Language in all-female groups', in Coates and Cameron (eds), pp. 94–122 .

Coates, J. (1993), *Women, Men and Language,* London: Longman.

Coates, J. (1997), 'One-at-a-time: The organization of men's talk', in Johnson and Meinhof (eds), pp. 107–29.

Coates, J. (ed.), (1998), *Language and Gender: A Reader,* Oxford: Blackwell.

Coates, J., and D. Cameron (eds) (1988), *Women in their Speech Communities: New Perspectives on Language and Sex,* London: Longman.

Collins, R. (1990), *Television: Policy and Culture*, London: Unwin Hyman.

Connor-Linton, J. (1991), 'A sociolinguistic model of *successful* speech act construction', in Verschueren (ed), pp. 93–112.

Coppock, V., D. Haydon and I. Richter (1995), *The Illusions of Post Feminism,* London: Taylor and Francis.

Corson, D. (1997), 'Gender, discourse and senior education: Ligatures for girls, options for boys?', in Wodak (1997b), pp. 141–62.

Cos, J.P.i (1997), 'Masculinities in a multilingual setting', in Johnson and Meinhof (eds), pp. 86–106.

Crawford, N. (1995), *Talking Difference: On Gender and Language,* London: Sage.

Davis, W. (1998) *Implicature: Intention, Convention and Principle in the failure of Gricean theory*, Cambridge: Cambridge University Press.

Deuchar, M. (1988), 'A pragmatic account of women's use of standard speech', in Coates and Cameron (eds), pp. 27–32.

Dijk, T. A. van (ed.) (1997), *Discourse as Social Interaction*, London: Sage.

Duranti, A. (1988), 'Ethnography of speaking: Towards a linguistics of praxis', in Newmeyer (ed.), pp. 210–28.

Duranti, A. (1991), 'Four properties of speech-in-interaction and the notion of translocutionary act', in Verschueren (ed.), pp. 133–50.

Duranti, A., and C. Goodwin (eds) (1992), *Rethinking Context,* Cambridge: Cambridge University Press.

Eades, Diana (1993), 'The case for Condren: Aboriginal English, pragmatics and the law speakers', *Journal of Pragmatics* 20: 141–62.

Eckert, P., and S. McConnell-Ginet (1994), 'Think practically and look locally: Language and Gender as a community based practice', in Roman et al. (eds), pp. 432–60.

Eckert, P., and S. McConnell-Ginet (1995), 'Constructing meaning, constructing selves: snapshots of language, gender and class from Belten High', in Hall and Bucholtz (eds), pp. 469–508.

Enkvist, N. E. (1985), 'Coherence and inference', in U. Pieper (ed.), *Studia Linguistica et Synchronica,* Berlin: Mouton de Gruyter, pp. 233–48.

Fairclough, N. (1989), *Language and Power,* London: Longman.

Fairclough, N., and R. Wodak (1997), 'Critical discourse analysis', in Dijk (ed.), pp. 258–84.

Fishman, P. (1998), 'Conversational Insecurity', in Cameron (ed.), pp. 253–8.

Geis, M. L. (1995), *Speech Acts and Conversational Interaction,* Cambridge: Cambridge University Press.

Georgakopoulou, A., and D. Goulsos (1997), *Discourse Analysis: An Introduction,* Edinburgh: Edinburgh University Press.

Goodwin, C., and A. Duranti (1992), 'Rethinking context: an introduction', in Duranti and Goodwin (eds), pp. 1–42.

Gorayska, B., and R. Lindsay (1993) 'The Roots of Relevance', *Journal of Pragmatics* V. (19): 301–23.

Graddol, D., and O. Boyd-Barrett (eds) (1994), *Media Texts, Authors and Readers: A Reader,* Clevedon: Multilingual Matters.

Graddol, D, and J. Swann (1989), *Gender Voices,* Oxford: Blackwell.

Green, Georgia (1989), *Pragmatics and Natural Language Understanding,* Hillsdale, NJ: Erlbaum.

Grice, P. (1989), *Studies in the Way of Words,* Cambridge, MA: Harvard University Press.

Grundy, P. (1995), *Doing Pragmatics,* London: Arnold.

Hall, K., and M. Bucholtz (eds) (1995), *Gender Articulated: Language and the Socially Constructed Self,* London: Routledge.

Halliday, M. A. K., and R. Hasan (1976), *Cohesion in English,* London: Longman.

Harding, S. (1986), *The Science Question in Feminism,* Ithaca, NY, and London: Cornell University Press.

Harris, R., and T. J. Taylor (1997), *Landmarks in Linguistic Thought* 1: *The Western Tradition from Socrates to Saussure,* London: Routledge.

Harris, S. (1995), 'Pragmatics and Power' *Journal of Pragmatics* 23: 117–35.

Hennessy, R. (1993), *Materialist Feminism and the Politics of Discourse,* London: Routledge.

Hepworth, J., and C. Griffin (1995), 'Conflicting opinions? "Anorexia nervosa", medicine and feminism', in Wilkinson and Kitzinger (eds), pp. 68–85.

Holmes, J. (1986), 'Functions of *you know* in women's and men's speech', *Language in Society* 15: 1, 1–22.

Holmes, J. (1993), 'New Zealand women are good to talk to: An analysis of politeness strategies in interaction' speakers', *Journal of Pragmatics* 20: 91–116.

Holmes, J. (1995), *Women, Men and Politeness,* London: Longman.

Jary, M. (1998), 'Relevance theory and the communication of politeness', *Journal of Pragmatics* 30: 1–19.

Johnson, S. (1997), 'Theorizing Language and Masculinity: A Feminist Perspective', in Johnson and Meinhof (eds), pp. 8–26.

Johnson, Sally, and Ulrike Hanna Meinhof (eds) (1997), *Language and Masculinity*, Oxford: Blackwell.

Johnstone, B., K. Ferrara and J. Mattson Bean (1992), 'Gender, politeness and discourse management in same-sex and cross-sex opinion-poll interviews', *Journal of Pragmatics* 18: 405–30.

Kaplan, C. (1998), 'Language and Gender', in Cameron (ed.), pp. 54–64.

Kasher, A. (ed.), (1998a), *Pragmatics: Critical Concepts*, Volume II: *Speech Act Theory and Particular Speech Acts*, London: Routledge.

Kasher, A. (ed.), (1998b), *Pragmatics: Critical Concepts*, Volume IV: *Presupposition, Implicature and Indirect Speech Acts*, London: Routledge.

Kitzinger, C. (1998), 'Feminist psychology in an interdisciplinary context', *Journal of Gender Studies* 7(2): 199–209.

Kopytko, Roman (1995), 'Against rationalistic pragmatics', *Journal of Pragmatics* 23: 475–91.

Kotthoff, H., and R. Wodak (eds) (1997), *Communicating Gender in Context*, Amsterdam: Benjamins.

Kramarae, C., and D. Spender (eds) (1993), *The Knowledge Explosion: Generations of Feminist Scholarship*, London: Harvester Wheatsheaf.

Lakoff, Robin (1995), 'Cries and whispers: The shattering of the silence', in Hall and Bucholtz (eds), pp. 25–50.

Lane, Chris (1993), 'Yes, I don't understand: Yes, no and European-Polynesian miscommunication in New Zealand', *Journal of Pragmatics* 20: 163–88.

Lavandera, Beatriz R. (1988), 'The study of language in its socio-cultural context', in Newmeyer (ed.), pp. 1–13.

Levinson, S. (1983), *Pragmatics*, Cambridge: Cambridge University Press.

Lovering, K. M. (1995), 'The bleeding body: adolescents talk about menstruation', in Wilkinson and Kitzinger (eds), pp. 10–31.

Lury, Celia (1995), 'The rights and wrongs of culture: issues of theory and methodology', in Skeggs (ed.), pp. 33–45.

Magalhaes, M. (1995), 'A critical discourse analysis of gender relations in Brazil', *Journal of Pragmatics* 23: 183–98.

McConnel-Ginet, S. (1998), 'The sexual (re)production of meaning: A discourse based theory', in Cameron (ed.), pp. 198–212.

McNay, L. (1992), *Foucault and Feminism*, Cambridge: Polity Press.

Meinhof, U. H. (1994), 'Double talk in news broadcasts: a cross cultural comparison of pictures and texts in television news', in Graddol and Boyd-Barrett (eds), pp. 212–23.

Meinhof, U., and S. Johnson (1997), 'Introduction', in Johnson and Meinhof (eds), pp. 1–8.

Mey, J. L. (1993), *Pragmatics: An Introduction*, Oxford: Blackwell.

Mills, S. (1997), *Discourse*, London: Routledge.

Mills, S. (ed.) (1994), *Gendering the Reader*, London: Harvester Wheatsheaf.

Moores, S. (1993) *Interpreting Audiences*, London: Sage.

Moores, S. (1994), 'Texts, readers and context of reading: developments in the study of media audiences', in Graddol and Boyd-Barrett (eds), pp. 256–72.

Murray, S. (1992), 'Review of Deborah Tannen, *You Just Don't Understand: Women and Men in Conversation*', *Journal of Pragmatics* 18: 507–21.

Newmeyer, Frederick J. (ed.) (1988), *Linguistics: The Cambridge Survey, Volume 4, Language: The Socio-Cultural Context*, Cambridge: Cambridge University Press.

Ochs, E. (1992), 'Indexing gender', in Duranti and Goodwin (eds), pp. 335–58.

Press, A. (1991), *Women Watching Television,* Philadelphia: University of Pennsylvania Press.

Pribram, D. (ed.) (1988), *Female Spectators,* London: Verso.

Recanati, F. (1987), *Meaning and Force: The Pragmatics of Performative Utterances*, Cambridge: Cambridge University Press.

Recanati, F. (1993), *Direct Reference: From Language to Thought,* Oxford: Blackwell.

Roman, C., S. Juhasz and C. Miller (eds) (1994), *The Women and Language Debate: A Sourcebook*, New Brunswick, NJ: Rutgers University Press.

Rundquist, S. (1992), 'Indirectness: A gender study of flouting Grice's maxims', *Journal of Pragmatics* 18: 431–49.

Sarangi, Srikant K., and Stefan Slembrouk (1992), 'Non-co-operation in communication: A reassessment of Gricean pragmatics', *Journal of Pragmatics* 17: 117–54.

Sbisa, M. (1995), 'Speech act theory', in Verschueren et al. (eds), pp. 495–505.

Schiffrin, D. (1994), *Approaches to Discourse*, Cambridge, MA, and Oxford: Blackwell.

Searle, J. R. (1969), *Speech Acts: An Essay in the Philosophy of Language,* Cambridge: Cambridge University Press.

Searle, J. R. (1971a), 'What is a speech act,' in Searle (ed.), pp. 23–54.

Searle, J. R. (1998), 'How Performatives Work', in Kasher, pp. 519–40.

Searle, J. R. (ed.) (1971b), *The Philosophy of Language,* Oxford: Oxford University Press.

Simpson, A. (1997), '"It's a game!": The construction of gendered subjectivity', in Wodak (1997b), pp. 197–24.

Skeggs, B. (ed.) (1995), *Feminist Cultural Theory,* Manchester: Manchester University Press.

Smith, N. V. and D. Wilson (eds) (1992), *Lingua: Special Issue on relevance theory* V. 87.

Sperber, D., and D. Wilson (1986, 1995), *Relevance,* Oxford: Blackwell.

Sperber, D., and D. Wilson (1987), 'Precis of *Relevance: Communication and cognition*', *Behavioural and Brain Sciences* 10: 697–754.

Stacey, J. (1995), 'The lost audience: methodology, cinema history and feminist film criticism' in Skeggs (ed.), pp. 97–118.

Stein, Dieter (ed.) (1992), *Co-operating with Written Texts: The Pragmatics and Comprehension of Written Texts*, Berlin: Mouton de Gruyter.

Strawson, P. F. (1998), 'Presupposition', in Kasher (1998b), pp. 5–7.

Talbot, M. (1997), '"Randy Fish Boss Branded a 'Stinker'": Coherence and the construction of masculinities in a British tabloid newspaper' in Johnson and Meinhof (eds), pp. 173–87.

Tannen, D. (1989), *Talking Voices: Repetition, Dialogue and Imagery in Conversational Discourse,* Cambridge: Cambridge University Press.

Tannen, D. (1992), *You just don't Understand,* London: Virago.

Tannen, D. (1994), *Gender and Discourse,* Oxford: Oxford University Press.

Tannen, D. (ed.) (1993), *Gender and Conversational Interaction,* Oxford: Oxford University Press.

Thomas, J. (1985), 'The language of power: towards a dynamic pragmatics', *Journal of Pragmatics* 9: 765–83.

Thomas, J. (1995), *Meaning in Interaction,* London: Longman.

Troemel-Ploetz, S. (1994), '"Let me put it this way, John": Conversational strategies of women in leadership positions', *Journal of Pragmatics* 22: 199–209.

Trudgill, P. (1974), *The Social Differentiation of English in Norwich,* Cambridge: Cambridge University Press.

Try Again Productions (1990), 'What makes ordinary people feminist', in the *Ordinary People* series. © Channel Four Television.

Urmson, J. (1998), 'Performative utterances', in Kasher (1998a), pp. 502–11.

Verschueren, J. (1995), 'The pragmatic perspective', in Verschueren et al. (eds), pp. 1–19.

Verschueren, J. (1999), *Understanding Pragmatics,* London: Arnold.

Verschueren, J. (ed.) (1991), *Pragmatics at Issue: Selected Papers of the International Pragmatics Conference, Antwerp August 17–22 1987,* Amsterdam: John Benjamins.

Verschueren, J., J. Ostman, and J. Blommaert (eds) (1995), *Handbook of Pragmatics Manual,* Amsterdam: John Benjamins.

Walby, Sylvia (1990), *Theorizing Patriarchy,* Oxford: Blackwell.

Walter, Natasha (1998), *The New Feminism,* London: Little, Brown.

West, C. (1994), 'Rethinking "sex differences" in conversational topics: It's not what they say but how they say it', in Roman et al. (eds), pp. 363–82.

West, Candace, Michelle M. Lazar and Cheri Kramarae (1997), 'Gender in discourse', in Dijk (ed.), pp 119–43.

Widdowson, H. G. (1995), 'Discourse analysis: a critical view', *Language and Literature,* 4(3): 157–72.

Wilkinson, S., and C. Kitzinger (eds) (1995), *Feminism and Discourse,* London: Sage.

Wodak, R. (1997a), 'Introduction: some important issues in the research of gender and discourse', in Wodak (1997b), pp. 1–13.

Wodak, R. (ed.) (1997b), *Gender and Discourse,* London: Sage.

Yule, G. (1996), *Pragmatics,* Oxford: Oxford University Press.

Zoonen, L. van (1994), *Feminist Media Studies,* London: Sage.

INDEX

201